THE ECONOMIC CHALLENGE OF THE ARABS

The economic challenge of the Arabs

GIAN PAOLO CASADIO
Institute of Economics
University of Bologna

SAXON HOUSE LEXINGTON BOOKS

Published by
SAXON HOUSE, D. C. Heath Ltd.
Westmead, Farnborough, Hants., England.

Jointly with
LEXINGTON BOOKS, D. C. Heath & Co.
Lexington, Mass. USA.

ISBN 0 347 01067 9
Library of Congress Catalog Card Number 75-35111
Printed in Great Britain by Butler and Tanner, Frome and London

Contents

List of tables

Foreword

Professor Casadio attempts to describe and analyse the problems and prospects of economic co-operation between the industrialised West and the Middle East at a time when the energy crisis in particular has created an unprecedented consciousness about the significance of the nature of the relationship of these two major centres of the world. The fundamental premise underlying his analysis is the simple but important proposition that the states of these two major subsystems need each other. The Middle East needs to co-operate with the industrialised West because its single most important source of revenue, that is oil, is a depleting and non-renewable natural resource which is at present the only major means that it can use to meet aspirations for industrial, social and economic development. On the other hand, the industrialised West needs the Middle East because at the present time it is dependent on Middle Eastern oil for its economic well-being and continued prosperity, although it is determined to reduce this dependence in the long run.

Granted this mutuality of present needs between the industrialised West and the Middle East, the author examines cogently the two principal approaches to the problems of economic co-operation between the states most particularly concerned. He recognises realistically that several Western and Middle Eastern states have already forged substantial bilateral ties and will probably continue to do so, but he is basically unsympathetic with bilateralism as the dominant pattern of relationship in the long run. The reasons for this are numerous. For example, bilateralism runs the risk of repressing international trade, particularly if it takes the form of bilateral agreements, encourages unrestrained competition and hence unavoidable friction, prompts excessive investment and thereby ruinous overproduction as a result of lack of co-ordination, provides insufficient guarantees and incentives to private business, and underestimates the fact that some investment requirements far exceed the capabilities of national enterprises.

Professor Casadio favours a kind of multilateral approach to the problems of economic co-operation that would result in the increase of trade and investment opportunities between the industrialised West and the Middle East with the twofold aim of shifting gradually from the West to the Middle East the production of 'first stage' basic commodities produced by energy-based industries on the one hand, and a gradual removal of imports levied by the West on the semi-finished and finished manufactures of the Middle East on the other. Whether or not one would agree with the particular type of mechanism that is suggested for the realisation of this basic twofold objective, the overall analysis in this study deserves serious attention, partly because of the author's ability as a European to take into account the indigenous social, economic and technical problems and prospects of Middle Eastern societies.

As a political scientist, I am tempted to bring this Foreword to a conclusion by suggesting that the larger question transcending, but by no means diminishing, the problems of economic co-operation between the industrialised West and the Middle East is political. The fundamental question within both areas is whether the political will is strong enough to overcome not only impediments to economic co-operation, but also to promote the common interest in the preservation of Western and Middle Eastern ways of life. At a time when Middle Eastern states have found an opportunity for the first time in their modern history to realise their aspirations of economic, social and political development by means of their newly found resource and financial power it is important, it seems to me, to encourage the forces of moderation throughout the area as a means of withstanding the onslaught of radicalism from within. And at a time when pessimism, self-doubt, economic crisis and political confusion seem to prepare the ground for the successful bid for power by forces of radicalism, particularly from within, it is important for the Atlantic community to heed the admonition of Alexander Solzhenitsyn. 'Totalitarianism,' he warns, 'is born from a weak and ill-prepared democracy.'

Rouhollah K. Ramazani
Edward R. Stettinius Jr Professor of Government and Foreign Affairs,
University of Virginia

Preface

We are not rich. We just happen to have a lot of money.

Abdel Rahman Al-Atiki, Kuwait Minister of Finance.

Oil resources are giving the Arab peoples a historical opportunity for developing and creating new sources of national wealth. If we let this opportunity go we would be condemned to remain poor and underdeveloped countries forever.

Nicolas Sarkis, Director of the Arab Petroleum Research Centre in Beirut.

There must be a fundamental change in economic relations between the rich and the poor states, and new contacts must be established in the fields of investment, trade and technology. In fact, all relations between rich and poor countries must be reviewed.

Jan Pronk, Minister for Development Co-operation, The Netherlands.

As Doctor R. Mabro (Fellow of St. Anthony's College, Oxford) says, 'between oil producers and consumers not only the gap in understanding remains wide, but both sides have not yet come to grips with the far-reaching implications of the economic and political changes brought about by the oil revolution of late 1973'. Thus, considering that the industrialised West and the Middle East are to a considerable extent natural partners, this book outlines the forms of a constructive action which might lead to a different relationship not only between Western countries and Middle Eastern nations but also between industrial nations, developing countries and producers of principal commodities. The plan of the work (which takes into consideration twenty-two developing nations of the Middle East and North Africa) is divided into two parts, comprising on the whole eight relatively independent chapters giving the reader a complete analysis of the principal problems posed by the oil crisis.

I would like to thank in particular Professor R.K. Ramazani who, since 1964, has pioneered a vigorous co-operation between the industrialised West and the Middle Eastern nations and has kindly agreed to write the foreword; Professor N. Andreatta who, as Rector of the University of Calabria, sponsored a seminar on industrial co-operation with the Arab nations in 1974; K. Maksoud, the director of the Central Administration for Industrial Planning and Technical Research in Cairo; K.K. Abdulnour, head of the planning division of the Industrial Development Centre for Arab States (IDCAS) in Cairo; M. M. Abdelmagio', Assistant Secretary-General of the Arab Economic Unity Council; A.N. Abdel-Hamid, adviser of the Arab International Bank for Trade and Development; B. El Din Hamdi of the European Arab Bank in Cairo; Professor S. Makdisi of the American University of Beirut (AUB); B. Dajani and E.T. Ghantus of the Union of Arab Chambers of Commerce in Beirut; Sabbah Al Haj and Y. El-Zein of the Center for Economic, Financial and Social Research and Documentation in Beirut; R.K. Kabbani of the Beirut Chamber of Commerce; O. Giusti, Deputy Director of Banco di Roma in Beirut; Z. Najjar of the Kuwait Chamber of Commerce; Minister G. Zampaglione and C. Bartoloni of the Italian mission in Kuwait; G. Amin and G. Zaccaria of the Kuwait Fund for Arab Economic Development; Ambassador M. Bucci, head of the Italian mission in Damascus; R.M. Abbar, the Director-General of the industrial studies and development centre in Riyadh; Mrs. E. Collard, Th. D. Mullins and J.H. Khoury of the *Middle East Economic Digest* (MEED); N. Al-Khatib and G. Leclerq of the Economic Commission for Western Asia (ECWA); A. Clo' of Montedison in Milan who went through Part I of the manuscript with the closest attention; Mrs. J. Borum of American Friends of the Middle East Inc.; and the staff of D. C. Heath Ltd., particularly Mrs. Mathias who edited the manuscript, and Miss Jenny Blake, editorial assistant.

Very useful to the book was my participation in the 'Third Conference on Industrial Development for Arab States', organised by IDCAS in Tripoli, Libya, 7-14 April 1974; the 'Seminar on Economic Co-operation between Italian Industry and the Arab Nations', organised by the University of Calabria and IPALMO (Institute for Italian relations with developing countries) in Cetraro, Italy, 11-14 July 1974; the international meeting on 'Co-operation and Security in the Mediterranean', organised by IPALMO in Palermo, 27-29 April 1975; the seminar on 'The Middle East and the Crisis in Relations among Industrial Countries', organised by the Atlantic Institute for International Affairs in Paris, 15-16 May 1975; and the seminar 'The 1975 Middle East Business Strategies

Conference', organised by MEED and AMR International Inc. in Brussels, 1-2 June 1975. Documents prepared by ECWA, FAO (for the regional conferences for the Near East), the Arab Planning Institute and Kuwait Economic Society also proved to be very valuable.

Field work was carried out during 1974 in Libya, Egypt, Kuwait and Lebanon.

Needless to say any omission or inaccuracies that may have occurred are due entirely to the author.

G.P.C.
Institute of Economics
University of Bologna, Italy
July 1975

PART I

THE IMPACT OF HIGHER OIL PRICES

1 Oil power

1.1 The transfer of real wealth

In terms of oil resources and financial power, the oil-exporting countries of the Middle East and North Africa have become major economic forces – almost overnight. The region, in fact, is the world's leading supplier of oil (accounting in 1974 for 42·5 per cent of world output). Oil reserves, in addition, are estimated at more than 300 billion barrels (approximately 62·3 per cent of the world's proven supply in 1974 including those of the communist bloc). In particular, huge reserves (56 per cent of the 1974 world total) are concentrated in the Gulf area – Saudi Arabia alone accounting for 24 per cent of the world total in 1974. The region, moreover, also accounts for a major share of natural gas reserves (36·5 per cent of the world total in 1974).

Thus the vulnerability of the developed countries is great; particularly for Western Europe and Japan – which in 1974 fulfilled respectively some 85 and 90 per cent of their petroleum needs from the Middle East – and also for the United States, whose direct and indirect purchases from Arab sources in early 1975 attained about 28 per cent of US oil-product imports compared with 18 per cent in early 1974.[1]

Additionally, an increase of around 470 per cent in the posted price of petroleum between October 1973 and January 1974 (along with further nationalisation of concessionaires) has created a major world monetary force. During 1974 the oil revenues of the countries of the region soared to $US 70·7 billion, against $US 8·7 billion in 1972 and $US 4·6 billion in 1970. Furthermore, in 1974 the oil-exporting nations of the region had already accumulated nearly $US 28 billion of non-gold reserves, mostly as dollars and some other foreign exchange, a sum which exceeds the $US 20 billion combined reserve held by eight of the Common Market countries. The fact that the petrodollar wealth of the Middle East might amount to $US 200–250 billion by 1980, instead of the earlier estimated $US 600 billion, does nothing to diminish the importance of this transfer of real wealth from the industrialised world.

1.2 The gazelles and the lions

The dangers of excessive transfer of economic power to the oil-exporting countries of the Middle East have been greatly stressed by the Western World. The US Government in particular has said that any attempt to maintain price levels by cutting production would provoke an economic and political backlash from the consuming states which would consider such action as an 'unfriendly act'. And though this term was later watered down to 'a counterproductive measure', the implication was that some form of military or economic action might be taken against the nations of the Middle East.

Thus, in a *Business Week* interview in January 1975, Secretary of State Kissinger stated that the United States might intervene militarily against Middle East oil producers if they threatened 'strangulation of the industrialised world'.

Similarly, despite the recognised need to recycle petrodollars in Western industry, to avoid squeezing their economies, the Western nations have been reluctant to allow investment in industry by the oil producers (whose wealth, it has been stressed, is based on a monopolistic rent of between 50 and 60 times the actual costs of dredging up oil from the desert). Thus *The Economist* has deemed it absurd that 'North America, Western Europe and Japan (which, between them, possess about 60 per cent of the world's industrial power) will agree through a decade to be halted in their economic growth by the Arab potentates which, between them, rule about 1 per cent of the world's population'.[2] And the *New York Times* stated that: 'From a political, social and national security standpoint, foreign control over major industries in the West (such as Iran's purchase of a 25 per cent stake in the Krupp group's steel subsidiary), especially by states with limited experience in world affairs and with driving national ambitions, gives obvious cause for concern'. [3]

The United States, which is considering laying down some basic guidelines for foreign investors, has already barred Kuwait and Iran from buying large blocks of stock in two defence contractors (Lockheed and Grumman), and some Arab businessmen from acquiring a large shareholding in two banks (First National Bank of San Jose and the Community National Bank of Pontiac). Critics of such investment have not spared those Arab nations which boast friendly relations with America. Thus Professor M.A. Adelman of MIT states: 'The US Government persists in identifying Saudi Arabia – the cartel leader – as a friendly country, even though they financed the war against Israel and then proceeded to wage an even more effective economic war against the

United States'. [4]

At the same time the international oil companies have been accused of being hostages of the Arabs and forced to operate at their beck and call. For example, the Senate subcommittee on multinational corporations, in an investigation of Aramco and its impact on US foreign policy, stated: 'The Arabian American Oil Co. undertook an extensive propaganda and lobbying campaign designated to dilute support of Israel by the United States, acting on the instructions of King Feisal of Saudi Arabia in May 1973'.[5]

1.3 Real power still lies with the industrial nations

To a great extent the dangers from the Arab oil world have been exaggerated, confirming that '90 per cent of oil business is just politics'. Before the outbreak of the Yom Kippur War, oil was underpriced. During the period 1950–70, oil prices deteriorated (in real terms) by about 50 per cent. Thus, for twenty years the oil-producing countries subsidised the West's industrial development. And while it is true that the oil-exporting countries of the Middle East have benefited from the spectacular increases of October 1973 to January 1974, we should bear in mind that they are selling their sole worthwhile asset - one that will be gone forever in some forty or fifty years. Moreover, it is not only the increased oil revenues which weigh heavily on the consumer nations, but also the substantial excise duties and similar taxes levied on oil and other oil products by the governments of those countries (around 8 per cent of their budgetary revenues). 'Thus, a large fraction of the profits are used for development . . . in the developed countries,' says Algerian President Boumedienne.

On the other hand, the direct oil-related inflationary impact is equal on average to only 2·4 per cent, as H. S. Merkelin, Director of the International Institute of the University of Dallas, points out. So it is on the domestic scene of the Western nations (i.e. to a disproportionate increase in money supply; deficit spending; exorbitant wage settlements; etc.) that one must look for the main cause of the inflation which now characterises modern industrial societies.[6] In fact, not only did the price-level increase begin long before the upswing in oil costs, but inflation has produced huge price rises in almost every commodity, including both raw materials and the manufactured products exported by industrialised countries. The oil-exporting countries, therefore, acted responsibly when, in December 1974, they decided to freeze the official price of oil for the first nine months of 1975; with soaring inflation and further depreciation of the dollar, this amounted to a significant cut in real terms.

The power enjoyed by the oil-exporting countries of the Middle East – as discussed later in Part II – is more imaginary than real. Real power, in effect, still lies with the industrial states. Middle Eastern nations have to face many problems which impinge on the oil-price question since their future survival depends on the use of petroleum and what they receive for it, in order to build their still backward economies. To accuse OPEC (Organisation of Petroleum Exporting Countries) of being a cartel with great economic and political power is merely to sabotage the co-operation between oil-exporting nations and industrial countries. The real cartel – which American courts have been denouncing for over twenty years – remains that of the international oil companies, the sole institutions which can enforce effective production control on a world scale.

Even though international oil companies no longer own large parts of the oilfields of the Middle East, their profit margins are restricted and the major companies still enjoy the best position in the purchase and distribution of Middle East crude oil. This was exemplified in their biggest-ever profits during the oil-price rise of 1973–74. In effect, their real strength lies in the 'downstream' oil circuit; in addition to their petrochemical complexes, tanker fleets and petrol-station services, they control around 60 per cent of the refineries of the world.

Of course the Arabs and Iranians are building up their own refineries, petrochemical factories and tanker fleets. These projects, however, cannot play any major role during the next ten years. In fact, in 1974 the Arabs sold directly only about 19 per cent of their oil production, that is, around 173 million tons out of a total production of 910 million tons. Meanwhile, the multinationals – as well as establishing new ties with the oil-producing countries of the Middle East to raise the means for their own investments – are able to diversify their sources of oil and enter the field of alternative energy (coal, tar sands, nuclear energy, etc.).[7]

In effect, despite the huge cost of petroleum imports sustained in 1974 by consumer countries, the industrial nations are realising that they can learn to live with expensive oil. In fact, as a result of the continuing decline in world oil consumption (through energy conservation policies, especially in the area of fuel for the home), reorganisation of international trade in oil (to depend more on non-OPEC countries) and increasing production of previously neglected domestic areas (through improved geophysical techniques, including promising deep-drilling techniques in the Po valley), the thirteen member nations of OPEC are forced to hold back from the market an increasing amount of their potential production, in order to maintain current prices.

The more oil the OPEC countries hold back from the market, the more income they must forgo. Thus, reversing previous catastrophic forecasts, new calculations (by the Morgan Guaranty Trust and others) suggest that the net investment surpluses of OPEC countries may have already reached a peak and that, by 1980, their combined surplus might be eliminated altogether because of the huge orders they have placed, at inflated prices, for imports of capital goods, military hardware and services.

It was therefore no surprise when, on 8 February 1975, the US Treasury Secretary, W. Simon, said: 'There is no reason for anxiety about the level of investment by OPEC countries in American enterprises'.

The rise in petroleum prices is seen to have some long term advantages, however, in revaluing rival resources (e.g. coal, natural gas, nuclear energy), in encouraging a worldwide search for oil, and in promoting the use of new 'miracle' energy supplies (solar energy, nuclear fusion, tidal power, geothermal power, energy from waste, etc.).

1.4 A basic reconsideration of US energy policy

The key to the fundamental shift in the world oil situation lies in America's change from an exporter to an increasingly large importer of petroleum rather than in the emancipation of producing countries. By 1980 the United States could be importing as much as eight to ten million barrels of oil a day from the Middle East.[8]

To face this situation the American Administration has worked out a new energy strategy. In particular, under 'Project Independence', the US is setting the basis for a major development of domestic energy sources which could guarantee almost complete independence in the next decade. Renewed investments of the major oil companies in oil resources and the attainment of the threshold of economic convenience in other energy sources (especially oil shale and tar sands) can be obtained, however, only through a large increase in domestic prices. But a successful outcome of this strategy could have been imperilled by the liberalisation of lower-price oil imports (blocked since 1958), as introduced by President Nixon in April 1973. It was, therefore, imperative that international prices be aligned to US domestic prices, independent of market conditions. Thus, the very purpose of the embargo – nothing but a bluff since the US always had crude-oil supplies – was to aggravate an oil-shortage 'psychosis', then favour the increase of oil prices.[9]

'Though the crisis which gripped Western Europe, Japan and North

America in 1973–74 now seems to have waned', says Senior Vice-President of the Sun Oil Company of Canada, R. Hennigar, 'no guarantee exists that we won't have to grapple with a similar situation sometime in the future. It is, therefore, imperative that the oil industry has a fairly stable environment in which to work.' Not surprisingly, the 'Kissinger Plan' – echoing in part the formula enunciated in November 1974 by Assistant Secretary of State, T. Enders, and submitted to the International Energy Agency in February 1975 – proposed that industrialised countries adopt a firm minimum price for imported oil. Thus it was hoped to create stable investment conditions for development of costly alternative sources of energy. In addition, President Ford intended to decontrol American crude-oil prices (so as to allow prices to move closer to the international level of $US 11 per barrel) and to gain windfall profits for home producers.

Thus, with the official delineation of the new US energy policy the era of cheap oil was ended, and the industrialised world will have to endure relatively high oil prices for years, though at a lower level of dependency and not necessarily quite as high as in 1973–74.

Notes

[1] M.C. Jensen, 'US Oil Imports from Arabs Increase', *International Herald Tribune,* 21 December 1974.

[2] Quoted in *The Economist,* 17 November 1973.

[3] 'The Oil Money', *The New York Times,* 20 July 1974.

[4] Quote in *The International Herald Tribune,* 13 January 1974.

[5] M. Mintz, 'Aramco Oil, On Faisal's Orders', *International Herald Tribune,* 7 August 1974.

[6] 'The Inflationary Impact of Rising Crude Oil Price', *The Arab Economist,* September 1974.

[7] A. Murcier, 'La Nouvelle stratégie des Sept Soeurs', *L'expansion,* February 1975.

[8] J. E. Akins, 'The Oil Crisis: This Time the Wolf is Here', *Foreign Affairs,* April 1973.

[9] A. Clo', *Politica energetica americana e prezzi del petrolio,* a publication of IPALMO, Rome 1974. For a careful analysis of the energy crisis in Western Europe, see A. Clo' and R. Prodi, *L'Europa e la crisi petrolifera,* Institute of Economics, University of Bologna, March 1975.

2 The diplomacy of resources

2.1 An irreplaceable product

The search for alternative oil sources and the further development of technology will doubtless proceed on all fronts. Yet such moves offer little hope of short-term relief. In the short and medium term, petroleum is irreplaceable. Many of the now defunct coal mines cannot be reopened, nor is labour easy to find for them, even if wages are high. Natural gas derives mainly from the oil-producing countries, is difficult to transport and its heat value is 5 per cent of that of oil. Nuclear energy cannot be supplied in a large quantity during the present decade and perhaps not until 1985–95. 'We are disappointed in nuclear energy', declares C. King Mallory III, Deputy Assistant Secretary for Energy and Minerals at the US Department of the Interior. 'It has been the repository of billions of research and development dollars during the past twenty-five years, but has been able to supply only 1 per cent of our energy needs to date. In addition, the supply of high-grade uranium ore has turned out to be not all that abundant.'[1] Exploitation of the shale oil of Colorado, of the tar sands of Athabaska and of heavy Venezuelan oil are more expensive than Arab petroleum. And the construction of barrages in tidal estuaries, geothermal heat systems and solar energy are all sources which cannot be readily developed.

Moreover, pollution and environmental damage raise new and largely unexplored problems in connection with the massive use of nuclear energy and the realisation of other scientific possibilities. In effect, the development of alternative energy resources – such as those planned by 'Project Independence' – only gives way to unprecedented environmental hazards. Significant here is the fact that the Alaska pipeline has been approved, that oil refineries are being built along the coast of New England, that as many as 5000 oil wells are contemplated in the off-shore area near the most popular beaches around Los Angeles, that air-pollution rules are less and less respected, and that the safety rules in nuclear installations are now less stringent.[2]

It would, therefore, be irresponsible to rush ahead without careful study and public debate and to barter our long-term future for short-term gains. In fact, at least for the next twenty years, petroleum will remain the dominant source of energy.[3] The EEC Commission report on the adoption of a new strategy for energy resources in Europe states that: 'Petroleum will remain for a long time a fundamental element of our energy supply. In 1985 – despite recourse to other sources – petroleum will still account for 41 per cent of the EEC energy supply.' Moreover, neither nuclear energy nor synthetic oil could ever replace petroleum as a raw material (i.e. for manufacturing petrochemicals, lubricants, etc.). Thus, the Federal Energy Administration believes that 'the United States can never again be free of dependence on foreign oil' and the National Academy of Sciences estimates that 'the United States will run out of oil and natural gas in twenty-five years', casting serious doubts on the White House programme for achieving energy independence.

An added difficulty is the soaring cost of developing alternative sources of energy to Middle East oil. These have already had a sharp regressive impact on the development of tar sands and shale-oil facilities in North America and raised serious doubts on the feasibility of rapidly expanding nuclear-power contribution as well as prompting a review of development potential in the North Sea. Therefore, despite recent oil discoveries (in southern Mexico, the Voring plateau near the Lofoten Islands, South-East Asia, Australia, China, India, etc.), the Middle East and North Africa will remain the world's leading source of energy supplies to the industrialised world for at least the next ten years.

Energy is a problem and will remain a problem that will take considerable efforts to solve. All countries should therefore try to work together to overcome the difficulties of these next ten years. Producer and consumer nations could thus avoid a confrontation which neither would win. A Western attack on Arab oilfields would invoke a world catastrophe. Petroleum at source is far easier to destroy than to seize by force. And attempts to pull oil prices down excessively, to enforce rigorous restrictions to the free movement of capital or to refuse to supply certain goods (e.g. foodstuffs) to the Arab nations would lead to consequences far more drastic for those taking such action than those against whom the action is directed.

In fact, the bargaining power of Middle East oil-exporting countries is shared with other states. Thus, contracts for the export of natural gas from Holland have already been tied to oil parity (i.e. price increase of 10 guilders per ton of crude automatically implies a 0·6 per cent increase per m^3 of natural gas). The Norwegians (the Arabs of the North), as well as failing to take part in the oil-sharing mechanism of the International Energy Agency, have – for political reasons and national security – virtually barred foreign oil companies from gas and oil exploration along the vast continental shelf of northern Norway. And in the contract for the sale of North Sea gas to Britain by Petronord (the Franco-Norwegian consortium working the Norwegian part of the Frigg gasfield) not only have very stringent conditions been laid down, but escalation clauses have been included, linking the agreed price to prices of other fuels and to other indices. Tough conditions have also been imposed by Canada (which has started phasing out crude exports to the US), Australia (which, in addition to export controls, has embargoed exports of uranium and natural gas) and the USSR (which, as well as raising the price to Eastern Europe by 120 per cent from 1975 to January 1976, is pressing for further increases in order to develop its abundant but remote Siberian and Uralian energy resources).

As to oil prices generally, the industrial countries seem to underestimate the degree of OPEC solidarity. In fact, it should come as no surprise if the Arab nations cut production rather than lower prices for they know their oil to be depletable. Attempts to drive a wedge between states with revenues exceeding internal absorption capacity, such as Saudi Arabia, and those who need the bulk of their incomes to sustain the living standards of their expanding population have so far failed.

The tendency to pass from exaggerated pessimism to euphoria is equally unhelpful. The oil surplus created at the beginning of 1975 is largely the result of higher oil prices, the mild winter in Europe and the worldwide economic slowdown. With an upturn in economic activity, and perhaps a cold winter, consumption could quickly recover.

At the same time it is now clear that the Middle East nations (notably Iran and Saudi Arabia, the two major oil-exporting countries) are more interested in taking their places among the rich nations than in opposing them. In particular, they are trying to encourage a growing interdependence between themselves and the West, investing in Europe and America in such a way as to ensure that the industrialised countries will remain oriented to Middle East development needs for a long time to come. Said H. H. Sheik Jaber Al Ahmed Al-Sabah, Heir Apparent and Prime Minister of Kuwait, 'We fully realise that any international monetary disorder or world economic recession will be detrimental to the interests of all countries including the oil producers.'[4]

'The Arab oil states are the victims of international financial chaos,' explained the Lebanese oil expert Marwan Iskandar. 'They have already suffered financial losses (estimated at over $US 600 million between 1968 and 1972) when their cash balances accumulated in currencies were devalued or when other funds and ventures folded.'[5]

'If the Arabs were to use part (or even all) of their surpluses to buy real assets in the developed countries,' said Elias S. Saba, an Arab economist, 'then these surpluses – as they stand today and as they are visualised in the foreseeable future – will remain a small fraction of the stock of wealth of the industrialised world. Nothing approaching "Arab control" is anywhere near possible. Furthermore, such purchases are likely to prove temporary because of the exhaustible nature of oil and the accelerating absorptive capacity of the Arab World in its attempt to build its own capital stock. Fears of this nature most likely reflect the understandable, but unjustifiable, resentment by members of one of the world's most exclusive clubs to admit any new members at such short notice.'[6]

In effect, since the producing countries spend most of their oil revenues on their own development, industrial countries have a real, but not insoluble, transfer problem in the short term. They feel non-deflationary pressure since export demand 'takes up' those resources freed when spending declined because of oil products and energy supplies attracting a higher proportion of domestic expenditure. As J. Tumlir, head of the Intelligence Division of the GATT Secretariat, points out: 'The one-and-for-all increase in the oil price represents 1–2 per cent of industrial countries' GNP, that is about one-half of their annual GNP growth capacity; and, after the inevitable structural adjustment, growth capacity of these economies would remain unaffected.'[7]

2.2 Co-operation between producers and consumers

The only realistic – and mutually advantageous – solution to the oil problem is to start a new form of economic partnership between producer and consumer countries. Such a partnership must have a global character, in the sense that it must not be limited to oil only, but that oil should be inserted into a complete context of economic relationships which comply with the developmental requirements of producing countries. If it is imperative for industrial countries to have sure supplies of oil at reasonable prices, it is equally urgent for producing countries to attain a true economic take-off and acquire a place in the great flows of international trade. Too often the oil industry, instead of becoming the engine of an economic take-off, has been maintained in a separate position from the economic context of producing countries.

On the contrary, it should represent the initial point of a smooth evolution (for the development of manufacturing industry, agriculture, the training of professional and managerial classes, etc.). 'Fundamentally, our strategy is designed to use our financial resources for the development of our own economies,' said Abdulatif U. Al-Hamad, Director General of the Kuwait Fund for Arab Economic Development. 'I believe we can establish a mutually beneficial relationship between the Arab countries and the potentially most dynamic force in international economic life, namely, the investment operations of the so-called multinational corporations, provided we succeed in persuading them that we shall no longer acquiesce to being reduced to mere exporters of raw materials, markets for industrial goods, or docile source of finance. We have the manpower required, the materials, a substantial part of the markets and the money. They have the technology, the patents, the managerial know-how, the marketing networks and the right contacts'.[8]

2.3 Bilateral deals

At present, the new economic partnership between producer and consumer countries is limited to the context of national solutions (conclusion of bilateral agreements), while a multilateral effort would be appropriate between the OPEC bloc and the OECD countries.

In spite of US misgivings the Japanese and European governments are clearly aiming at increasing the import of crude oil by direct deals with the oil-producing countries. Although the cost works out at slightly more ($1 per barrel more, in fact) than that of crude oil imported through the international companies, from the point of view of security of supply the governments' objective is to raise the present share of supply by direct deals. Thus for instance, Japan aims at an increase in oil imports from 5 per cent to 40 per cent of Japanese imports of crude oil. Government to government deals are also bypassing the international money and capital markets. Thus for instance, Japan, France and Britain have signed long-term agreements with Saudi Arabia and Iran, with these countries depositing substantial sums with the Banks of Japan, France and England.

Bilateral deals are attractive to the Arabs because they guarantee that customers pay for oil by boosting Arab development, and to the consumer countries because they avoid large deficits in their balance of payments (exporting goods instead of foreign currencies). Moreover, bilateral agreements may be so constructed as to avoid price uncertainties for both parties. In particular, instead of the bitterness associated with a unilateral increase in oil price, there is a spirit of mutual co-operation and advantage – though the problem of 'indexing' also remains in such deals. Additionally, bilateral agreements – which are also current in East–West relations – may open up investment opportunities in real assets which would otherwise not be possible, and provide some guarantee against restrictive regulations *vis-à-vis* Arab investments and provide for needed commodities and technology. Thus, even the United States – which condemned these deals as 'selfish' – has signed $US 10 billion and $US 15 billion agreements respectively with Saudi Arabia and Iran for the supply of goods, machinery, arms and technology (the largest international transactions ever arranged, even the Marshall Plan involving far smaller commitments).

Bilateral agreements also carry serious risks, however, and may:

1 Favour barter deals.
2 Produce cut-throat competition and cause international friction, especially among importing countries.
3 Lead to excessive investments which turn into ruinous overproduction (owing to lack of co-ordination between governments).
4 Fail to grant sufficient guarantees and concrete incentives to businessmen.
5 Neglect the fact that some investments require much greater means than the resources of national enterprises.
6 Fail to allow an industrial group to divide the risks between countries with different political tendencies when it cannot associate with competitors to expand other markets.
7 Concentrate capital investments in paper assets which, unless well structured and well designed, are vulnerable to depreciation, refutation and even default.

Thus, although in the short term bilateral agreements can be expected to mushroom (especially if a multilateral solution is not agreed on quickly), in the long run they are less likely to find favour. In fact, Arab governments have lost political leverage, e.g. by setting aside European restrictions on arms sales in the Middle East, since Britain and France have rescinded their arms embargoes and no transfer clause on weapons seems likely to be enforced.

Some bilateral contracts, in effect, constitute, to some extent at least, mere public relations. As one paper puts it: 'the tale of a thousand and one factories'. But few such deals are firm contracts, as yet only outline agreements.

Another difficulty of bilateral agreements stems from capital flows tending to concentrate in a few countries, with adverse effects on others (particularly many less developed countries).

2.4 A multilateral solution

It would seem best, therefore, to phase the bilateral approach gradually into a multilateral solution. In particular, by a concerted effort in the Paris forum between industrialised countries, oil-exporting states and other developing nations, an international scheme could be negotiated under which:

(a) The governments of the oil-exporting countries would commit themselves to provide industrial countries with a major share of their oil consumption (for instance 60 per cent) at an assured price (but at a lower level than the current one) for some definite period (e.g. five years) subject to renewal. This would operate on the basis of a multilateral export quota system (modelled on the arrangements for sugar, as agreed in the Lomé Convention between the EEC, African, Caribbean and Pacific states)[9] and be managed by the national oil companies of the two blocs of countries (to exclude any manipulation by international oil companies).

In return, the governments of the industrial countries would commit themselves to pay for the agreed oil supplies with a planned volume of goods and services (foodstuffs, industrial equipment, technology transfer, technical assistance, etc.) meeting the developmental requirements of oil-exporting countries, and to open their own markets gradually (e.g. by 10 per cent of the whole consumption every five years) to the imports of oil-derived products. In addition, the negotiated price levels of the scheme would be kept in an appropriate relationship every year; the scheme's net proceeds from oil would be exclusively used for the purchase of the goods and services agreed on; the eventual loss of earnings under the plan (for both blocs) would not be compensated automatically but would first be reviewed by a mixed commission; eventual disputes would be entrusted to the World Bank International Centre for the Settlement of Investment Disputes; heavy fines as well as reimposition of import restrictions on oil-derived products would be applied to those oil-exporting states which do not comply with the engagements undertaken. Thus, a kind of international oil-clearing agreement would be defined, so that the advantages of bilateral deals could be maintained in a multilateral and co-ordinated context.

(b) A corporate joint venture would be instituted, whereby oil capital would be combined with engineering and organisational know-how of firms from industrial countries. Thus the institutions and the enterprises of the countries participating in the international oil-clearing agreement would be granted guarantees against political risks; additional import facilities in the markets of the industrial countries for the goods (notably oil-refined products) exclusively produced by the ventures; attractive fiscal facilities (especially for 'cross-partnership'); and liberal interpretation of antitrust laws. This multilateral scheme should, then, be integrated with other international arrangements to finance oil payments deficits as well as permit the exploitation of 'synthetic' fuel and 'miracle' energy resources (e.g. fusion and solar power).

In fact, the transfer problem posed by oil payments (which, by 1980, may still amount to the staggering figure of $US 250–300 billion), and the enormous capital needed to develop costly forms of energy, pose structural and technical difficulties which have to be overcome. In effect the Eurocurrency markets – though well equipped to manipulate major funds (in 1974 about $US 21 billion went into Eurocurrency deposits out of a total flow of petrodollars of around $US 55 billion) and while giving the desired anonymity to investors – have three main disadvantages:

(1) Oil-exporting countries seek liquid investment in the short term, while oil-importing countries want medium term commitment.

(2) Movement of floating capital produced by changes in exchange rate are not compatible with equilibrium in the medium term.

(3) The private market is not able to solve the problems of those countries whose situation is quite difficult. In addition, with its more restrictive monetary policy, the US capital market – though now fully accessible because of the abolition of controls – acts as an intake pump for Eurodollars, thus reducing the possibility of financing deficit countries. Also inadequate is the action of intergovernmental institutions (such as the swap network among central banks, as well as the IMF drawing rights and standby loans). In addition to the IMF's pilot oil-financing scheme for 1974 (known colloquially as Witteveen I, and to which nine oil exporters committed just over $US 3·6 billion mostly for use by developing countries, with small amounts going to Italy and New Zealand), a major step forward has been the creation of a new 'oil facility' with the IMF (Witteveen II) endowed with $US 6 billion for 1975; this is intended to supply the needs of industrial countries and not – as under Witteveen I – mainly those of the least developed countries. In particular, the new facility borrows from oil exporters and industrial countries with strong reserves (at only a fraction below the average short term rates in leading financial centres) and reduces the interest rate for the least developed countries through a special debt servicing subsidy. Furthermore, while the Common Market countries have activated their own mini-recycling scheme (borrowing $US 3 billion from the OPEC countries under a collective guarantee), a 'solidarity fund', open to all members of

the OECD and acting as a 'safety net, to be used as a last resort' has been established.

However, despite its advantages (acting impartially and automatically in raising and relending funds; bringing the OPEC countries face to face with the consequences of their oil pricing policy; being set up quickly and easily), the IMF recycling facility involves a limited sum ($US 6 billion) of a temporary nature. And the practical working of the other two mechanisms is doubtful. A Community loan can be floated only by unanimous decision of the EEC's ministerial council, and recipients are obliged to adhere to stringent economic conditions. The OECD solidarity fund facility cannot be brought into operation at short notice since the scheme requires legislation in most countries (and the US Congress has already expressed open criticism); the $US 25 billion Fund is for two years only, and only half of it can be lent at any time; quotas and voting right are linked not to the amount of oil money that any country receives but to its economic size (based on GNP and international trade), thus the United Kingdom and Italy would have to contribute fairly heavily, though they are obviously two of the first potential borrowers; loans are subject to 'appropriate economic policy conditions'; and the United States, which would have between 25 and 30 per cent of the quotas, would thus have too great a say as to whom the funds would go and when.

It is therefore necessary to go much further than the defensive co-operation of the OECD countries, and think in terms of more constructive initiatives which would make it possible - in a manner profitable to both oil producer and consumer countries - to lessen the difficulties connected with absorption of oil capital and the financing of costly alternative energy resources. In particular, two other international mechanisms should be set up:

(a) *a new system of (partial) payments for petroleum* whereby oil-exporting countries would receive in (partial) payment for certain quantities of oil (within the category of surplus capital) index-linked bonds to avoid inflationary bias. In particular, according to Dr. R. E. Mabro, Fellow of St Anthony's College, Oxford, 'bonds constructed as a form of investment for producers to finance future imports at the end of the oil era, not instruments of mutual compensation, and to be indexed to the price of a basket of goods and services representative of Arab future imports'.[10] Such payment would be achieved through double or multiple guarantees involving the IMF, on the one hand, and one or more member countries on the other, depending on the amount of the loan and the period concerned.

(b) *a new international investment fund* which would collect a part of the funds which the oil producers wish to invest in real assets in the OECD area and channel them towards outlets which would be profitable for the investors. Adequate safeguards and guarantees would be provided (such as fair compensation for expropriated ventures, removal of existing barriers to movement of foreign capital) but with a healthy restraint on maximum holdings (to allay fears of disruption in developed countries; to prevent oil producers from crowding the US market to the detriment of Europe and Japan; and to leave the Arabs sufficient oil money for their national and regional developments).[11]

Within such an international investment fund, the co-ordination and pooling of large-scale national research efforts could be promoted, to develop energy forms such as fusion and solar power, in which the oil-exporting countries could also have the opportunity to share, by investment participation, as with Iranian interests in the North Sea.

2.5 Stabilising world commodity markets

Successful producer action to raise oil prices has had a strong impact on the commodity world, in economic as well as political terms. In fact, in April 1974 the UN General Assembly proclaimed the right of the developing nations to control their natural wealth and to industrialise on the basis of the local processing of their raw materials – first and foremost for their own economic and social development. Thus, Venezuela nationalised the country's iron-ore industry, previously controlled by two American companies and second only to petroleum in export revenues; Peru nationalised the Cerro de Pasco Co., one of the most important mining companies in Latin America; Mauritania nationalised Miferma, the corporation which works the copper mines of Akjout; Togo nationalised the Mining Company of Benin; and Jamaica took a majority stake in the local subsidiary of Kaiser Aluminium.

Moreover, several developing nations have tried to emulate the OPEC example. In particular, seven bauxite countries (Guinea, Australia, Guyana, Jamaica, Sierra Leone, Surinam and Yugoslavia), producing between them some 63 per cent of world production, agreed to set up the International Association of Bauxite Producers, to manufacture aluminium and assure that the multinationals do not work to the detriment of any member state; Algeria, Italy and Spain agreed a price-setting arrangement for mercury; Zambia, Chile, Peru and Zaire, accounting for 70 per cent of copper exports and constituting the Intergovernmental Council of Copper Exporting Countries (CIPEC), have cut back production to boost declining world copper prices; twenty

Latin American nations (including Cuba) established a cartel to protect the world price of sugar; Cameroun, Ghana, the Ivory Coast, Nigeria, Togo and Brazil established the Cocoa Producers' Alliance (COPAL); coffee producers decided to withhold part of their production and set up a multinational organisation (Café Suaves Centrales) to regulate price and supply, with support from Colombia, Brazil and Venezuela to finance a 'buffer' stockpile; Morocco, the biggest world exporter of phosphates, joined forces with smaller producers (Senegal, Algeria, Tunisia and Togo) to maintain high prices throughout the world and promote the use of phosphatic fertilisers. And eleven iron-ore exporting countries have agreed to set up an organisation of exporting countries.

To keep the Third World in the OPEC camp, the OPEC states have rapidly expanded their aid commitments. Thus, in 1974, OECD estimated that the total amount of OPEC aid reached almost $US 7½ billion (as defined by the criteria applying to Western aid, i.e. exclusively from high-interest loans and military assistance). The amount of OPEC aid is even higher if we include items not included in the OECD computations – substantial purchases of World Bank bonds, contributions to the new aid mechanisms such as the IMF oil facility and the UN Special Emergency Fund, and the concessionary sale of oil, notably to India and Bangladesh. While in 1974 OPEC aid (2 per cent of its combined GNP) proved to be more generous than that provided by the West (0·3 per cent of combined GNP), even more important, 40 per cent of OPEC aid disbursements (compared with only 8 per cent of Western aid) went to the thirty-three poorest countries: the so-called Fourth World (mainly the Sahel countries, some East African and Central American nations, and the Indian subcontinent).

Moreover, it is the Arab states and Iran which are doing most to try to offset the impact of higher oil prices on the poorer nations. (Kuwait, Saudi Arabia and the Emirates have emerged as the world's top donors in proportion to GNP.) In 1974 this was achieved through:

(a) existing international monetary and development institutions such as IMF and the World Bank;

(b) new regional bodies such as the Arab Bank for African Economic Development; the $US 200 million Special Arab Fund for Africa; the $US 900 million Islamic Development Bank; the $US 340 million Arab Fund for Economic and Social Development; and the Saudi and Iraqi Development Funds modelled on the Kuwait and Abu Dhabi Funds which have also extended their activities to non-Arab developing nations, by increasing their capital to $US 3·4 billion and $US 500 million respectively);

(c) the expansion of trade ties, notably Brazil bartering soya, sugar and cotton in exchange for oil; South-East Asia, which is complementary to West Asia in many ways - Singapore, for instance, depends greatly on Middle East oil refining; India, which can provide the manpower and the market for fertiliser plants installed in the Middle East; etc.;

(d) bilateral or tripartite investment deals, e.g. the establishment of Iranohind, a new shipping line run jointly by Iran and India; the setting up of a joint tanker shipping company between Iran and Pakistan; the creation of a Kuwaiti–Brazilian investment company for agricultural and industrial projects; Libyan investment in a Zaire copper-mine development; Iraqi investment in Malaysia for the manufacture of rubber-based goods; a fertiliser plant jointly owned by Abu Dhabi and Pakistan, with Pakistan's share being contributed by Saudi Arabia; and a company jointly owned by Guinea, Saudi Arabia, Kuwait, Libya and Egypt to mine the Aykoye bauxite deposits in Guinea.

However, the most important consequence of the oil crisis for the developing nations might prove to be that OPEC - at the instigation of Algeria as a leader not only of the oil-exporting countries but of the whole Third World - has formally advocated that any dialogue between energy consumers and energy producers should include the producers of all raw materials. This will cover the trilateral conference organised by the French President G. D'Estaing.

In fact, further OPEC aid and other international mechanisms (like the second IMF oil facility; the Third Window of the World Bank designed to add about $US 1 billion a year to the financial resources available to almost fifty of the poorer countries, at subsidised, below-market interest rates; the new International Agricultural Development Fund designed to assist the poorest countries with imports such as fertilisers, pesticides, cereals and the development of food production) would prove inadequate if the external base of the developing countries were seriously undermined by a collapse in commodity prices, concomitant with increasing costs of manufactured goods imports, increased fertiliser and cereal prices and reduced export earnings because of stagnation in the industrialised world.

Thus, as suggested above, other major raw materials should be included with oil in a stabilisation of prices by a system of multilateral commitments between buyers and sellers. Within the Lomé Convention, the EEC and forty-six developing nations have already agreed to stabilise the foreign exchange earnings of twelve essential commodity groups (e.g. groundnut, coffee, cocoa, leathers and skins, tea, sisal and iron ore) and of several derivatives.

Of course, some industrial countries are reluctant to extend their commitments to commodities other than oil because:

1 The world faces no serious shortage of raw materials in the foreseeable future.
2 Cartels in minerals seldom hold together for long and are not generally successful (CIPEC cutbacks, for example, failed to achieve a price fall for copper).
3 Investments in raw materials can be placed in more 'secure' countries such as Canada, Australia and South Africa.
4 Certain commodities have synthetic substitutes (Hoechst, for instance, claims that it has developed a soluble sugar substitute, and the French aluminium giant, Pechiney-Ugine-Kuhlmann, claims to have developed a process that will dispense with bauxite).

The implications of short-term economic disruptions for a number of 'sensitive' products (e.g. iron ore, tin, cotton, vegetable oils, and coffee) should not be underestimated. The vulnerability of Japan and the EEC is great, since they respectively import 90 and 70 per cent of all raw materials. And the United States has a growing dependency, importing about 15 per cent of raw material requirements, but already obtaining 100 per cent of its natural rubber and coffee from abroad, 93 per cent of its manganese, 92 per cent of cobalt and graphite, 91 per cent of chromium, and more than 50 per cent of its platinum, tin, nickel, antimony, bismuth, mercury and zinc. In fact, a major collapse in the terms of trade of primary commodities is likely to mean that 'mini-OPECs' are set up for several commodities, with a resulting establishment of consumer cartels, which might lead to international friction. Moreover, the United States could be tempted to use its enormous latent power as a major exporter of wheat, feed grains, oilseeds and fertilisers, and as a dominant holder of stockpile supplies whose release could seriously disrupt the world commodity markets.

A better course for both sides is therefore to participate in intelligently managed negotiations, producers and consumers alike needing the 'relative stability' founded on fair contractual bases – even if this stability were to cost something. Modelled for example on the mechanisms established by the Lomé Convention, a multi-commodity stabilisation operation could be negotiated in the GATT forum, in the framework of the Tokyo Round (with the active assistance of UNCTAD), under which:

(a) medium and long term intergovernmental contracts would be concluded for the most sensitive commodities, the importing countries –

in return for a commitment to buy minimum proportions of their requirements - assuring guaranteed outlets at agreed prices for a fixed period, (say five years, subject to renewal). Moreover, all the least developed countries concerned would obtain freer access for their processed goods on the markets of the industrialised world. This would be achieved through extension of the GSP (Generalised System of Preferences), the removal of non-tariff barriers and the provision of export incentives, while heavy fines as well as reimposition of import restrictions on processed products would be applied to any exporting countries deliberately evading supply commitments undertaken. A committee representing both the least developed and the industrial countries would meet every year to keep the negotiated prices in appropriate relationship to the imports of the developing countries. But maximum year to year variation of prices would be limited to specified percentages.

(b) for some other commodities, a minimum level of export revenues would be guaranteed by the importing nations, provided that:

(i) each product represents an appreciable percentage of a developing country's total exports;

(ii) the system's financial endowment is limited to a fixed amount periodically subject to revision;

(iii) financial transfers in lean years would be awarded on condition that developing nations' export revenues drop by a certain percentage;

(iv) reimbursement would be made during commodity booms, with the exception of the poorest nations.

(c) closer regulation of futures trading would be adopted in the major world commodity markets. This need has already been recognised by the United States in legislation establishing a commodity futures trading commission to regulate futures markets in commodities produced in developing countries as well as those domestically produced, and to curb malpractices which seriously upset market performance. In addition, a solidarity fund of $US 10–15 billion, to be financed mainly from OPEC grants and loans and voluntary contributions from the industrial nations, is also needed:

(i) to set up large fertiliser plants to fulfil the major needs of developing countries at 'cost of production';

(ii) to establish a grain reserve of at least 10 million tons to meet emergencies (floods, droughts, blights, earthquakes) and restore a modicum of stability to food prices;

(iii) to improve and extend the compensatory financing facility of the IMF (intended to smooth out fluctuations in total exports of primary producing members and thus compensate for fluctuations in specific commodity exports);

(iv) to institute a stockpiling policy for some key commodities, as advocated by UNCTAD's integrated programme[12], to counter rapid deterioration of prices or downturns in demand and, in some instances, to replenish dangerously low levels of world stocks.

Finally, an international investment scheme jointly operated by the developed countries, OPEC members and other developing nations could facilitate tripartite ventures involving Western technology and know-how, oil funds, and the potentially massive agricultural and mineral resources of many developing countries. Thus, in addition to firm guarantees against political risks, duty-free access to the markets of the industrialised world would be granted for the resulting processed products.

Notes

[1] 'Energy Developments, Energy Finance and Political Choice', a speech delivered at the World Energy Finance Seminar organised by the *Financial Times* and the *Oil Daily,* 7–8 October 1974.

[2] G. Taix, *La crise de l'énergie: aux portes de l'enfer atomique,* Société d'études et de publications, Paris, 1975.

[3] D. Cook, 'Supply of Enriched Uranium is Committed for the Decade', *International Herald Tribune,* 4 October 1974; OECD, *Energy Prospects to 1985,* Paris, 1974.

[4] Speech delivered on opening 'Seminar on the Investment Policies of the Arab Oil Producing Countries', Kuwait, 18 February 1974.

[5] M. Iskandar, *The Arab Oil Question,* Middle East Economic Consultancy, Beirut, 1974.

[6] E.S. Saba, 'The Role of Arab Funds in the Money and Capital Markets of the World, Seminar on Investment Policies', Kuwait, February 1974.

[7] J. Tumlir, 'Oil Payments and Oil Debt in the World Economy', *Lloyds Bank Review,* no. 113, London, July 1974.

[8] 'Arab Funds and International Economic Co-operation', address given to the European Institute of Business Administration, Fontainebleau, France, 20 November 1973.

[9] Under the Lomé Convention, the Antilles and Guyana, Mauritius, Fiji, Swaziland, Congo/Brazzaville, India, the British Honduras, Madagascar, British Africa and Surinam will send the EEC up to 1·3 million tons of sugar a year until 1980 and maybe beyond. The special

price of £260 per ton held until the end of 1975; the countries involved now get a price indexed to the EEC's own support price.

[10] R.E. Mabro, 'Problems of Investment', Seminar on Investment Policies, Kuwait, February 1974.

[11] R. Mabro and E. Monroe, 'Arab Wealth from Oil: Problems of its Investment', *International Affairs,* January 1974.

[12] UNCTAD, *The Role of Multilateral Commitments in Commodity Trade,* Geneva, December 1974; FAO, *The Long-Term Contract,* Rome, 1953.

3 A complex but interdependent world

3.1 Restructuring the international system

It would be foolish for the industrial countries to underestimate the consequences of the oil crisis and to assume that, after an interval to restructure their industrial set-ups and build some production sites overseas, the old process of international economic relationships and thus the former pattern of internal growth could continue without substantial change.

Nevertheless, the oil crisis has brought about only a limited shift in the international commodity and money markets, and the oil-producing countries are likely to remain underdeveloped for many years to come.[1]

The challenges posed by the current changes in world economic and financial relationships - which the oil crisis of October 1973 has accelerated - will have to be met, therefore, if the Western World wants to survive.

Despite the growth in prosperity of the industrialised world during the last twenty-five years, the development of the West has succeeded only in creating islands of prosperity which have absorbed the greatest part of the world resources and condemned large areas to stagnation and degradation. The drift from the land and the migration from south to north have increased the imbalances between town and countryside, between developed and underdeveloped areas, while the development of the world economy is organised, on a selfish basis, by a minority.

To bypass the current crisis, the West has to move quickly to an era in which the industrial nations, along with oil-producing countries and the other developing states, will co-operate to build a new international economic order characterised by peace among all nations. This era will be marked by the ending of post-war domination by the United States and the Soviet Union, with many more countries - even quite small ones - again exerting leverage on the international system. Before a more autonomous and balanced pattern of economic and social growth can be achieved, it is essential, however, to confront three basic problems:

1 The establishment of a progressive international division of labour involving a massive transfer of labour-intensive manufacturing jobs and

energy-based industries to the developing world.

2 The protection of a relative but substantial national economic independence.

3 A fairer distribution of income between nations, regions and social classes.

Relocation of industry does not merely mean exporting Western pollution to the poorer countries. Rather, it should reduce the flow of migrant workers to the advanced countries, and lower consumer prices by transferring manufacture into lower-wage regions. Above all, it must imply that industrial countries will not continue to export everything, including Arab processed oil, but instead allow the developing world to build a relatively autonomous and self-sustained economy so that it can join the world economic system.

National economic independence is to be protected both through diversification of the industrial base and of international economic relations, and - by a concerted effort at international level - through curbing the growth of cartels and control of the giant multinationals which are major contributors to economic instability and have grown beyond the reach of traditional government controls. While even the US economy has become the North American division of the giant corporations, their world liquidity levels (estimated at over $US 300 billion, five times as much as the 1974 capital surplus of the OPEC states) prevent governments from controlling global money supplies and, particularly, global banking transactions. To assert control over these corporations, tax and antitrust laws must be changed and the corporations themselves must be required to disclose more data to the various governments, including information on foreign investment in the enterprise, above a certain level. In addition, governments must assume direct control over essential industries. Thus, since October 1973, it has become clear that, in the framework of their relationships with the oil-producing nations, the governments of consumer countries must modify their previous role and abide by a new set of rules co-ordinating all the essential stages of the oil industry, from the import of crude oil to the processing and marketing of oil products. The governments of the producing countries have already taken over majority control of crude-oil production. And continuation of the international oil companies' role of middlemen between producers and consumers would constitute no real guarantee for the West. While occasionally converging with those of producer countries, the aims of the oil companies do not necessarily coincide with those of the consumer countries, in regard to security of supply at relatively stable prices. When a crisis occurs, the consumers suffer immediately, and are obliged to pay higher prices for a product that they cannot do without, while the giant corporations increase their profits. The oil companies cannot be held responsible for the pricing policy of the firms of industrial countries and, therefore, cannot guarantee the terms of trade covering oil and industrial goods. Only governments can enter agreements whereby those terms of trade are duly considered. Moreover, it is intolerable that countries largely dependent on imports are supplied almost exclusively by corporations having their decision-making centre in a competitive country. It is equally naïve to think of replacing the major oil firms by national companies, which, in their turn, might follow sectional interests, as witnessed in the unprecedented criminal charges of illegal price-fixing and productive curtailment made in several countries (notably France and Japan). The energy policy, as well as the policies relating to other key raw materials, must be determined by governments alone, under rigorous scrutiny of the respective parliaments. In particular, governments should have the right to set the prices which the companies pay for crude oil and the prices they can charge for oil products, allowing only a fair return on their investments, i.e. for their technical but subordinate role.

Along with the setting-up of solidarity funds such as the envisaged OPEC Fund and the Third Window of the World Bank, industrial relocation will raise the incomes of the poorer nations and more employment, and consequently more spending power, will be achieved through items produced locally, and mainly by labour-intensive methods.[2] However, *an equitable distribution of income* can be attained only through a polyvalent growth model, centred on the revitalisation of neglected sectors, such as agriculture, and the massive development of small- and medium-size enterprises. At the same time, there must be a new pattern of community living, based on new housing, culture and health care, with public transport facilities and crime prevention. Likewise, in the interest of society at large, the business system must be restructured, in the knowledge that the individual's drive for his own interests will not necessarily work towards community welfare. In particular, there must be heightened responsibility within industry as to the effect of technology, and also greater commitment to planning of a global scale. Additionally, a new conception of the social relationships within the firm must be achieved in order to restructure the system of profits and penalties and define the workers' role, in respect of their increased responsibility.[3]

3.2 The adjustment problems

Tremendous problems of adjustment arise from the problems discussed above. So far as a new international division of labour is concerned, there is one major, and recurring, difficulty: developing countries are primarily interested in extending their own industrial base, while the firms of the industrial countries focus on the overall economics of integrated operation. Thus, for example, the Japanese expressed interest in helping to build a refinery in Iran provided that, in return, they would receive the refined products. On realising that the Iranians wanted these products to supply a local petrochemical plant, the Japanese lost interest. Similarly, the direct-reduction steelworks which the Germans are helping to build in the Middle East is conceivable if the steel, or a fair part of it, is exported to Europe for finishing and later manufacture. Since it is in Europe that the market exists, it makes less sense for the Middle East nations to try to pass on to the next stages of manufacture. The same rationale applies to chemicals.[4] Nevertheless, it is by a 'diplomatic' approach to the use of resources, as suggested earlier, that the industrial countries and the developing nations can carry out the long-delayed and inevitable economic transformation whereby the transfer of industries and jobs is the result of long-range international planning. In this way, redundancies and business closures, as well as possible world gluts in the eighties, can be dealt with constructively, to avoid a breakdown in the world's trading system. With this in mind – and as suggested by L. Emmerij, Director of the WEP (World Employment Program) – an effective way of helping the Third World would be to provide aid for the donor countries in order to cope with problems of industrial adjustment.

Moreover, it is clear that a global understanding on long-term international planning has to aim at a *better equilibrium in world markets* and assure larger outlets for the exports of developing countries. Despite the gradual preferences and easing of selective tariffs, the trade policies of the OECD countries still include a wide array of non-tariff barriers which are often applied whether or not the products exported by developing nations compete with domestically produced articles. Similarly, the governments of the developing nations, instead of linking import savings with infant industry protection, could perhaps simplify their import procedures and curtail the use of import protection in sectors where imports could promote domestic investment and production.

Thus, through a concerted effort, e.g. in the framework of the Tokyo Round, the international community should seek new rules of multilateral surveillance over now sacrosanct domestic policies such as farm price supports, subsidies, and export arrangements permitting, for example, American exporting firms to postpone indefinitely payment of taxes on half of their export earnings. Also needed are new standards to regulate protectionist measures which cope with 'market disruption'. For instance, orderly methods of trade adjustment could be implemented, as in the market-sharing system current between the United States and Mexico for processing strawberries. Alternatively, representatives of governments, industries and trade unions of the countries involved could meet, with the object of improving the market situation by agreement on restriction of direct and indirect subsidies, provision for the exchange of information, and by discussion of the problems of market access and the potential for expansion of markets, etc.[5]

However, while the concern about access to raw materials, stimulated by the energy crisis, must be dealt with primarily in the context of a system of multilateral contracts, some amendment of the GATT rules covering export controls should also be considered, if the risk of international economic conflict is to be reduced. Thus, for example, export controls should be the subject of advance notification and consultation, with adequate compensation where export taxes are introduced unjustifiably.[6]

Equally, a concerted international effort is necessary to write *a new monetary constitution for the world,* with the aim of developing a system of reserves and settlements to replace the dollar standard and of providing an orderly adjustment of current-account positions, so as to combat inflation and prevent deflation; similarly, capital flows should be channelled to areas where investment opportunities exceed local savings; incentives for disequilibrating capital movements should be removed; there should be investment of substantial sums by countries that run prolonged current-account surpluses; and an increased use of credit arrangements such as *ad hoc* swap arrangements, IMF loans and related facilities.

All these needs were emphasised by the oil crisis. In the Committee of Twenty in June 1974, only a limited agreement was possible on the basket-SDR guidelines for floating and the setting-up of an SDR 3 billion oil facility. In January 1975 the interim committee of the Boards of Governors of the IMF agreed to continue the oil facility (on an expanded basis of SDR 5 billion); to subsidise the interest burden of loans contracted by the thirty-three poorest developing countries; to increase by 32·5 per cent the IMF quotas (bringing the size of the Fund up to SDR 39 billion); to modify the Fund's operational rules, in order to make all currencies usable at the Fund's discretion by eliminating members' *de facto* veto power; and to double the quotas of the major oil exporters whilst those of other lesser developed countries were to remain constant. In addition, for the first time, the United States agreed to abolish an official price for gold and allow national monetary authorities to buy and sell gold.

Other important amendments of the IMF's articles, however, still arouse serious difficulties. The system of flexible exchange rates, introduced in March 1973, has not succeeded in moderating inflation. Indeed, by weakening monetary discipline, the floating-rate system has contributed to the extreme inflationary bias. Nor has the floating-rate system prevented unemployment from rising in many countries, despite the increased autonomy of monetary policy that floating rates were expected to provide. In addition, the US concession of abolishing the official price of gold and allowing national monetary authorities to buy and sell gold (presumably at market prices) has provoked reaction from the oil-exporting countries which are afraid that such a decision, if implemented, might nullify the effect of the increase in oil prices. For if gold at market prices is to be used in payment for oil imports or as collateral against borrowings, and if the industrial nations keep their gold reserves at their present dollar value, the revaluation of gold to market prices will mean an increase in international liquidity by something like $US 180 billion, given the present official market price of gold and with current gold reserves. From this increase, the industrial nations would receive $US 150·6 billion, enough to pay for their oil over the next three to four years. Hence, at a stroke, the world's industrialised nations would have solved their oil problem and loaded the oil producers with unwanted holdings of gold.

A reformed system of exchange-rate management, as well as precise aid commitments to the least developed countries, on the plus value eventually obtained from the gold stocks, are therefore imperative. Moreover, a large liquidity pool combined with a meaningful multilateral system of sanctions (managed by a revitalised IMF) is required to discipline the upsurge in international money supply, the activities of the international banks (which do not provide convenient information sources) and of recalcitrant deficit/surplus countries. Otherwise, we may well witness the onset of a revolt against paper money at the international level leading to retrogressive developments, such as a return to barter (which, in fact, is already becoming one of the most rapidly growing elements of world trade even for the sophisticated traders of the West), together with the non-convertibility of currencies and the creation of monetary zones based on a few key currencies.

International co-operation on a wholly new scale is equally needed to solve *the inflation–unemployment dilemma* so that the policies which are used to achieve a viable equilibrium in one country are not vitiated by offsetting action by other countries. In fact, the need for competitive adjustment policies induced the OECD countries, in May 1974, to accept the pledge that they would refrain from introducing or intensifying import restrictions. However, measures to cut imports have been adopted (Israel imposed a 40 per cent import deposit; Denmark raised indirect taxes on a large number of items; Finland imposed a 15 per cent import surcharge; Australia limited the imports of textiles and clothing; and the EEC banned imports of beef), while other restrictive actions (for cars, shoes, textiles, etc.) are envisaged by other countries. Further international co-operation is therefore essential, especially as the incentive for competitive policies could be greatly intensified by a serious recession, and deficit countries might feel obliged to spread deflation round the world by unduly deflating their own economies. In particular, as suggested by *The Economist* (18 January 1975), the best way to strengthen the defence against restrictive measures is by

> . . . explicit agreement that each big country undertakes the internal restimulation that would be appropriate if the world is to aim, for instance, at a 2 per cent stimulation of gross world product. If any country with a strong balance of payments feels it cannot undertake such a stimulation - because it offended its anti-inflationary rectitude - then it should have some obligation to follow its anti-inflationary policies in ways that did not export slump to other peoples (namely it should upvalue its currency or permit the original scarce currency clauses of the IMF charter to operate so that special import licences be imposed against some exports of its goods). If any country, such as Britain or Italy, wanted to mop up its unemployment more strenuously than a 2 per cent on gross world product formula would allow, then Britain and Italy could have a mixture of rights and obligations to undertake the extra restimulation in a way that improved its balance of payments and did not spread more inflation to the rest of the world. The rights could include special dispensation to devalue or even to impose some import controls, i.e. the obligations that Britain and Italy could not borrow still more abroad without new wage–price controls.[7]

Another major task is to *reconcile an enlightened nationalism with an enlightened internationalism,* at a time when the spirit of national identity has become very strong. Indeed, the international division of labour – and the consequent movement between countries of people, capital and technical know-how – must reflect the opportunity of all nations, both developing and developed, to share effectively in the benefits of economic prosperity and to reclaim control of their national destinies. It is no surprise that, as a result of the events of October 1973, the worldwide oil business, long dominated by a handful of integrated international operators, is now breaking up into national oil companies owned and run by the governments of both importing and exporting countries that can negotiate directly among themselves. Even in the United States, the AFL–CIO suggests that the oil companies be made into government-regulated utilities, subject to stringent regulation, and the Atlantic Council insists on the creation of a powerful Energy Supply Authority which would assume complete responsibility for energy supply actions. Equally significant is the major policy action taken by the Japanese Government to revise the nation's antimonopoly law to curb the proliferation of cartels; the action undertaken by the US Justice Department to break up the American Telephone and Telegraph Company (the world's largest privately owned corporation); the bold move of the EEC Commission against the so-called 'seven sisters' (accused of violating Article 86 of the Rome Treaty by abusing their collective monopoly status in Holland), which delineated their rights and duties and emphasised participation of local public and private interests with foreign investors, reconciling national development goals and priorities with the interests of international co-operation.

Moreover, small developing countries should be urged to unite, to build indigenous technical capability, to introduce economies of scale and, more generally, to put stronger emphasis on their common interest. Although such action has already emerged (e.g. the Caribbean Free Trade Association, the Arab Common Market, the Latin American Free Trade Association and the Andean Pact), vast sources of bargaining power in the developing countries remain untapped. To some extent, therefore, as P. Streeten, a Chatham House expert, argues[8] national self-interest will have to be sacrificed if the developing nations wish to match the power and skills of the transnational corporations and achieve a transfer of technology on acceptable terms.

Finally, another central problem is to reconcile material progress with improvements in *the quality of life* and to bring increasingly important social affairs into the sphere of international co-operation. As E. van Lennep, OECD Secretary-General, declared: 'We cannot go on accepting the damage caused by economic growth and then build up increasingly vast bureaucratic machines to repair this damage. We must, on the contrary, work towards a new quality-oriented process of growth which will make welfare one of the central objectives of the growth process itself'.[9] In particular, the methods of organising production must reflect the right of workers both to an adequate income and to satisfying work. Equal opportunities must be produced for urban and rural sectors. Industrial democracy must be promoted, and new approaches introduced to prevent disease, stimulate educational and occupational opportunities, and curb crime. Further, through pollution control and various social charges on employers, it is necessary to minimise the adverse impact of quality-oriented national policies on world trade and investment. Although the different economic, social and physical conditions make complete harmonisation impossible, international agreement and rules of conduct can be drawn in accordance with guidelines and standards agreed, with flexible consultation procedures.

3.3 A gap in understanding splits the Atlantic

A reformed world economic system requires the three centres of world economic power - the United States, Western Europe and Japan - to assume joint responsibilities in reordering their relationships. In fact, if economic differences drive them apart, no major international economic initiative can succeed.

There are, however, considerable obstacles to new forms of co-operation that will allow the industrial countries jointly to assume economic policy responsibilities hitherto largely discharged by the United States. Since the 1967 Kennedy Round, controversy over trade, agriculture, investment, the economic burden of defence, and international monetary policy, has become at times more strident, and has led more frequently to confrontation than to negotiations. Despite compromises such as the Atlantic Declaration of June 1974, the establishment of an emergency oil-sharing mechanism in the event of another embargo and the French change of attitude towards co-operation with the IEA's efforts, the events of October 1973 have helped to drive nations towards mutual mistrust. For example, it has been alleged that 'America readily gave in to OPEC because increased oil prices were seen as a quick and easy way of slowing down the Japanese and European economies whose exports are bothering the United States mightily and which are more hurt by rises in oil prices than any other nations'.[10] Although such action is attributed to negligence rather than malicious intent Professor M.A. Adelman, of MIT, points out that 'the US has done more than any other country to help the (OPEC) cartel'.[11] In effect, the 'Kissinger Plan' (based on a guaranteed floor-price for oil and a $US 25 billion recycling facility set up outside the IMF and largely controlled by the United States) has embarrassingly confirmed that, except for Britain and Norway, Kissinger's America has more in common with the OPEC countries (and with the Soviet Union which also enjoyed considerable benefits from increased oil prices) than with Western Europe and Japan.

Furthermore, after the American attacks against the EEC common agricultural policy, Europeans were bewildered to learn that, according to the US Secretary of State, a common floor-price on oil imports to industrial countries might have been protected by a system similar to that of the CAP. Clearly, the proposal to create consortia (with a reasonable degree of equalisation among Western partners) is a much wiser option to prevent a monopoly of alternative energy sources being added to a crude-oil monopoly.

Mutual mistrust has in addition been deepened by:

(i) the military alert of 24 October 1973 (which Kissinger promised to explain but never did);

(ii) the ambiguous threats of military action to seize the oilfields (when, at the same time, 2,000 marines experimentally disembarked on the coasts of Sardinia, and American mercenaries were being recruited by those very same Arab countries which, according to Kissinger, it might have become necessary to attack);

(iii) the coincidence that US administration interests have corresponded to those of the major oil companies (e.g. the State Department tried, as revealed by J. Sawhill, former Director of the Federal Energy Administration, to block an independent study on the role of multinational oil companies, a study that was actively resisted by the companies);[12]

(iv) increasing relegation of European policy to a subordinate role, the point of gravity of European energy policy having been moved from Brussels to Paris in the International Energy Agency;

(v) the priority conferred on *détente* with the Soviet Union (as spectacularly apparent in the mammoth Russian cereal purchases that sent international wheat prices soaring, in 1972 and 1975)[13] and by the European Security Conference (to be considered no more than a replay of Yalta);

(vi) the sour taste left all over Europe by the so-called 'arms deal of the century' (the $US 2 billion sale of 350 American F-16 to four NATO countries) since what is at stake is not only more dependence on the United States even for basic military equipment but the decline of any future prospect of European political union, which is hard to conceive without a vigorous defence programme;

(vii) the restrictive congressional plan to control all foreign investors wishing to buy more than five per cent of the shares of a US corporation with assets of more than $US 1 million (America having built its own prosperity by investing abroad, particularly in Western Europe and, at the same time, American industrialists installed in the German Federal Republic refusing to apply the German system of worker participation in their factories);

(viii) the systematic imposition of countervailing duties against European imports at a time when the GATT multilateral trade liberalisation talks had begun in Geneva and when no damage to the US domestic industry had been proved, as required under GATT rules;

(ix) the fact that the US Treasury has allowed exorbitant and strategic fluctuations in the value of the dollar against most major currencies in order to conclude huge trade deals - notably with Iran and Saudi Arabia - and obtain a lion's share of the petrodollars.

Kissinger has certainly been a very able man and a very efficient negotiator. However, under his guidance, the United States has given exaggerated priority to American interests, causing serious division and disarray in the Western World. We can affirm that US foreign policy towards Western Europe, in particular, has been a disaster in the last few years.

The attempt to impose a new 'pax Americana' by exploiting the oil crisis to defeat European economic nationalism and using the divisions between European governments has widely provoked anti-American sentiment, notably in Greece, Turkey and Cyprus, has expanded communist influence in Portugal, Italy, France and Spain and strengthened the presence of the Soviet Union (which, despite *détente,* still desires to be politically predominant in Europe). Even Greece, where the electoral victory of Caramenlis is a bright spot, has withdrawn from NATO, breaking the Atlantic Alliance's southern flank, while Portugal's Azores base may soon become unavailable to the United States as a military springboard. Cyprus, in its frustration, may turn to Russia for help that it believes unobtainable in the West, and President Makarios has expressed support for a Soviet proposal to call an international conference on the problem. In fact, as J. R. Schaetzel, former US Ambassador to the EEC, points out, 'instead of supporting European unity other than with cheapened language, Kissinger's studied neutralism changes to hostility when the Europeans show signs of actually uniting, as they have attempted in the new dialogue between the European Community and the Arabs'.[14]

To avoid further deterioration of Atlantic ties, which could move Western Europe to a neutral, but communist-influenced, position such as Finland's, drastic reappraisal of Euro-American relationships must be based on genuine common interests. Kissinger's statement, 'Either we lead or no one leads,' is inaccurate; its real meaning is that so far the United States has accepted only those actions which suited American interest. With the exception of the Kennedy Round, Atlantic co-operation has not reflected a discussion between equal partners, but only American decisions (in respect of which European governments have often rivalled each other to comply, in order to satisfy immediate specific interests).

Recognition of Western interdependence requires the United States to abandon any attempt to disrupt the process of European unification in an Atlantic free trade area, and also gives unequivocal support for intense but progressive European nationalism. As Sir Christopher Soames, Vice-President of the European Commission, has stated: 'Nationalism has been one of the great motive forces in European history, and although many terrible crimes and follies have been committed in its name, it is and will remain a fundamental element in the sense of identity of our peoples, especially in France and the German Federal Republic since – as was recognised by Sir Winston Churchill in his famous Zürich speech – "there can be no revival of Europe without a spiritually great France and a spiritually great Germany".'[15]

A stronger Europe would, of course, imply more economic competition for American enterprises and the remaking of world rules of commerce, investment and money, less geared to American specifications. Such an adjustment, however, should not excessively worry our partners on the other side of the Atlantic. For, while the forces and stimuli of fair competition constitute the basis on which the Western World is built, the United States – which must learn to redefine its power and political relationships in ways relevant to the new realities – is in no mood to maintain its leadership as a resolver of world problems, domestic affairs outweighing international problems more than at any time since the thirties. And improved Atlantic co-operation in the economic, technological, social and strategic sectors – on the basis of mutual confidence and respect – will more than offset wounded interests and become a stabilising factor for the whole international system. In fact, as far as the key problem of petroleum is concerned, we must discard the idea that America and Western Europe have divergent interests. Both partners need to diversify their sources of energy, to develop alternative resources and energy-saving technologies, and above all, to enhance co-operation with the Arabs and Iranians. For it is now estimated that American oil imports will not decline in the next five years as the White House has forecast. In fact US domestic production of crude oil has been declining since 1970, but even the arrival of oil from Alaska is expected to do little more than stabilise the level of US production.

In turn, Western Europe, in addition to demonstrating its sensitivity to the acute political and psychological problems of the United States, has to build its political will on new bases. In particular, the European political class - to be reinvigorated through the inclusion of younger and better-educated people - should be conscious of the absolute need to create common centres of decision-making, based on democratic principles and giving vitality and imagination to European policy, in order to meet the wish for international solidarity held by new generations to whom Europe now appears as an overcentralised and overbureaucratic construction. Western Europe, the United States and Japan should, moreover, work together to develop more co-operative efforts toward less developed countries, to promote a better distribution of incomes in the world, to fight poverty and unemployment, and to face the explosion of violence, etc. There should be a competent international forum to deal with trade, financing and development in an integrated manner. For it is only by recognising the interdependence of these problems that we can tackle the difficulties that beset the world community - not through piecemeal approaches that tackle one problem to the detriment of others. Additionally, there must be a new and flexible mechanism to solve the adjustment problems while avoiding excessive bureaucracy.

Prime attention has also to be given to the Middle East developing nations. The West has not only to accept the new, irreversible, economic realities created by the oil crisis of October 1973, but to support Arab/Iranian nationalism as the best guarantee against Russian influence in the region. As H. Heikal, former editor of *Al Ahram,* points out, 'Breaking the oil cartel's power would only mean that the West loses completely the enormous strategic value of the Persian/Arab Gulf area since Arab moderates would be swept out of power or become anti-West radicals'.[16]

Notes

[1] J. Aboaf, 'Iran seems Unlikely to Become Big World Economic

Power', *International Herald Tribune,* 4 March 1974.
[2] P. Harrison, 'A Conference to Share the Jobs', *The Financial Times,* 12 December 1974.
[3] Charles Goux, 'Pour une nouvelle orientation de l'activité économique', *Le Monde Diplomatique,* November 1974.
[4] 'The Year Arabia Discovered Money and Europe Discovered Arabia (and Iran)', *The Economist,* 11 January 1975.
[5] For a wider analysis see R.N. Gardner, 'The Hard Road to World Order', *Foreign Affairs,* vol. 52, no. 53, 3 April 1974.
[6] C.F. Bergsten, *Completing the GATT: Toward New International Rules to Govern Export Controls,* British-North American Committee, National Planning Association, 1974.
[7] 'All Turn Round', *The Economist,* 18 January 1975.
[8] *Ceres,* vol. 5, no. 2, March/April 1972.
[9] A speech made on 7 October 1974 to the Tokyo Symposium commemorating the 10th anniversary of Japan's membership of the OECD. See also Norman Macrae, 'Pacific Century 1975-2075?', *The Economist,* 4 January 1975.
[10] 'The Phoney Oil Crisis', *The Economist,* 7 July 1974.
[11] Statement addressed in a letter to *The Economist,* 7 December 1974. J.E. Akins refuted this thesis in another letter published by *The Economist* on 4 August 1974.
[12] M. Berger, 'State Department Tried to Block US Oil Study', *International Herald Tribune,* 17 August 1974.
[13] J. Trager, *Amber Waves of Grain,* A. Field Books, New York, 1973.
[14] J.R. Schaetzel, 'To Rescue Europe from the Precipice', *International Herald Tribune,* 9 September 1974.
[15] 'National Patriotism and European Patriotism', address given in Berne, 31 January 1975, to the Winston Churchill Foundation.
[16] 'Heikal Breaks Year-Long Silence', *International Herald Tribune,* 20 January 1975.

PART II

THE ABSORPTIVE CAPACITY OF THE ARAB WORLD AND ECONOMIC CO-OPERATION WITH WESTERN COUNTRIES

4 At the threshold of a great leap forward

4.1 Population and the labour force

The Middle East and North Africa embrace some twenty-two countries with an estimated population of about 200 million people.[1] The region covers much of the Arab World – whose population in 1971 was around 127 million. Turkey and Iran are largely non-Arab countries. Non-Muslim communities are also important in Lebanon and Cyprus. In terms of population, Turkey, Egypt, Iran, Morocco, Algeria and Iraq are the six largest nations. At the other end of the scale, there are a number of small states (Qatar, the United Arab Emirates, Bahrain, Oman, Kuwait and Cyprus), each with less than 1 million inhabitants, while several other countries (Mauritania, the Democratic Republic of Yemen, Libya, Jordan, Lebanon, the Yemen Arab Republic, Syria and Saudi Arabia) have between 1 million and 7 million inhabitants.

Although population density is generally low, it nevertheless conceals extremes. The major concentration occurs along the Mediterranean and the valleys of the Nile, Tigris and Euphrates which combine fertile land with an abundance of water and mild weather. The remainder of the region is less fertile, with a substantial portion of desert and uncultivable land. The Sudan apart, the demographic pressure on arable land is high, especially (but not exclusively) in the south where the ratio reaches a very high level in Kuwait and Saudi Arabia.

The region is characterised by a high rate of population growth, on average about 3 per cent per year, varying between a minimum of 2·1 per cent in Mauritania and a maximum of 9·9 per cent in Kuwait. *Intraregional migration* is largely accountable for the high national growth rates in the Gulf states. With current rates of growth, all the countries of the region are expected to double their populations within thirty years.[2] In the Gulf states rapid economic development and continuous immigration mean that the population is likely to be doubled in less than ten years.

Accelerated population growth will, of course, have an impact on the already high population densities. Thus, for example, in Lebanon continued current population growth would imply a population density of about 450 (as against the current 218 persons per square kilometre) by the year 2000. Moreover, the high rates of population growth adversely affect the growth rates of national product. Thus, in the extreme case of Kuwait, between 1965 and 1971, there was a negative (–2·1 per cent) growth rate in *per capita* national production; in this case, the high rate of population growth is largely the result of massive immigration streams (especially from Palestine, Iran, Pakistan, India and, to a lesser extent, Oman, Lebanon and Egypt). In 1972, non-Kuwaitis in fact constituted 57 per cent of Kuwait's total population.

Analysis according to age group indicates *the extreme youth of the region's population.* In almost all countries, the percentage of the population below 15 years of age is more than 44 per cent. However, most of the Gulf countries, where the population structures are strongly affected by immigration, diverge from this regional pattern. With the exception of Lebanon and the Syrian Arab Republic, the population segment above 65 years of age does not exceed 3 per cent.

Mortality rates have continued to decline during the past four years, largely because of better health care and improved sanitation. High fertility and a declining mortality rate are the main features affecting the age structure of the population throughout the region. These population characteristics have economic implications, since the proportion of potential workers (males of 14–65 years) is markedly lower in all countries of the region (between 20 and 30 per cent)[3] than is the average for the developing countries (42 per cent), the industrialised countries (45 per cent) and the world as a whole (43 per cent).

Setting aside emigration to oil-rich states and to European countries (especially from North Africa and Turkey), vast dislocations of population have taken place throughout the region, either through rural to urban migration, or through population movements resulting from the Arab–Israeli conflicts. In particular, all countries of the region have become increasingly urbanised, most cities and towns at least doubling in size over a decade or two, and some cities, e.g. Baghdad, Beirut, Cairo and Kuwait, having incorporated surrounding towns and extended outside their city walls. The spread of urbanisation is as yet uneven throughout the area. Apart from Bahrain, Kuwait and Lebanon, the most densely populated countries of the Middle East have less than 45 per cent of their populations living in urban centres, which leaves ample scope for further urbanisation over the next ten or twenty years. On the other hand, successive Arab–Israeli conflicts have resulted in growing numbers of Palestinian refugees throughout the region, enforced migration from the border areas of southern Lebanon to other parts of Lebanon and increased numbers of Syrian refugees from the Golan Heights. Of approximately 3 million Palestinians (1970), over 1 million lived in those parts of Jordan and the Arab Republic of Egypt occupied by Israel in 1967 (670,000 on the West Bank and 364,000 in the Gaza Strip); 340,000 resided in Israel and 900,000 in the East Bank of Jordan, while the remainder (649,000) were mainly spread over a number of Arab countries, with concentrations in Lebanon (240,000), the Syrian Arab Republic (155,000) and Kuwait (140,000).

From the economic standpoint, agriculture is the largest provider of employment, except for Kuwait and Bahrain where only a small fraction of the labour force is employed on the land. Services (largely operated by the various governments) represent the second largest sector in most countries of the region, especially in the Gulf area (Kuwait, Bahrain, the United Arab Emirates, Iraq, Saudi Arabia) and in Libya, Lebanon, Cyprus, Sudan, Egypt and Morocco. Manufacturing ranks third, accounting for about 21 per cent in Iran, 17·8 per cent in Lebanon, 14·1 per cent in Cyprus, 14 per cent in Kuwait, 12·3 per cent in Tunisia and 11·3 per cent in Egypt. Construction absorbs the fourth largest number (25·8 per cent of the work force in the United Arab Emirates, 17 per cent in Bahrain, 14·4 per cent in Kuwait, 12·5 per cent in Libya, 10·3 per cent in Saudi Arabia, 9·5 per cent in Cyprus) followed by commerce (17 per cent in Lebanon, 14·1 per cent in Kuwait, 12·6 per cent in Bahrain, 10·5 per cent in the United Arab Emirates). Oil (including mining) is the least important sector in employment, because of the heavily capital-intensive industry.

Table 4.1
The composition of the labour force in the Gulf states according to origin

Country	Year	Nationals	Expatriates	Expatriates as % of labour force
Bahrain	1971	37,950	22,351	37
Kuwait	1970	65,136	175,203	73
Qatar	1972	8,160	40,300	83
United Arab Emirates[a]	1972	7,940	37,235	82

[a] Figures for Abu Dhabi only.
Source: R.A. Mertz, *Education and Manpower in the Arabian Gulf*, Beirut, 1972.

In the last few years, employment has grown in all countries, but the regional imbalance is great. Shortage of skilled and unskilled labour is a feature of all major oil-producing countries, with the exception of Algeria and, to a much lesser extent, Bahrain. Unemployment, especially among the young (and particularly in agriculture), is dramatically high– even among the educated – in the densely populated poorer countries (e.g. Egypt, Morocco, Tunisia, Algeria, Turkey).

The number of persons engaged in technical skills and other key professions (engineers, doctors, teachers, accountants, etc.) is very small, even in those countries of the region which have become ultramodern and enjoy the reputation of entrepreneurial ability. Thus, in 1971, in Kuwait there were only 29 Kuwaiti doctors out of 581 and 56 Kuwaiti engineers out of 1,211. And 79 per cent of Kuwaiti civil servants were either illiterate or had completed only primary education.

Similarly, the educational level throughout the remainder of the working population is very low, with a scarcity of scientists and technicians, and a preponderance of graduates in literature, philosophy and law. Illiteracy (for males, varying from 25 per cent in Lebanon to 30, 46, 47, 49 and 61 per cent respectively in Kuwait, Bahrain, the Syrian Arab Republic, Jordan and Iraq) is a serious constraint on productivity in both industry and agriculture.[4]

Despite lack of data on income distribution, there is ample evidence of *intense economic dualism* and a widening gap between the technologically advanced and the traditional sectors. Thus, with the exception of Kuwait and Lebanon, none of the countries in the region has a GDP *per capita* in agriculture above 40 per cent of that in the combined non-agricultural sectors. In fact, emphasis on economic growth and industrial output has had a polarising effect, causing inequalities not only between urban and rural areas but between different regions. Moreover, social policies in education, welfare and employment have been designated corollaries to economic policies thus, in turn, accentuating disparities already present.

4.2 Three major groups of countries

The substantial acceleration of output in recent years[5] is enhanced by the extremely ambitious development plans of the twenty-two countries under review. These are identifiable in three major groups. The first group includes the major oil-producing nations whose highly 'transitional' economy is in something of a limbo between the underdeveloped and developed.[6] By their *per capita* income, growth rate of GNP, capital surplus, high savings rate, favourable balance of payments, high level of

Table 4.2

Labour force distribution according to the main economic sectors

Country		Agriculture, fishing, etc.		Manufac-turing		Petrol-mineral Sector		Construction		Transport, communications		Commerce		Other Sectors		Total employed
		Total ('000)	%	Total ('000)	%	Total ('000)	%	Total ('000)	%	Total ('000)	%	Total ('000)	%	Total ('000)	%	('000)
Morocco	1971	1,988·0	54·7	388·3	10·6	34·8	0·9	154·0a	4·2	100·4	3·0	260·3	7·2	705·2	19·4	3,631·0
Algeria	1969	1,337·0	60·8	130·5	5·9	15·5	0·7	85·0	3·9	129·0	5·9	200·0	9·1	302·0	13·7	2,199·0
Tunisia	1972	800·0	57·7	171·0	12·3	19·0	1·4	59·0a	4·2	43·0	3·1	83·0	6·0	212·0	15·3	1,387·0
Libya	1973	166·5	27·9	41·0	6·9	18·9	3·1	74·9	12·5	54·8	9·2	40·0	6·7	200·4	33·7	596·5
Egypt	1970–71	4,056·9	48·5	946·6	11·3	-	-	365·8	4·4	356·6	4·3	815·6b	9·7	1,823·5	21·8	8,365·0
Syria	1972	908·0	55·6	181·0	11·1	3·0	0·2	100·0	6·1	63·0	3·8	137·0	8·4	242·0	14·8	1,634·0
Lebanon	1970	101·7	18·9	95·6	17·8	-	-	35·0	6·5	38·2	7·1	91·6c	17·0	176·3	32·7	538·4
Turkey	1972	8,762·2	64·1	1,263·6	9·2	103·7	0·8	412·1	3·0	399·3d	2·9	737·1c	5·4	1,995·9	14·6	13,673·9
Cyprus e	1970	95·5	35·9	37·5f	14·1	4·9	1·8	25·3	9·5	12·0	4·5	25·0	9·4	65·8	24·7	266·0
Mediterranean area		18,215·8	56·4	3,255·1	10·1	199·8	0·6	1,311·1	4·1	1,196·3	3·7	2,389·6	7·4	5,723·1	17·7	32,290·8
Jordan	1970	115·0	32·9	21·0	6·0	3·0	0·9	7·0	2·0	11·0d	3·1	23·0c	6·6	170·0	48·5	350·0
Iraq	1972	1,434·7	55·3	160·0	6·2	16·5	0·6	69·0	2·6	154·0	5·6	155·0	6·0	603·4	23·3	2,592·6
Kuwait	1970	4·1	1·7	32·1	13·7	7·2	3·0	33·7	14·4	12·1	5·2	33·0	14·1	112·2	47·9	234·4
United Arab Emirates	1968	13·5	17·6	3·0	3·9	3·2	4·0	19·9	25·8	8·5	11·1	8·0	10·5	20·9	27·1	77·0
Iran	1972–73	3,659·0	40·1	890·0g	20·7	50·0h	0·5	710·0	7·8	-	-	2,740·0	30·0	80·0	0·9	9,129·0
Oman j	1972	124·0	82·7	-	-	5·0k	3·3	6·0	4·0	-	-	-	-	15·0	10·0	150·0
Bahrain	1971	4·0	6·5	4·1	6·8	4·3	7·1	10·4	17·0	7·7	12·7	7·7	12·6	22·8	37·3	61·1
Arabian Gulf area		5,354·3	42·5	2,110·2	16·8	89·1	0·8	856·0	6·8	193·3	1·5	2,966·7	23·3	1,009·3	8·0	12,594·1
Saudi Arabia	1966	464·7	46·2	41·0	4·1	25·6	2·5	104·0	10·3	44·0	4·4	95·7	9·5	231·6	23·0	1,006·6
Sudan	1971	5,920·0	80·0	370·0	5·0	-	-	44·4	0·6	44·4	0·5	155·4	2·1	865·8	11·7	7,400·0
Yemen Arab Republic	1972	1,688·0	76·2	12·0	0·5	-	-	-	-	289·0i	13·0	-	-	225·0	10·2	2,214·0
Red Sea area		8,072·7	76·0	413·0	3·9	25·6	0·2	148·4	1·4	377·4	3·7	251·1	2·4	1,922·4	12·4	10,620·6
Total		31,642·8	57·0	5,788·3	10·4	314·5	0·6	2,315·5	4·2	1,767·0	3·1	5,607·4	10·1	8,054·8	14·5	55,505·5

[a]Housing and public works; [b]Trade and finance; [c]Commerce and hotels; [d]Transport, communications and storage; [e]Figures based on the 1960 Census of Population, the 1962 Industrial Census and the Annual Survey of Industrial Population; [f]Industry, electricity, gas, water and sanitary services; [g]Manufacturing and mining; [h]Oil; [i]Services; [j]Estimates; [k]Oil, banking, commercial activities.

Sources: The Arab Planning Institute and Kuwait Economic Society, *Seminar on Investment Policies of Arab Oil Producing Countries,* 18–20 February 1974, Kuwait; H. J. Budig and H Süer, *Middle East and North Africa Market Review 1973–74,* Gower Economic Publications/Advertising Research and Marketing Services Ltd., *Food and Agriculture Sector Country Development Brief Series, Sudan Country Development Brief,* Food and Agriculture Organisation; *United Nations Inter-Disciplinary reconnaissance mission, Bahrain,* vol. 1, UNESOB July 1972.

employment and availability of social services, the economies of this group fall into the developed category. Underdevelopment, however, is evident in the near-total reliance on a single product, the inadequate indigenous supply of capital goods and consumer products, and the narrowness of the domestic market which limits ample productive investment opportunities.

The second group includes the relatively more diversified economies with an established agricultural sector, a manufacturing sector which already has some impact on the development process, a reasonably developed infrastructure and proximity to European markets. In addition, in most of these countries, planning has a liberal bias.

The third group includes the least developed countries, characterised by low *per capita* GNP (especially if the mining and oil sector is excluded), rudimentary industry, subsistence agriculture, inadequate physical infrastructure and a low level of education. Around 80 per cent of these populations depend on agriculture and fisheries for a subsistence livelihood.

4.3 The development plans of the major oil-producing countries

The major oil-producing countries fall into two categories:

(a) Economies having a relatively satisfactory infrastructure and a balanced sectoral base on which to structure economic growth and planning. Iran, Algeria and Iraq are included.

Iran Total investment in this, second-largest oil-producing country of the region is, under the fifth plan (1973–78), projected at almost $US 70 billion by 1978. GNP is expected to approach $US 52 billion in 1978, attaining a growth rate of 51 per cent in 1974 and settling down to an increase of 26 per cent for the remaining three years.

Growth is expected to reach 18 per cent per annum for the industrial sector, 16·4 per cent for services, 7 per cent for agriculture. Iran's basic objective is rapid development of alternative sources to oil as the basis of the economy. Thus, intensive industrialisation – especially in the fields of petrochemicals, cars and steel – will advance more rapidly than forecast, to attain a 17 per cent annual rise. Moves to modernise agriculture also have high priority. However, the growth rate in agriculture may not exceed in real terms 3 to 4 per cent annually, the emphasis being on expansion of agro-industrial units and on raising domestic levels of crop production, especially to attain self-sufficiency in meat, sugar, grains and other basic foods. Iran's ambition is to become the major industrial power in the region. Prime Minister Amir Abbas Hoveyda describes it thus: 'Within twenty-five to thirty years our standard of living will surpass Japan, our production of steel per head will bypass Europe and within ten years it will be higher than that of the USSR.'

Already, Iran is the biggest consumer market in the Middle East, imports alone rising by over 20 per cent a year. Iran is also becoming a major supplier of Middle East and African markets. The Shah's resolute and ambitious rule supports Iranian development, with formidable expansion of the armed forces.

Politically, Iran has presented itself as a friend of the Western industrial nations, never having joined boycotts against the United States, Holland or any other country, including Israel, though being in a position militarily and strategically to keep open the Straits of Hormuz. Iran alone, the Shah claims, has put forward comprehensive schemes to relieve the balance of payments problems of the oil consumers, including the hard-hit countries of the underdeveloped world.

Iran's weaknesses are a lack of port facilities, a shortage of about 400,000 workers (mainly technical and managerial) and its agriculture, which only recently has received adequate attention. Also pressing is the need for closer integration of planning in different sectors of the economy to avoid bottlenecks seriously impeding overall development. Furthermore, the coolness displayed by the Shah's Arab neighbours – suspicious of renewed Persian imperialism – could produce intensified rivalry in the region, though the common interest in maintaining high oil prices has improved relations with the Arab World as was evident in the Shah's visit to Cairo, early in 1975, and above all, in the agreement resolving border conflicts with Iraq.

Algeria The total investment of DA 110 billion in the 1974–77 four-year plan – almost four times the investment target in the previous plan – places Algeria among the top countries in the Middle East development stakes. This record figure is, of course, the consequence of the increases in receipts from oil (production expected to reach 59 million tons by 1977) and from gas (25 milliard m^3 will be exported by 1977, while total reserves are at nearly 3,000 billion m^3).

Since rapid industrialisation is the keystone of Algeria's development strategy, the new plan again gives priority to the industrial sector, consolidating projects begun in the heavy industries during the previous plan. Projects aimed at improving infrastructure (particularly in communications and services in the commercial and technical sectors) and the neglected social services are also important. In addition, although consumer and luxury goods will continue to be discouraged, projects to increase the production of food processing and light industries will be introduced.

Economic performance – which in the eighties could make Algeria Africa's 'socialist Japan' – is one of the most successful in the developing world. Algeria has been able to gain control over both its natural resources and its development. The State now controls about 90 per cent of industry and 70 per cent of the work force. Foreign investment is limited to the hydrocarbon sector where Sonatrach – the state oil and gas company – holds a majority of 51 per cent in a number of joint ventures formed with foreign oil companies to explore and exploit oil resources. Further, the emphasis put by the planners on building an ultramodern and outward-looking industrial base by 1980 looks well placed to break the country from its underdevelopment cycle. Already there are three oil refineries with a fourth under construction which will bring capacity up to 13 million tons a year. Three gas liquefaction plants exist at the moment. A fourth will be completed in 1974 and two more are planned. Three petrochemicals centres are also being built. A large plastics industry began operation two years ago, and a wide range of fertiliser products is being manufactured. In 1973, at Annaba, a heavy-industry steelworks produced 700,000 tons of steel and is expected to reach 2 million tons by 1977–78. In addition, other industrial units are being set up in the food, textile, pharmaceutical, paper and cellulose, porcelain and other fields.

Although Algeria's priority is on the basic industries, the new plan gives more emphasis to agriculture, which provides for the needs of 70 per cent of the population, particularly through the backward-linked, multiplier-effect industries (fertiliser and tractor plants, plastics manufacture, etc.). Agricultural development, however, is lagging behind, mainly because the Algerians have tried to run the large, integrated French estates as socialist collective farms, with the usual disastrous results. New land measures initiated in 1971 should enable peasants to participate in more lucrative farms.

Lack of semi-skilled labour constitutes a constraint to the speed of industrialisation. Algerian oil, moreover, is the most vulnerable to the drop in international demand, and Algerian gas has to compete in Europe with Soviet and Iranian gas.

Iraq In its 1976–80 plan, the government assigned a major role to rapid industrialisation, and it is interested in the transition of the country's economy from agriculture to an agro-industrial one. A thorough attempt is therefore being made to absorb rising oil revenues through an ambitious programme of industrial expansion. Investment in industry alone in the 1974–75 financial year has been set at ID 225 million

($US 775 million).

In keeping with socialistic objectives, the industries in Iraq should, on the one hand, be able to meet basic consumer needs and amenities according to a predetermined standard of living and, on the other, build up a self-sustained and self-reliant growth. This requires adequate growth of: (i) consumer industries; (ii) processing industries which convert the available raw materials into intermediate and finished products, thus achieving maximum return for the country's raw materials and providing adequate resources for future growth; (iii) technologically advanced engineering industries so that, in time, Iraq may be able to take care of its future industrial development and projects.

The economy is basically dependent on agriculture and mineral oil, sale of which provides the main resource. The industrialisation programmes – centred on the role of the public sector – therefore have to be based on proper utilisation of agricultural output and mineral oil. Iraq has reached the stage when the input–output relationship between agriculture and industry is such that further progress of agriculture itself depends on the development of industries which can, on the one hand, consume the output of agriculture and, on the other, provide the required inputs (machinery, improved implements, fertilisers, etc.) for agriculture.

Iraq at present exports large quantities of crude oil. Gradually, these exports should be increasingly replaced by fuels, fertilisers and other intermediates based on mineral oil. The aim is therefore to set up large refineries, fertiliser factories and petrochemicals complexes to manufacture polyesters, polyvinyl chloride, plastics, organic chemicals, pesticides and insecticides, and other industrial products. In addition to oil, natural gas and mineral deposits exist in abundant quantities, while geological surveys are in progress for metallic minerals. Iraq also lays stress on the development of consumer-goods industries so that the country is able to support, from domestic production, the demand for essential items such as housing, processed foods, clothing and other day to day requirements. Development of these industries would also help to create a base for large and capital-goods industries.

Another interest is the development of heavy and large engineering industries so that the technological development is available for Iraq to establish and run sophisticated projects on its own, instead of relying on imports. Iraq is planning an integrated industrial structure, taking into account inter-industry links, so that maximum internal and external economies are achieved, and waste avoided. Towards this end, the programme is to establish industrial complexes comprising groups of interrelated products, e.g. salt, caustic soda, paper and rayon fibre are taken as a group, so that their input-output relationships are utilised for speedy industrialisation and maximum economic benefit.

In selection of industrial projects, size and technology are matched in accord with the economy and working conditions to yield maximum economies of scale and high returns on investment. Each case is considered on its merits, and since the developmental strategy is to expand industrial exports in the long run, products must be able to compete in the international market. Equal importance is given to medium and small-scale industries which are essential, on the one hand, to feed the large industries with various items and, on the other, to meet local consumer requirements on a diversified basis. Although the government is anxious to use available resources and oil revenues for accelerated growth, Iraq does not encourage the setting up of foreign projects. The emphasis is more on technical collaboration than on foreign financial interests and ownership. However, Arab nationals from other countries are allowed financial and investment interests.

Lack of properly qualified, skilled workers and the rigidities of the socialist industrial organisation constitute the other main constraints in the speedy economic growth of the country. Politically, the end of the Baghdad–Tehran confrontation in the northern Kurdish regions of Iraq marked the beginning of Iraq's cautious emergence from isolation towards a more active role in the Arab world and a softening towards the West. In fact, between 1968 and 1974, the growth of imports (mainly from Western Europe, Japan and the United States) has been phenomenal: from $US500 million to nearly $US6 billion. Thus, considering its potential wealth in agriculture and industry, plus oil reserves second only to those of Saudi Arabia, the new Iraq can no longer be treated as the outcast of the Arab world.

(b) Despite economic dynamism due to the rapid expansion of energy-based industries and their trading centres, other economies are constrained by manpower limitation, small domestic markets, scarcity of water and natural resources other than oil and gas, and a modest agricultural sector. These features characterise Saudi Arabia, Kuwait, Bahrain, Qatar and the Emirates – which all follow a fairly flexible and pragmatic planning approach. Although endowed with water resources and having more imperative planning, Libya is also included here.

Saudi Arabia The largest producer and exporter of oil in the region, with 25 per cent of proven global reserves, Saudi Arabia is moving rapidly from underdevelopment and stagnation to economic dynamism and advanced technology. Total investment under the second five-year plan

Table 4.3

Claims on resources, 1972

Country	% of GNP allocated to			% of total government expenditure	
	Consumption	Capital formation	Total government expenditure	Defence and internal security	Education
Morocco	72·7	13·1[a]	14·4	2·3	25·0
Algeria[c]	52·4	35·5[b]	16·0	9·9	12·0
Tunisia[c]	64·6	21·0[a]	17·2	10·3	25·0
Libya	28·9	26·2[a]	23·6	5·9	10·0
Egypt[c]	66·1	11·3	25·6	32·4	10·0
Syria	65·0	14·6	20·4	75·0[d]	8·5
Lebanon	83·4	18·6[a]	10·2	21·7	19·7
Turkey[c]	70·5	16·5[a]	13·0	20·3	17·0
Cyprus	70·2	22·1	12·1	6·3	13·0
Mediterranean area	63·8	20·0	16·9	20·4	15·6
Jordan	76·1	15·6	27·6	41·9	6·3
Iraq[c]	53·6	15·3	23·8	40·0	19·4
Kuwait[c]	29·5	13·5	19·5	7·1[d]	13·0
Iran[e]	59·4	22·1	23·6	28·0[d]	8·9
Oman[c]	22·0	34·6	23·6	60·0[d]	5·1
Bahrain	76·6	15·5	17·7	21·0	25·7
Arabian Gulf area	52·9	19·8	21·9	33·0	13·1
Saudi Arabia	28·7	21·3	23·4	22·0[d]	10·0
Sudan[c]	63·3	11·6	25·1	18·2	10·6
Red Sea area	46·0	16·4	24·3	20·1	10·3
Total	57·8	19·3	19·5	24·5	13·0

[a]Gross capital formation; [b]Fixed capital formation; [c]Data for 1973; [d]Data for 1974; [e]GDP instead of GNP.

Sources: IMF, *International Financial Statistics;* H.J. Budig and M. Süer, *Middle East and North Africa Market Review 1973–74,* Gower Economic Publications, 1973; International Agency for Development, *The Near East and South Asia,* 1973; Centre for Economic and Social Research, *The Sudanese Economy,* Beirut, 1972; United Nations Inter-Disciplinary Reconnaissance Mission, vol. I, *Bahrain,* Beirut, July 1972.

(1975–80) is projected at more than $US 140 billion and the main emphasis is on the production sector. In order to diversify the economy, Saudi Arabia has launched a broad drive towards industrialisation. The biggest investment will be in energy-based industries, where Saudi Arabia is at great advantage both because of the immense energy resources and an almost unlimited supply of capital, both long and short term. The investment will encompass steel mills, aluminium smelters and petrochemical plants.

The new plan will also emphasise agriculture, to reduce dependence on food imports from about 60 per cent to about 20 per cent by the end of the century. Gigantic irrigation schemes are planned, as well as dams to conserve rainfall, and there will be nuclear-powered desalting plants along the Red Sea. In addition, Saudi Arabia is investigating the possibility of importing fresh water in supertankers returning in ballast after discharging their oil.

Construction of roads, airports and the expansion of communication facilities is also receiving a considerable share of project allocation since industrial development is hampered by the inadequacy of the infrastructure. Special emphasis is also given in the new plan to education and other aspects of social welfare, such as health and low-cost housing. Saudi Arabia is also planning to spend several billion dollars on defence equipment.

The government's new industrial policy is aimed at encouraging the private sector in industrial projects, with foreign capital and experience participating in the development of the country. Businessmen enjoy the full support of the government during all stages of preparation, establishment and operation of industrial projects. In fact, probably no other developing country offers so many investment incentives (tax exemptions, provision of industrial zones, loans, etc.). An industrial development fund with a capital of $US 141 million provides medium and long term interest-free loans to private manufacturing companies, to implement industrial projects. Ten years hence Saudi Arabia will probably be one of the most important trading partners of Western countries, and is already inundated with projects by all the major Western companies anxious to invest in a country with a plentiful oil supply.

The weak points of Saudi economy are an insufficiency of manpower and skilled labour at all levels, the existence of a relatively small market and the inadequacy of the infrastructure (modern ports, for instance, are needed to bring in the necessary equipment, as is a satisfactory transport network).

Kuwait The wealthiest Arabian Gulf state, Kuwait has a prosperous economy. Because of the heavy dependence on oil revenues (62·9 per cent of GDP in 1973), the government has ambitious plans to expand and diversify the industrial base. The most immediate areas of new activity are expected to be gas and petrochemicals. Thus, a liquefied propane plant and a large petrochemical complex are in the planning stages. In addition, the government intends to handle the marketing and shipping of LPG, petrochemicals and crude oil, and plans have been made to establish factories for, amongst other things, cement, air-conditioning units, industrial detergents and a solar energy company, as well as atomic power stations for water-distillation purposes. Thus, in the next five years, Kuwait will witness the start of many major industrial projects, which – together with large public works schemes (housing, roads, schools, hospitals, etc.) – should stimulate the economy as a whole. Business activity will also flourish in the services sectors, especially airways, shipping and transport, building materials, etc. Nevertheless, against Kuwait's positive features (vast sources of capital, abundant supplies of natural gas, access to a great variety of refined petroleum products, favourable geographic position, freedom to repatriate earnings and profits, duty-free imports of machinery and spare parts, tariff protection against foreign competition, etc.), foreign investors must consider the shortage of water, the absence of raw materials other than crude oil and natural gas, the smallness of the market, high labour costs and a paucity of technical and organisational skills, etc.

Potential for agricultural development is severely limited, as only 5 per cent of the land is suitable for farming. Agriculture concentrates on experimental stations and small-scale private farms. There is, however, a growing interest in livestock and poultry farming, commercial-scale production of vegetables in glasshouses, outdoor cultures, and hydroponics (a soilless, chemical-based growth system). Kuwait is an open economy, existing on free trade. Hence, Kuwaitis have moved on an international scale into banking, insurance, shipping, real estate, etc., creating widespread international connections.

Bahrain Diversification of the economy of this archipelago of thirty-three islands in the Gulf (of which only five are inhabited) is favoured by the abundance of high-quality natural gas, relatively inexpensive labour, modern transport and communication facilities, and the existence of liberal government policies. In particular, the strategy of diversification aims at developing energy-based and export-oriented industries, together with development of light industries (based on import substitution but with a regional perspective); also, at extending special services in the field of transit trade.

The most notable achievement – in addition to a large oil refinery – has been the establishment of one of the world's largest aluminium smelters (ALBA) by the Bahrain government and six other companies (British Metal Int., General Cable Corp., Kaiser Aluminium Bahrain, Electrokopper, Bretton Investment and Western Metals). The ALBA smelter, one of the most successful industrial ventures in the Middle East, draws its fuel from natural gas, and alumina from Australia under a twenty-year contract with prices fixed in terms of US dollars. With its assured supplies of cheap energy, ALBA (with 120,000 tons a year capacity) is in a position to capitalise on the world shortage of aluminium and to obtain the best price, since it produces some of the purest product. Ancillary industries associated with aluminium – in particular Bahrain Atomisers Int. which produces about 4,000 tons of aluminium powder a year – have also been established.

Other successful industrial enterprises are the Bahrain Flour Mill (owned by the Bahrain government, the Kuwait Flour Mill and private interests in Bahrain), Gulf Plastic Industries, the Bahrain Fishing Co., Maskati Brothers (paper products), several construction companies, an air-conditioning assembly plant and a company for underwater drilling. Among light industries, those engaged in the production of soft drinks and light engineering are dominant. New industrial projects include an aluminium extrusion plant, a vegetable processing factory, a paint factory and a detergent plant. Foremost of the projects is a joint-venture fertiliser plant with an annual production of 500,000 tons, of which India would buy all production surplus to Bahrain's needs.

Given the abundance of non-associated gas (estimated to be of a comparable size to those of the Dutch fields in Europe), the export of LNG is also planned, as is the development of opportunities such as the production of phosphatic fertilisers (importing phosphate rock from Jordan) and the exploitation of the very large deposits of manganese ore of good quality. The emphasis on establishing Bahrain as a trading centre depends on its central location in the Gulf, making Bahrain the ideal entrepôt port for the area. Indeed, with the island's long experience in trade and its sophisticated infrastructure and communications (greatly enhanced by the earth satellite station built in 1969), many foreign businesses and banks have already established Middle East headquarters there. Moreover, the port of Mina Sulman, which is to be enlarged, enjoys a good reputation for efficiency and speed in handling cargoes. The incentives of the free-zone area near Mina Sulman are also attracting foreign investments. In addition, the traditional role as ship-repairing centre is to be greatly improved by the construction of the OAPEC-sponsored dry dock, which, by 1976, will handle oil tankers up to 375,000 tons.

About Bahrain Dinar 100 million is to be invested in the economy over the next three years. Most goods and services will be imported, and the countries to win orders will be those that have made personal contacts in the area, have studied the needs of the market closely and can produce goods of high quality at competitive prices. Bahrain is, however, likely to face three serious problems: the depletion of its oil reserves (still accounting for 70 per cent of total government revenues); limited availability of underground water resources, despite the construction of desalting plants; and over-heavy dependence on food imports, since the possibility of expanding agricultural production is limited by small land surface and inadequate water supply.

Qatar Overwhelmingly dependent on oil incomes (accounting for 92 per cent of government receipts), the development plan of Qatar for the period 1972–82 aims at improvement of the infrastructure and an intensive industrialisation programme. Although tremendous efforts have been made during the past few years, massive expansion and modernisation of the infrastructure and of the social services and other facilities is needed before a full-scale industrialisation programme can be implemented. Thus, the government plans to spend large sums on roads, homes, a new airport, a new hospital and many other social facilities.

In the field of industry the goal is to build two types: industries which are viable for a small market (e.g. construction materials, foodstuffs, furniture, plastics and leather goods, etc.); and export-oriented industries which depend on natural gas as a source of energy or as an input raw material. Thus, an iron and steel mill with an output of over 300,000 tons a year is being set up in collaboration with two Japanese companies (Kobe Steel and Tokyo Boeki). An aluminium plant, a large oil refinery, a petrochemicals complex, a liquefied natural gas plant with an output of about 800,000 tons of LNG a year, and the expansion of the Uù Bab cement plant, as well as the ammonia/urea plant at Umm Said are also planned. Service industries are being improved as well. Work is being carried out on a power-desalination complex at Wakra which will have an output of 300 MW and will take ten years to complete. In addition, the Ras Abu central power-desalination plant has recently been expanded and the Diha electricity network is being improved.

Agricultural development is limited by climatic conditions. But the development of hydroponics, combined with the expansion of glasshouse vegetable production, should make the country self-sufficient in food by 1980; Qatar already exports to other Gulf states an annual average of

1,000 tons of carrots, tomatoes and aubergines. Fishing also offers good prospects.

Despite the incentives offered, Qatar's economic growth is hampered by shortage of skilled and unskilled labour, too small a domestic market and limited availability of natural resources other than oil and gas. Foreign participation in Qatari commerce and industry is strictly controlled.

United Arab Emirates (UAE) Formed in December 1971, the Emirates is a federation of seven Sheikhdoms (Abu Dhabi, Dubai, Sharjah, Ajman, Um al Quaiwan, Ras al Khaimah, Fujairah) which vary widely in area, population and resources. The wealthy oil-producing Emirates of Abu Dhabi and Dubai (the latter retaining its position of entrepôt and trading city-state for the Gulf) together account for about 60 per cent of the Federation's population and more than 90 per cent of its total known resources. In the Emirates of Sharjah and Um al Quaiwan, the production of oil started in mid 1974. The other three Emirates do not yet produce oil, and, being relatively poor, are heavily dependent on financial assistance, mainly from Abu Dhabi. Although the Union has not as yet overcome regional jealousies sufficiently to act as a single nation, the federal government has taken over the management of a unified currency (the dirham), the co-ordination of the oil policy, the armed forces, the postal services, and gradually, the running of schools, hospitals and other facilities (e.g. the electricity system). A national plan is envisaged by 1975.

The federal budget gives priority to improved communications and public utilities (water supplies and electricity production). Thus, the construction industry is benefiting most from the sudden surge in oil revenues. The stage is, however, also set for establishment of new industries, since the aim is to diversify the economy.

In particular, in Abu Dhabi the planned projects include a refinery, a cement plant, an LPG plant, and the establishment of petrochemicals complexes. Private enterprises have also entered the manufacturing field, producing soft drinks, dairy products, furniture and cement, and are engaged in poultry farming also.

Unlike Abu Dhabi, Dubai's rising oil income is being increasingly used to finance projects designed to expand the Emirate's trade and services capacities. Following the completion of Port Rashid with its 16 deep-water berths, Dubai has started another major project, namely the construction by 1977 of a huge dry dock capable of handling the largest oil tankers afloat. The project – estimated to cost $US 200 million – will be administered by the Dubai Dry Dock Co., which is 70 per cent owned by the government, with the balance equally shared by a private firm in

Dubai and an American company. An aluminium plant, which will cover the entire aluminium requirements of the Arab world and provide room for exports, is also being set up, in collaboration with a British company, British Smelter Construction.

In the other Emirates, manufacturing is little developed. In Ras al Khaimah a cement plant will attain a capacity of 250,000 tons a year, and elsewhere there are good possibilities for setting up modern fish processing factories.

Scarcity of water and poor soil limit the role of agriculture, which employs about 18 per cent of the economically active population (a proportion rising to 45 per cent in Ras al Khaimah and Fujairah). The FAO sees considerable commercial potential in concentrating on fresh vegetables, fruit, livestock and integrated fishing. Actually, agricultural production is confined to a few oases, experimental farming (notably successful for strawberries and flowers), and specially favoured localities in some parts of Ras al Khaimah and Fujairah. In addition, Sadiyat Island encompasses the Arid Lands Research Centre which is a joint project of the University of Arizona and the government of Abu Dhabi for vegetable growing and agricultural research. In fact, the output of Sadiyat is estimated to meet a large proportion of the requirements of the town of Abu Dhabi.

Besides an expanding production of oil, the UAE are keenly active in trading with a cosmopolitan population anxious to implement the development projects made possible by considerable yearly increases of public expenditure. The main constraint is a shortage of labour intensified by new restrictions on immigration (mainly Pakistani, Iranian, Indian and Baluchi workers).

Libyan Arab Republic The five-year plan (1976–80) of the Republic is a tremendous effort towards diversified economic growth. Since petroleum accounts for 60 per cent of GNP and 98·8 per cent of total exports, the aim is to build the non-oil sector to create a varied economy capable of laying down a broad and solid economic base that can gradually replace oil as a source of finance. Top priority is thus given to basic productive sectors.

In the field of agriculture (3·1 per cent of GDP), efforts are concentrated in four large projects for 553,000 hectares (2·1 per cent of the country's land area): El Jafara plain, El Jabel El Akhder, Fezzan, El Kufra-El Saris. The government, in particular, wants to reduce dependence on food imports. This aim is greatly favoured by large underground water resources, in contrast with most countries of the Gulf. Great importance is also attached to animal husbandry (cattle, sheep and poultry).

With industry, priority is given to food processing industries; building and construction materials; engineering metallic industries; chemical industries based on locally available materials, and providing the production requirements of other sectors; petrochemical industries (there are huge reserves of high-quality gas and oil) based on production of broylene and ethylene gases and of nitrogen fertilisers; oil refining (50 million tons); and the establishment of an iron and steel complex (7 million ton output envisaged) on the basis of natural gas and iron ores locally available (reserves of iron ores are estimated to be six times more important than those of Mauritania). The setting-up of nuclear power stations is under consideration since the country also has uranium. To balance growth, the plan is investing heavily in schools, hospitals, roads, housing and other social projects.

The most serious constraint is the critical lack of skilled manpower at every level (14·5 per cent of the total labour force is foreign, mainly Tunisians and Egyptians); moreover, the regime is unwilling to educate and employ women. A further problem lies in the desire to combine traditional Arab and Islamic religious instruction with a mastery of modern science and technology. Also a disadvantage is the austerity of the intensely nationalist military and the technocrats. Delays and red tape are also considerable in negotiating public-sector investments, since these have to be approved by a few overworked civil servants who often have below them virtually no one capable of evaluating or implementing projects.

Despite these difficulties, Libya offers ample opportunities for economic co-operation, all the more so, as Libyans - though tough and demanding - are willing to pay cash. All goods sold to Libya must be labelled in Arabic. Direct contacts with the state corporations (especially in the spheres of public works and of agriculture) are quite important. Two specific organisations (the Industrial Research Centre and the General Organisation for Industrialisation), with headquarters in Tripoli, are in charge of the execution of industrial projects. Imports of certain foodstuffs (rice, wheat, flour, tea, barley) is entrusted to the National Supply Corporation. Equally, the General Corporation for Imports and Sale of Agricultural Machinery and Tools and the National Pharmaceutical Co. each enjoy a monopoly in agricultural machinery and pharmaceutical products.

4.4 The development plans of the diversified economies

The second group of relatively more diversified economies can be divided

Table 4.4

Population (mid 1974), GNP at market prices (1974 $US), and average annual growth rates (1974)

Country	Area ('000 sq. km.)	Population ('000)	GNP (million $US)	GNP per head ($US)	Growth Rates: Population	Growth Rates: GNP	Growth Rates: GNP per head
Mauritania	1,030	1,207	220	182	1·4	5·0	4·5
Morocco	445	16,660	3,332	200	2·6	5·6	2·8
Algeria	2,328	15,960	10,199	639	3·0	7·0	4·0
Tunisia	164	5,760	2,200	380	2·2	14·3	11·9
Libya	1,760	2,240	11,176	4,987	3·6	15·0	11·9
Egypt	1,000	37,000	9,250	250	2·2	-6·0	-8·6
Syria	185	7,200	2,500	340	3·2	13·3	9·9
Lebanon	10	3,000	2,380	786	2·5	7·0	4·4
Turkey	781	37,900	13,700	519	2·5	8·8	6·0
Cyprus	9	645	751	1,164	0·9	7·2	7·0
Mediterranean Area	7,766	127,572	59,708	943	2·4	7·7	5·3
Jordan	98	2,600	804	310	3·1	7·2	4·0
Iraq	435	10,700	8,155	760	3·1	12·4	9·3
Kuwait	16	1,000	12,217	12,217	9·3	12·0	2·7
Iran	1,648	32,200	44,000	1,366	3·0	34·0	31·0
Oman	212	650	1,360	2,106	3·0	30·0	27·0
Bahrain	0·6	240	500	2,083	2·9	10·0	7·0
Qatar	22	167	1,722	10,313	9·5	37·0	27·5
United Arab Emirates	84	310	3,489	11,255	9·5	28·0	18·5
Arabian Gulf Area	2,515·6	47,867	72,247	5,051	5·4	21·3	15·9
Saudi Arabia	2,150	7,870	24,510	3,113	2·9	19·7	16·4
Sudan	2,500	17,500	2,506	143	2·6	4·7	2·1
Yemen Democratic Republic	335	1,600	225	143	2·7	n.a.	n.a.
Yemen Arab Republic	195	6,300	674	107	2·2	6·0	3·7
Red Sea Area	5,180	33,270	26,915	876	2·6	10·2	7·4
Total	15,461·6	208,709	158,870	2,291	2·9	13·0	9·5

Source: *Arab Projects and Development*, Beirut, Lebanon.

Table 4.5

The economic structure of GDP at factor cost, 1973

Country	Economic structure of GDP at factor cost (%)			
	Agriculture, fishing, etc.	Manufacturing	Mining and quarrying	Other sectors
Morocco	31·0[a]	14·0[a]	20·0[ab]	35·0
Algeria	8·9[a]	13·3[a]	18·6[a]	59·2[a]
Tunisia[d]	14·5[a]	15·0[a]	8·7[ae]	61·8[a]
Libya	3·1	1·7	62·2	33·0
Egypt[d]	28·8	22·7[f]	–	48·5
Syria	21·9[g]	19·5[fg]	–	58·6
Lebanon[h]	9·2[a]	25·0[a]	–	65·8[a]
Turkey[d]	30·9[i]	20·0[i]	–	49·1[i]
Cyprus	17·6	11·7	6·3	64·4
Mediterranean area	18·4	15·9	11·6	45·6
Jordan	18·0	11·0[f]	–	71·0
Iraq[d]	15·8	9·7	37·1	37·4
Kuwait[d]	0·3	2·9	64·5[j]	32·2
Iran	16·6	20·0	25·4	38·0
Oman[d]	11·6	0·2	65·0	23·2
Bahrain[d]	1·0	2·4	71·7[k]	24·9
Arabian Gulf area	10·5	7·7	43·9	37·8
Saudi Arabia[d]	4·1	7·3	58·4	30·1
Sudan[h]	38·0	13·0[f]	–	49·0
Yemen Democratic Republic[d]	21·0	4·8	24·8	49·4
Red Sea area	21·0	8·4	27·7	42·7
Totals	16·6	11·0	25·1	47·3

[a] GDP at market prices;
[b] energy and mines;
[c] gross capital formation;
[d] data for 1971;
[e] including energy, power and water;
[f] manufacturing and mining;
[g] net Domestic Product;
[h] data for 1974;
[i] net GDP at factor cost;
[j] crude oil and natural gas;
[k] plus oil refining (the proportion of oil sector to GDP accounted for only 37·7 per cent in 1972).

Sources: IMF, *International Financial Statistics;* H. J. Budig and M. Süer, *Middle East and North Africa Market Review 1973–74,* Gower Economic Publications; *Le Maroc en marche: 1973–77, Plan du décollage;* The Arab Planning Institute and Kuwait Economic Society, Seminar on Investment Policies of Arab Oil Producing Countries, February 1974, Kuwait; *Food and agriculture sector country development, Brief Series, Sudan,* Country development brief, Food and agriculture organisation; United Nations Economic Commission for Western Asia, *Preliminary report on the social situation in the ECWA region;* Sultanate of Oman, General Development Organisation, National Statistics Department, *Statistical Year Book,* first issue, 1972.

into two categories:

(a) Large, densely populated states where, despite the prime role of the public sector, a pragmatic approach prevails in planning, since the private sector is encouraged. Egypt, Turkey and Morocco are included.

Egypt The decennial plan (1973–82) is divided into two detailed phases (1973–77 and 1977–82) and aims to double income to Egyptian £5,735 million (assessed in 1972 terms) and to create 3 million jobs. Investments during the ten-year plan are estimated at a total of Egyptian £8,400 million. During the first five years of the plan, investments will amount to Egyptian £3,221 million and the annual growth rate reach 6·5 per cent with respect to GNP and 4 per cent with respect to *per capita* income.

The high priority (33–7 per cent of total investment) given to the industrial sector (22 per cent of GNP in 1974) reflects Egypt's potential for development in this field. In particular, parallel with the expansion of agro-based industries (especially textiles and clothing), there are good prospects for development of selected resource-based industries (fertilisers, cement, petroleum, steel) and of engineering. Thus, with assistance from the USSR, the Helwan iron and steel complex will be expanded from 0·3 million to 1·2 million of steel products; a $US400 million oil refinery is to be built in the free zone of Alexandria; a $US130 million fertiliser plant, at Talkah, and an aluminium smelter, at Aswan – again with assistance from the USSR – will be built to take advantage of the power available from the High Dam.

Foreign participation is being sought in a great variety of projects, including the tourist sector. Despite difficulties at El Morgan field, the prospects for crude petroleum – Egypt's real hope – are bright, because of recent discoveries both on the Red Sea and in the western desert, and, more important, due to an expected rise in exploration activity. Construction of the SUMED pipeline, entrusted to an Italian consortium, will by 1976 link the southern part of the Gulf of Suez with facilities west of Alexandria. Natural gas production is also to be increased (10 million tons by 1982). Local naphtha surpluses will be utilised by the petrochemicals industry (plastics, synthetic rubber and fibres) according to the plans prepared by the General Organisation for Industrialisation. Emphasis is also given to exploitation of phosphates, iron ore, salt and, to a lesser extent, kaolin, talc, manganese and asbestos.

Alongside this programme is the plan to build and rebuild the citics of the Suez Canal (Port Said, Ismailia, Suez and environs) and the demolished factories. Improvement of the infrastructure is also planned, to accompany the reopening of the Canal and the reconstruction of industrial utilities adjacent to it. There will also be replacement of major units of public utilities in main cities, and expansion of housing units in both city and countryside.

Despite the growing industrial base, the agricultural sector (30 per cent of GNP, 68 per cent of total active population, 60 to 65 per cent of export earnings) is still the mainstay of the Egyptian economy, especially with cotton and rice (more than 50 per cent of export earnings). Much of the effort is concentrated on measures to introduce higher-yielding varieties of crops, such as wheat and cotton, and on improvements to the co-operative marketing system, and consolidation of fragmented land holdings under common rotation, especially where cotton is concerned. In addition, measures are being considered to increase the number of crops marketed in whole or part through the co-operative network, and to increase regional specialisation in crop rotations. Main investments in agriculture are directed at tile-drainage projects, the improvement of newly reclaimed lands, irrigation in the eastern desert (south of the present limits of delta cultivation). A spectacular project in the north, aiming to create an immense dam, larger than Aswan, by means of nuclear explosion, is also envisaged.

The heavy burden of military expenditure (estimated at no less than 30 per cent of the budget) constitutes a severe constraint on the economy. Thus, peace in the Middle East is of paramount importance to the country. Other problems are the predominant role of the public sector which has been expanded excessively in the last twenty years, and a burdensome bureaucracy. At present, however, President Sadat is attempting to run the economy in a more decentralised way, allowing the private sector to play a large role ('denasserisation'). Moreover, to attract foreign investment, the government has created an industrial free zone on the Mediterranean coast and near Cairo (where manufacturers can import and export free of duty or government controls); five years' tax exemption is also granted, and guarantees given against nationalisation or other non-trade risks. To back up these guarantees, Egypt has signed a convention with the World Bank for international arbitration on any disputes concerning foreign investment. Given Egypt's other advantages (which include abundant and skilled labour, a large domestic market, a managerial class, mineral resources, a reasonably developed infrastructure, proximity to European and Middle East markets, and eligibility for Arab finance), these concessions are designed to attract European, Japanese and American companies to bring instant, 'Brazil type' industrialisation, which could lead the economic development of the whole Arab World.

Turkey The core of the development effort envisaged in the third five-year plan (1973–77) – which includes long-term strategy up to 1995 – is a policy of more rapid and intensive industrialisation concentrated mainly in Istanbul and Izmir. The structural change in the composition of domestic output in favour of industrial goods (which account for 19·7 per cent of GNP) is to be brought about through the intermediary and capital-goods industries, especially the chemical, petrochemical, machine manufacturing, metal goods, motor vehicle, electric and electronic industries. Fertilisers are also accorded top priority. For iron and steel, it is hoped to attain self-sufficiency by expanding, with Soviet aid, the existing mills at Iskenderum, Eregli and Karabuk and erecting a new 700,000 tons/year capacity crude-steel plant. An oil-refining and chemical complex at Tarsus is also envisaged. To improve employment and increase export earnings, emphasis is also given to the thriving textile and clothing industries, raising spinning capacity so that two-thirds of cotton production can be processed locally. Other developments are expected in the remainder of the manufacturing sector (especially for glass, paper and other consumer durables).

Since the manufacturing industries face, in some cases, shortages of raw materials and, almost universally, shortage of power, special attention is given to improving ties with Arab countries (especially Saudi Arabia). Oil production is, in fact, modest (3·4 million tons in 1972), while crude imports amounted to $US 1 billion in 1974. In addition, it is planned to levy substantial transport royalties and supply a guaranteed minimum quantity of crude at fixed prices on construction, by a Turkish–Iraqi joint venture, of the Kirkuk–Dortyol (Iskenderum) oil pipeline. Moreover, the proposed Iran–West Europe natural-gas pipeline could be routed through Turkey instead of the USSR, while plans for development of nuclear energy are pressing ahead. Oil exploration is also being intensified, particularly in the promising areas of the Aegean Sea where, however, a confrontation with Greece seems possible. Turkey is rich in minerals and is among the world's leading producers of chromium (mainly sold to the US) and, though to a much lesser extent, of copper, marble and magnesium. However, iron ore and coal resources are insufficient.

The inadequate attention given to agriculture (which will receive only 12 per cent of total investments of the plan) is only exceeded by the difficulty of implementing improvements (e.g. land rcform, extension of irrigation, substantial increase in fertiliser consumption, eradication of endemic foot and mouth disease, introduction of intensive animal husbandry, new high-yielding techniques, education for farmers, and improved marketing). Agriculture (which still employs 66 per cent of the labour force, produces 31 per cent of GNP and accounts for 75 per cent of total exports) in fact has great potential (especially for such items as cotton, tobacco, cereals, fruit and vegetables, livestock and forestry products, etc.), while substantial imports place a heavy burden on the balance of payments (500,000 tons of wheat and barley were imported, mainly from the US, during the 1973–74 season). External constraints, such as the ban imposed on the recruitment of foreign labour by the German Federal Republic (which could force workers to return home), the oil and food import bill, and the probable reduction of exports directed to Western Europe (because of the recession), all make it imperative to diversify outlets, with emphasis on the Middle East markets. Wide-ranging agreements have already been established with Libya (covering a joint investment bank, a joint tanker fleet, a joint armament industry and the supply of crude oil and manpower).

On the domestic front, however, a firmer balance must be established between the state and the private sectors, the former accounting for virtually 100 per cent of domestic production in several important industries, the viability and efficiency of which have long been questioned. This would avoid the difficulties inherent in ambiguous projects such as the so-called 'people's sector', which should provide facilities for investment of small savings in regional industries; in particular, of funds generated abroad, the principal sources of invisible income. The five-year plan lays down the criteria for foreign investment approvals, although these are of course subject to revision by the government of the day. Accordingly, foreign investment (unless wholly export-oriented) must introduce new technology as well as capital; product prices must be competitive in the international market and provision must be made for exports; projects must be specific as regards products or activities, and monopolies are not permitted. Finally, investments must be either wholly export-oriented or in priority fields.

Morocco The fundamental aim of the ambitious third plan (1973–77) is that of organising national development within a liberal system which nevertheless assigns the state a leading role in attracting and encouraging private enterprise (particularly by means of a generous investment code), both in infrastructure development and in sectors in which private enterprise and investment are inadequate or unsuitable, particularly the social sector. Highest priority is given to agriculture, which represents 31 per cent of GNP and employs 68 per cent of the population. Thus, the plan foresees the opening-up of 1 million acres of irrigated land through the building of more dams, and the redistribution of almost 1 million acres among landless peasants, grouped into co-operatives (520,000 acres of the remaining French and Spanish land were nationalised in 1973).

Phosphates are the other mainstay of the nation's economy, providing 20 per cent of GNP and 65 per cent of export earnings. Having sold phosphates at around $US 14 a ton since 1962, Morocco raised its price to $US 63 a ton, yielding revenues in 1974 of over $US 1 billion ($US 163 million in 1973). Thus, the phosphate boom is to the Moroccan economy what oil is to other Arab states. The state phosphate organisation plans to boost production to 26 million tons by 1977 (19·5 million in 1973) and to control the world price of fertilisers, Morocco exporting 37 per cent of the world shipment (the largest exporter) and being the third largest producer (reserves estimated at more than 50 billion tons). Morocco is also building a phosphoric acid refining plant and phosphate fertiliser plant at Safi, while the USSR is helping to open up a new mine, with rail and road links, and a new port to serve it. In addition, Morocco is increasing production of other important mineral resources such as lead, zinc, manganese (sixth largest producer), iron and cobalt (second largest exporter). While the search for oil continues, Morocco can exploit gas and shale oil (3·5 million tons per year for over fifty years).

In the manufacturing sector, priority is given to the promotion of agro-industries (sugar, processed fruit, etc.) and the establishment of export-oriented labour-intensive industries making parts of manufactured goods (clothing, electronic components, etc.) for the EEC markets. The plan lists a number of industries in which the government seeks to encourage private investment; they include pharmaceuticals, household appliances, dairy foods, construction materials, paper and hosiery. Any project with a high labour content will receive particular encouragement, as the plan sets a target of 95,000 new industrial jobs.

Close to Europe and routes to the United States, Morocco possesses the essentials for sustained economic growth, in terms of natural resources, power and water supplies, an adequate infrastructure, cheap and trainable labour, and entrepreneurship; generous incentives, including a ten-year tax holiday, are another feature. Since publication of the plan, foreign multinationals have paid increasing attention to the potential of Morocco. The enthusiasm engendered by the phosphate boom is, however, still tempered by anxiety over the instability of King Hassan's regime, the difficulty of dealing with local bureaucracy, the policy of Moroccanisation (although the 50 per cent local-ownership proviso applies only to new industries producing for the domestic market, while export-oriented industries can be 100 per cent foreign-controlled), the very high birth rate in the cities (4·4 per cent), and the difficulties of a political settlement in Spanish Sahara (where at Bou Craa a major phosphate-producing competitor is established).

(b) Smaller states where planning is generally merely indicative of targets. In addition to Lebanon, Jordan, Cyprus and Tunisia, Syria is included in this category, since the current economic liberalisation there is softening the rigidities of the development plan.

Lebanon The six-year plan (1972-77), while only a guide to development action, includes a public-sector investment programme of £L1,740 million, and aims at a 7 per cent annual growth rate, more equal distribution of income and education services, a high level of employment, balanced development of the various regions, and a reduction of the economy's heavy dependence on trade and services (65 per cent of GDP in 1974). The plan thus seems to aim more at curing some economic ills than co-ordinating various economic activities. Moreover, it seems to offer no clear indications as to areas of emphasis.

Substantially following a *laissez-faire* policy, Lebanon is a relatively prosperous city-state (Beirut dominating the country) and a focal distribution centre for all countries in the Middle East. (Only low import duties are levied on Lebanese exports to Arab countries and, in some cases, total exemption is allowed.) The economy's rate of expansion - vigorous in the fifties (7 per cent in real terms) and remarkable in the sixties (5 per cent) - is now at risk. In fact, since 1973 the Lebanese economy seems to have reached a turning point which, due to a neglect of fundamental and structural problems, could have serious implications for the Arab World's most successful experiment in democracy. In particular, with the improving performance of neighbouring countries, a lack of oil and mineral resources, and the rising expectations of the populace, the economy is subject to additional pressures which require the adoption of a new political, economic and social policy, attaching more importance to the future. With this in mind, the outlook for the industrial sector - now contributing 25 per cent of GDP - could be favourable, especially since Arab money coming to Beirut is being invested in industrial enterprises (especially food products, chemicals, plastics, wood, paper and paper products, hides and skins, and cement).

As well as its liberal economic policy and advantageous geographical position, Lebanon can provide skilled and unskilled labour at relatively low cost, funds to finance feasible industrial projects, advanced internal and external transport facilities and communications, and low-cost electric power, fuel oil and gas oil (because of preferential agreements with oil-rich Arab countries).

Another field of great potential growth is the agricultural sector now providing only 9 per cent of the GNP. In particular, extended irrigation in the fertile Bekaa Valley would allow more animal feedstuffs to be produced and thus encourage production of meat and dairy products. Equally, southern Lebanon (once border clashes with Israel are settled) could be developed greatly, with major irrigation projects. Moreover, with its tradition of banking experience, Beirut could maintain its role as a leading financial centre, as well as attracting Arab and other foreign investments which enjoy traditional good treatment, together with the facilities of the free zone of the Beirut port. Furthermore, while exploiting the existing quantities of high-quality shale oil (215 milliard barrels), the government could find it worthwhile to undertake further prospecting for petroleum, both on and off shore.

Syria Syria's future is built on the development of the Euphrates dam to which the largest share of resources ($US 400 million) was allocated in the third five-year plan (1971–75). This gigantic project, scheduled for completion in 1975 is to produce 2·5 billion kWh electricity a year (three times the previous production) and will irrigate more than 1·5 million acres of land (doubling Syria's irrigated area). Thus, the basis for the industrial take-off will be achieved, while, with water assured, Syria should be able to achieve solid prosperity as a small agricultural country selling to the countries of the region as well as in the world market. In fact, the northern half of Syria is potentially one of the richest producing areas in the world. The parts irrigated by the Orontes River around the towns of Homs and Hama have qualities akin to those of the best farming areas of Iowa and Illinois. The climate and soil, moreover, are right for the growing of cash crops whose values are now mounting on world markets. Some of the best reputed cotton in the world – one of the mainstays of the Syrian economy – comes from this area. Wheat, vegetables and fruits are also abundant.

In addition to the Euphrates dam, several agricultural development projects are being implemented or under consideration, e.g. the use of fertilisers and cultivation of Mexican wheat varieties. And priority has been given to increasing production of a few cash crops such as wheat, cotton and sugar beet.

Despite two recent devastating wars, the economy appears to be going ahead at high speed, partly because of economic liberalisation under the Assad regime. Although the public sector continues to lead in economic development, many incentives are offered (notably a large duty-free zone where foreign investors can build factories and benefit from tax exemption and other facilities; foreign participation in development projects in the private sector and relaxation of exchange controls on hard currencies).

While the country remains largely dependent on the USSR and other socialist countries for economic and military aid, President Assad is turning to the West, also, for help in its development projects. A little less than half the public sector's investment under the new plan is earmarked for development of industrial and mineral resources. The major industrial projects relate to expansion of the cotton textiles, fertiliser and cement industries, and the development of plants for steel rolling, tractor assembly, glass making and battery manufacture. Although the country is still at a fairly early stage of industrialisation, a new industrial policy is aimed at export-oriented industries and diversification of the industrial base; this should encourage consumer-goods production and introduce intermediate and basic industries and, hopefully, heavy industry as well. Thus, for instance, the aim is for output of cotton yarn to reach 80 per cent of cotton production against the current 55–60 per cent, and projects for increasing export production are being implemented.

Plans are also being made to exploit deposits of phosphates, rock salt and iron ore. And priority is being given to raise production of petroleum from 7·9 million tons in 1973 to 15 million in 1975. Two new refineries at Barias (with Rumania and Japan respectively) are planned. Production of phosphates (begun in 1971 with 300,000 tons) is expected to attain 1 million tons in 1975.

The country's economy is unlikely to achieve complete stability, however, until the financial difficulties imposed by the burden of military expenditures are resolved. Some 75 per cent of the budget is estimated to be spent on such use. In addition, entrepreneurship suffers the disadvantage of working under a government which is basically authoritarian.

Jordan The investment priorities of the five-year development plan (1976–80) represent a bold attempt to emulate the impressive performance of the economy before the 1967 War. Emphasis is on transport facilities, agriculture and irrigation, the mining industry and electricity, and education. Thus, the Hassa–Aqaba railway, by which phosphates are transported to the sea, is being improved under a $US 5 million contract. Aqaba, where port facilities are to be enlarged and modernised, is also being linked by rail to Hijaz. And a new international airport is being built outside Amman.

The main focus on agricultural development (with fruit and vegetables contributing heavily to export earnings) is the Jordan valley scheme financed by the Kuwait Fund, IDA (of the World Bank Group), the USA, the German Federal Republic and the Abu Dhabi Fund.

Zarqa is the centre of a new power project, and industrial development – restricted by lack of local fuel and mainly concentrated on small concerns producing food or clothes – is aimed at rapidly increasing the production of phosphates (from 700,000 to 2 million tons a year within 1975), at cement and petroleum refining (from 780,000 to 2·9 million tons a year by 1975 at the refinery of Zarqa), establishment of a steel-tube plant, an integrated fertiliser complex, a ceramics plant and the urbanisation of the East Ghor valley.

Despite its weak position due to the Arab–Israeli conflict and the loss of the West Bank (which contributed an estimated 40 per cent of GNP), economic prospects are encouraging because of the world price rise in phosphates (estimated reserves 1,000 million tons), the exploitation of copper deposits in Wadi Araba (estimated copper reserves 55 million tons), the tourist boom and financial aid from abroad (notably the US, Saudi Arabia and Kuwait).

Although the public sector plays an important role, Jordan's economy (largely service-oriented) is essentially based on a free market. Investment incentives and guarantees make it an attractive place in which to invest funds because of the many untapped opportunities and the excellent relations developed with the tremendous expanding markets of the Gulf states. Apart from the mining industry, however, the small Jordanian market can hardly sustain sizeable capital and intermediate goods industries, let alone production of consumer goods. A sensible move would be to emphasise agro-based and construction-related industries. Although Jordanian businessmen are reluctant to enter industrial ventures, the Jordanian authorities are participating actively in various joint ventures, particularly where heavy capital injection is required (e.g. the cement and phosphate industries).

Cyprus Development prospects were seriously disrupted in 1974 when the Turkish invasion inflicted heavy damage on the economy, with Turkey assuming occupation of the most important sector, including the main areas for cultivation of citrus, olives, carobs, meat, eggs, milk and cereals, as well as most of the facilities for tourism and industry. In addition to the serious loss of production, the refugee problem (some 226,000 people displaced out of a population of 620,000) has proved expensive, though substantial international aid was mobilised. Thus, Greek Cypriots face difficult problems and will have to wait many years before recovering a decent standard of living. The situation is particularly unfortunate since, economically, Cyprus was generally proceeding well, especially in tourism, mining (pyrites, copper, chrome, asbestos, etc.) and in manufacturing (particularly, light industries export-oriented towards Europe – the most important market – and African countries, especially Libya and Tanzania). In addition, a water development project, the biggest of its kind in Cyprus, was under way in the Paphos district to increase agricultural production.

Politically, the island's *de facto* partition has been at fault, since Cyprus could set the pattern of a mutually advantageous coexistence between Muslims and Christians and could play an active role of non-alignment in the Mediterranean. Thus, if it becomes inevitable that the Greek and Turkish communities are divided geographically, it is important for their future coexistence that a common economy is organised by giving Turkish Cypriots a vested interest in an independent Cyprus.

Tunisia Tunisia's fourth economic and social development plan (1973–76) aims at a substantial acceleration of economic growth to improve the drastic employment situation (Tunisia's central problem in the years to come) and the country's financial position. The economy is dependent on agriculture which in 1974 supported about 50 per cent of the population and represented 23 per cent of GDP. Although agriculture will play a much less important role than in the final years of the third plan, it has been assigned a key position to provide adequate supplies of foodstuffs and raw materials to the important food processing industry, which is mainly geared towards exports, especially for the production of olive oil, and, to a lesser extent, wheat flour, fruit juices, canned vegetables, sugar, etc.

The industrial sector – including mining, energy, manufacturing and construction, and public works – accounted in 1973 for about 23·7 per cent of real GDP at market prices. The largest branch of industrial activity is manufacturing (centred on Tunis, Sousse, Sfax, Gabes and Bizerte), in particular, light industry (textiles, clothing, leather, etc.) which could become a decisive factor in Tunisia's growth. Establishment of light industry is, in fact, a major priority of the new plan since such industry could absorb some of the rapidly growing labour force, produce substitutes for imported goods and obtain substantial export earnings.

A substantial part of industrial growth is due to the increasing revenues from production of crude petroleum (4 million tons in 1974; 10 million tons expected by 1976), now the most important earner of foreign exchange. With the expected increase in oil production, Tunisia is planning a number of oil-based projects, and there is already an oil refinery with a capacity of 1·2 million tons of crude oil a year. A second refinery is planned with a capacity of 7 to 10 million tons of crude. Tunisia has also been approached by Japanese, French and US firms to consider the development of petrochemicals industries, including synthetic fibre production and the production of nitrogenous fertilisers. Natural gas will also be available within the next few years. Agreement has been reached with Algeria and Italy on the construction of a gas pipeline from the Algerian gasfield at Hassi R'Mel, to Italy across Tunisia.

Despite their low quality, phosphates are emerging as the second most important earner of foreign exchanges. Thus, the fourth plan allocates phosphates 70 per cent of the investment of the mining production. A second phosphoric acid plant was due for establishment in 1975, thus replacing output of phosphate rock by exports of phosphoric acid. Iron ore has declined in importance, and output of lead, zinc and salt is very small. But the prospects for fluorspar are more favourable. Tunisia looks forward to a period of relative prosperity – a growth rate of 18 per cent in real terms was attained in 1972 – because of increased earnings from petroleum, phosphates and olive oil, its proximity to Europe, its good record of relations with foreign business interests, and its cheap and skilled labour force. Since the days of over-intensive collectivisation under Ahmed Ben Salah, Tunisia, in addition to adopting a liberal policy, has become something of a fiscal paradise, especially for foreign investors seeking to set up export industries.

4.5 The development plans of the least developed countries of the region

The third group of the least developed countries is also divisible into two categories:

(a) Economies with abundant natural resources (petroleum, massive mineral deposits, etc.).Mostly these are yet to be exploited, and there is promising potential for industrial and agricultural development, etc., though subject to very pressing constraints (e.g. guerrilla fighting, droughts, shortage of skilled manpower, inadequate infrastructure). The Sultanate of Oman (whose relatively high *per capita* GNP represents only about $US 140 if the oil sector is excluded), the Republic of Mauritania and the Sudan are included here.

Oman Although impressive economic achievements have been attained since mid-1970 (when isolationism ended), Oman is the least developed country of the Gulf subregion. With the oil sector accounting

Table 4.6
Planned rates of growth

Country	Reference period of development plans	GNP	Population	GNP per head	Agriculture	Manufacturing	Exports	Imports
Morocco	1973–77	7·5	2·5	3·1	3·6	11·0	10·0	8·0
Algeria	1974–77	10·0	2·2	7·8	3·0	19·0	20·0	21·0
Tunisia	1973–76	8·8	2·2	5·3	6·2	10·2	8·0	13·3
Libya	1976–80	11·0	4·5	6·0	16·0	26·0	7·0	12·8
Egypt	1973–77	6·9	2·7	4·2	3·5	24·5	9·0	4·0
Syria	1976–80	16·0	3·2	12·8	10·0	17·8	6·5	5·0
Lebanon	1972–77	7·0	3·0	4·0	5·0	8·3	7·3	6·7
Turkey	1973–77	7·9[a]	2·6	5·4	3·8	11·3	9·4	7·1
Mediterranean area		9·4	2·9	6·1	7·4	16·0	9·7	9·7
Jordan	1976–80	8·0	3·0	5·0	6·4	14·0	16·2	8·2
Iraq	1976–80	7·1	3·4	3·6	7·0	12·0	2·8	5·2
Iran	1973–78	16·6	2·9	12·1	7·0	18·0	10·0	19·0
Arabian Gulf area		10·1	3·1	6·9	6·8	14·7	9·7	10·8
Saudi Arabia	1975–80	15·0	2·9	10·1	4·0	14·0	7·8	13·4
Sudan	1975–80	5·8	2·8	3·0	10·0	15·0	n.a.	n.a.
Red Sea area		10·4	2·8	6·5	7·0	14·5	7·8	13·4
Total		9·9	2·9	6·5	7·2	15·0	9·1	11·3

[a]Gross Domestic Product
Source: National Development Plans for the respective countries.

for 95 per cent of fiscal revenues and 98 per cent of total foreign exchange earnings, modern manufacturing is almost non-existent, while agriculture, employing about 80 per cent of the population, is still largely of a subsistence nature. There is also a critical shortage of adequate housing, school and health services, and other basic amenities. Oman's absorptive capacity is also subject to pressing constraints. In particular, the implementation of a programme of major development projects is handicapped by unsatisfactory knowledge in almost every sector of the economy, lack of an institutional framework geared to economic development, and by shortage of skilled and semi-skilled manpower.

Military expenditure has had major priority. In 1974, half of Oman's oil earnings (which stand at nearly $US 1 billion) was committed to defence and security matters, and most of the State's other financial resources were concentrated on the fight against the guerrillas of the Popular Front for the Liberation of Oman (PFLO) which is opposing the government in Dhofar, the region bordering Democratic Yemen. Thus, while, during 1970–73, development expenditure concentrated on the infrastructure (roads and ports) and social facilities, most of the new development projects (especially the setting-up of an ammonia factory, a natural-gas liquefaction plant, a few date processing plants, and a large cement factory) which aimed at diversifying the economy (in the industrial as well as in the agricultural and mining sectors) were postponed to 1976.

Yet, in terms of population, area and resources, Oman is one of the most promising countries in the Gulf subregion. Agriculture, in particular, offers vast scope for growth, as the country is endowed with abundant groundwater resources and fertilisers can be produced locally. Climate and topography point to a variety of crops (aside from the traditional crops such as limes and dates). The production of cereals introduced on an economic scale, increased livestock and grazing, and technical assistance programmes drastically improve the low productivity mainly due to bad farming practices and ignorance of the proper application of fertilisers and insecticides.

Oman has potential, too, for industrial development (notably of industries based on agricultural and fishing resources, oil refining, building materials, cement, and a number of other small and medium-scale factories whose establishment may be justified in terms of the availability of resources, skills, size of the domestic market and opportunities for export to neighbouring countries. Massive mineral deposits also exist (especially of high-grade copper, manganese and asbestos), although exploration is still in its infancy. Furthermore, Oman could seek to revive its trading role, using its strategic position, as in the past when the Sultanate was the most powerful state of the Arabian peninsula.

Mauritania The third four-year plan (1974–77) of Mauritania concentrates on economic development and the expansion of lay education. Mineral exploitation is to be the main area of progress, Mauritania being potentially one of the larger ore-producing areas of the world. At Kedia n'Ijil, near the salt deposits of the north, exceptionally rich deposits of iron ore are being mined by Miferna, the giant mining concern now controlled by the government. Iron ore is the main export, and its production (8·6 million metric tons in 1972) represents more than a third of GDP. Implementation of the plan would result in exports of 12 million tons a year. Another increasingly important export is copper, obtained from equally rich deposits at Akjoujit which are being exploited by a company combining Mauritanian, French and World Bank interests. Production of copper (begun in earnest in 1971 and 1972) has reached 5·2 million tons. Foreign investors are being sought for a range of new mining projects. A new state mining group, SNIM, is investigating the potential for sulphur, rare earths, iron ore, phosphates, etc., for which foreign capital is needed, while there are long-term hopes of mining gypsum, nickel, lead/zinc, diamonds, etc. A number of international oil companies are engaged in prospecting both on and off shore. The increasing gains of the mining sector are outweighed by losses due to the disastrous drought which has afflicted the country for four consecutive years (1971–74) and threatens to alter the entire social structure of the population, which is now gathering around townships and oases.

The development of agriculture - at present basically subsistence - is severely limited. Apart from occasional oases in the Sahara, the only arable area in this enormous country is in the Senegal valley, where 130,000 settled farmers grow crops of millet and sorghum. But production falls short of estimated Mauritanian needs by 50 per cent for cereals, 20 per cent for pulses and 40 per cent for oils and fats. The major expenditure planned in agriculture is for irrigation schemes, dams and modern palm plantations.

In the manufacturing sector (which in 1970 accounted for only around 2 per cent of GDP), priority is given to a sugar factory, a sawmill, a plaster factory, a dairy, a tomato concentrate factory, a flour mill, a textile complex and an iron smelting centre. President Daddah is shifting his sights away from France towards its North African Arab neighbours. Thus Mauritania has left the franc zone (establishing its own national currency, the ouguiya) and refashioned the old cultural, defence and economic co-operation agreements with France. In December 1973,

Mauritania was admitted to the Arab League. President Daddah is convinced of the need for a liberal policy. Thus, the existing code of investment encourages private enterprise and allows 100 per cent repatriation of profits after tax.

Sudan Although a resourceful country endowed with vast lands capable of cultivation, the Sudan - the largest country of the region and, indeed, of Africa - ranks among the poorest of developing nations. The principal problems impeding development are the shortage of financial resources, skilled manpower and capital equipment, an inadequate infrastructure, shortage of groundwater, soil erosion, the traditional attitude of nomads to livestock, and uneven distribution of labour. Thus, the interim action programme for the five years from 1973–78 has five basic priorities: (a) transport (particularly roads, initially the Khartoum–Port Sudan highway which will open up the rich Gezira scheme); (b) expansion in agriculture (on which more than 80 per cent of the population is dependent, directly or indirectly, and which provides 98 per cent of foreign income): the aim is particularly towards increased and diversified production and self-sufficiency in most imported products (wheat, sugar, tea and coffee, etc.); (c) exploitation of livestock whose enormous potential (in an area of around 80 million acres of grazing land) is largely untapped and could provide a suitable foundation for food, milk, shoe, fodder and tanning industries and fattening schemes; (d) promotion of agro-industrial projects such as sugar, textile, flour, jute products (sacks), canned products, the paper industry, etc; (e) training and management, with emphasis on technical and agricultural education.

The fundamental need of the Sudan is to win back the confidence of both foreign and domestic capital investors. Thus, although the public sector plays a leading role in development, the Nimeiri regime has given substantial incentives to private investment (in particular generous tax and capital repatriation terms for foreign investors, with exemption from customs duties, allocation of land for construction of enterprises, guarantees, and further facilities for projects deemed to be of national strategic value). Moreover, many of the industrial enterprises nationalised in 1970 have since been returned to private ownership. Sudan's affiliation with the World Bank Centre for Settlement of Investment Disputes is another incentive.

Economic prospects are now bright because of the higher prices for cotton (about 60 per cent of export earnings) and other commodities (such as soya beans, sugar cane, tobacco, etc.), increased financial aid from the Gulf states (who believe that the Sudan could become the breadbasket of the Arab world), better relations with Egypt, and the reintegration of the south (devastated by the civil war which raged for more than eight years until the peace agreement of 1972). Encouraging, also, are the mineral findings. Two commercial gold operations are firmly established and a salt industry based on solar evaporation of Red Sea water has gradually been developed. Reserves of chromite in the Red Sea area are estimated at 1·5 million tons. And recent geological studies have revealed surface deposits of iron ore, copper and gypsum, while positive results have been recorded in petroleum research.

(b) Economies emerging into the twentieth century after centuries of feudalism, and relying heavily on foreign aid. Natural resources are scanty and most of the population is engaged in the largely rudimentary agriculture. The Yemen Arab Republic and the People's Democratic Republic of Yemen (currently 'Democratic Yemen') are included in this category.

Yemen Arab Republic Infrastructure development is the real goal of the first three-year plan (1973–76), which aims to transform an economy fundamentally dependent on an underdeveloped agricultural sector accounting for about 74 per cent of the value added to GNP and employing over 90 per cent of the population. In particular, YR 292 million (out of YR 936 million) have been allocated for transport, especially port improvement (at either of the country's existing ports), since a lack of adequate docking facilities results in an unreasonably high cost per ton for transportation, supplies arriving in small coastal tankers from 600 to 3,000 ton capacity. Expansion of road networks is also stressed; according to 1972 data, there are only 569 km. of asphalt roads and 1,000 km. of minor roadways. In addition, the telecommunication network linking the isolated provinces with the capital is earmarked for extension and the two airports of Taiz and Al Hudaydah are to be consolidated. Special emphasis is also given to essential services, particularly to extending the existing waterpipe network of Taiz, to implementing studies for the sewerage system, to constructing a pure water system in Saana and Hodeidah, and to implementing the programme for water drilling and tank erection in the rural areas.

Plans for developing the industrial sector (accounting for only about 3 per cent of GNP) have been conceived to aid the development of agriculture. A leading project is the proposed industrial complex in Saana to be built with the assistance of the World Bank and UNIDO. Numerous light industries (factories for canning agricultural produce, skin tanning, cotton ginning, sugar refining, salt mining, etc.) are also envisaged, while the Saana textile mill and cement factory will be expanded. Great importance is also given to prospecting for oil and minerals, for which Shell Petroleum Company's reports tend to be encouraging.

In the agricultural sector, centred on cotton (the main cash crop), coffee, vegetables, tobacco, sorghum and maize (especially in the Tiham coastal plain and in the lower mountain regions), the government intends to encourage cultivation of wheat and soya beans in the highlands and sugar cane in the Tihama; also, to build dams and pilot farms, to carry out soil analysis and agricultural extension programmes in the southern highlands, to develop animal husbandry introducing Friesian cattle to the highlands, to improve the fishing industry, and to establish an agricultural loan unit as a start towards an agricultural bank providing loans for agricultural development projects.

The future of the YAR would seem to encompass steady but unspectacular progress - since the country is emerging into the twentieth century after centuries of feudalism - with heavy reliance on foreign aid, especially from Saudi Arabia. The country is afflicted by a scarcity of rainfall, and economic growth is only just beginning, following a protracted and bitter civil war. The government encourages foreign investment, pursuing an open-door policy. Any venture, however, must absorb local raw materials, train the local labour force, satisfy domestic consumption and create exports (to increase the inflow of foreign currencies and reduce the burden of the import balances).

People's Democratic Republic of Yemen The economy of the Republic, both poor and severely deficient in its infrastructure, centres around service activities (wholesale and retail trade, public administration, oil refining and bunkering at the port of Aden, etc.) as well as a largely rudimentary agriculture in which most of the population is engaged. A severe recession occurred in the five-year period ended 1972. The decline of GNP reflected the adverse effects of the closing of the Suez Canal on entrepôt trade, financial services, bunkering and other services provided through the port of Aden. Moreover, drought reduced the value added in agriculture by almost 60 per cent, while adoption of substantial fiscal measures led to a sharp cutback in consumption and investment expenditure. Great hopes are, therefore, vested in the new five-year plan (1974–79) - providing a total investment of 92 million dinar - since it aims at establishing an industrial and agricultural foundation on which it is possible to build up the material basis for changing the old, underdeveloped, society.

Priority in the industrial section is given to shoe manufacturing, tanning, plastic products, tomato paste, fishmeal, matches and cigarettes, textiles and cement. Great importance is also attached to geological research, particularly in oil and mineral prospecting. The Republic intended to start producing commercial quantities of petroleum by 1975.

As for agriculture, the government aims to rely on better techniques such as crop rotation, more intensive use of fertilisers, scientific research, introduction of better-quality seed and improved husbandry with regard to cattle, sheep and poultry; also, soil improvement schemes such as the use of irrigation and drainage networks, dams and floodwater control and other measures to control soil erosion.

The plan also includes a series of measures to improve the infrastructure, especially the air and sea communication networks. Great emphasis is given to modernisation of the port of Aden, which, with the reopening of the Suez Canal, could again flourish as an entrepôt and bunkering centre on the route to the Gulf and Indian Ocean. The projected financing of investments indicates a high degree of dependence on external aid, mainly from the USSR, China, the Arab countries, the United Nations and the IBRD. Virtually all capital movements require prior approval by the Exchange Control Committee. However, external borrowing by non-resident firms operating in the country is exempt. Remittance of profits abroad is permitted up to a level of 50 per cent of net profits. Repatriation of the original investment is allowed after five years from the start of operation of the enterprise, at a rate of 25 per cent of investment value per annum.

Notes

[1] Demographic data are inadequate in the Middle East. An up-to-date reliable guide is J.I. Clarke and W.B. Fisher, *Populations of the Middle East and North Africa,* University of London Press, 1972. The *Population Bulletins* of ECWA (formerly UNESOB) are also useful.

[2] UN Economic Commission for Western Asia, *The Social Situation in the ECWA Region,* ECWA/HR/74.1, March 1974, p. 3.

[3] It is, however, suspected that such low rates are due to underestimation of the female labour force. UNESOB, *Long-Term Perspectives in the Development of Selected Countries of the Middle East with special reference to industrial and labour force structures in the year 2000,* September 1971, p. 42.

[4] UNESOB, *La croissance économique et le niveau de qualification de la population active dans divers pays du Moyen Orient,* a survey carried out by Saint-Joseph University, Beirut, April 1971.

[5] Some of the finest general surveys on the economic growth of the

Middle East and North Africa originate from UN specialised agencies, particularly the International Bank for Reconstruction and Development, the International Monetary Fund, the Economic Commission for Western Asia (formerly UNESOB), and the Economic Commission for Africa. Very useful, and often annually updated, are the following volumes: H.J. Budig and M. Süer, *Middle East and North Africa Markets Review,* Gower Economic Publications, Epping, Essex; Europa Publications, *The Middle East and North Africa,* London; *Studies on Development Problems in Selected Countries of the Middle East,* UN, New York; *Arab Economic Report* published by the General Union of Chambers of Commerce, Industry and Agriculture for Arab Countries, Beirut; *Rapport sur l'économie arabe* published by the 'Office Arabe de Presse et de Documentation', Damascus. Among the various journals the best sources include: the *Middle East Economic Digest* (London), *Middle East International* (London), *Middle East Studies Association Bulletin* (Washington DC), *Middle East Economic Survey* (Beirut), *Arab Oil and Gas* (Beirut), *The Arab Economist* (Beirut), *Middle East Economic Papers* published by the American University of Beirut. As far as statistics are concerned, in addition to publications of the UN specialised agencies, the report of the International Agency for Development (AID), *Near East and South Asia,* is also helpful, being frequently updated.

[6] R. El Mallakh, *Kuwait, Economic Development and Regional Co-operation,* University of Chicago Press, 1968, p. 237.

5 Persistent weaknesses in the region's agricultural economy

5.1 Major emphasis on production

Not only is agricultural production in the countries under review lagging behind targets, but the annual growth rate of agricultural output is far below the growth rate of any other sector of the economy and does not even match the annual increase in population. In fact, according to ECWA estimates,[1] during 1961–71 the rate of growth in gross value of agricultural production in the Middle East was a meagre 1·3 per cent per annum with *per capita* agricultural production actually decreasing at an annual rate of 1·6 per cent. Although agricultural production in individual countries fluctuates widely from year to year (owing to the arid and semi-arid conditions and variations in rainfall), overall performance in some countries has been rather disappointing, particularly in Jordan (partly because of war and civil disturbances), the Yemen Arab Republic, Mauritania, Algeria, Democratic Yemen and Syria, where – according to the FAO – *per capita* agricultural production during the period 1961–72 declined considerably or stagnated (as in Tunisia, Saudi Arabia and even Egypt).

In contrast, the somewhat better growth rate of Iraq and, to a lesser extent, of Iran is largely due to an expansion of the area under cultivation rather than to intensification of land use. The apparently satisfactory performance of Sudan, Morocco and Turkey is mainly due to increased production for export outside the region (mainly of cotton, tobacco and citrus fruit), while in cereals and sheep production, achievements have been quite small.

Despite considerable efforts, Libya (as well as the other small oil-rich states) remains overwhelmingly dependent on foreign food supplies. And the excellent growth rate of Cyprus is now impaired by the impact of 200,000 refugees.

More serious is the fact that those commodity groups which are lagging in performance, and are mostly vulnerable to fluctuations in rainfall, include cereals, grains and meat, the produce on which the great bulk of the farm populations of the review countries depend. By contrast, rice production under irrigation has expanded rapidly, especially in Egypt and Iran. Sheep production has remained virtually static (apart from Iraq, Iran and Sudan), while beef production has done little better. Poultry production has expanded on a commercial scale, especially in Lebanon, Jordan and the oil-rich states where other sources of animal protein are lacking locally.

As to processing crops, the production of oilseeds has made little progress (with the notable exceptions of sesame and cotton seeds in Sudan), though cotton production has expanded considerably, especially in Egypt, Iran, Sudan, Syria and Turkey. Sugar production increased in Turkey, Egypt, Iran and Morocco, while tobacco production has fared remarkably well in Turkey, Cyprus, Iran, Lebanon and Syria.

Vegetable crops (notably tomatoes, onions and potatoes), mainly sold within the region, have shown a significantly higher rate of growth in most countries (including some of the micro-states of the Gulf, but especially in Iraq, Egypt and Syria). Fruit production has also expanded rapidly, especially for apples (Lebanon) and citrus fruit (Egypt, Lebanon, Cyprus, Iran, Iraq, Turkey, Morocco, Tunisia, Algeria). The production of dates has stagnated, however, even declining in Iraq and Saudi Arabia.

Disequilibrium between demand and supply has increased food prices and forced many countries to rely more heavily on imports, notably grain shipments. Thus, the picture presented in Table 5.1 is alarming. In fact, between 1962 and 1972, total wheat and wheat flour imports of the countries under review showed a spectacular increase (especially to Egypt - by far the major importer - Saudi Arabia, Sudan[2], Algeria, Iran, Kuwait, Lebanon, Libya and the Yemen Arab Republic). Syrian and Tunisian exports fell, in addition, and those to Morocco and Algeria ceased. Many of the countries also import meat and meat products.

The situation worsened in 1973–74, when agricultural and food imports rose more rapidly at soaring prices. In fact, between July 1973 and May 1974, Saudi Arabia tripled its food imports; Iran bought a total of 2·5 million tons of wheat; Egypt renewed massive imports of wheat and wheat flour (and also corn, seed oil, tallow, soya bean meal, mixed feed and tobacco), buying from the United States and substantially from Australia; and Iraq imported considerable amounts of wheat from Canada and Australia. Demand is expected to rise at 4 to 5 per cent per annum during the coming ten years (because of population pressure and growth, increasing urbanisation and industrialisation, and rising incomes and living standards). But with production probably growing at an annual rate of between 1 and 3 per cent[3] the present trend (unless policies are

Table 5.1
Basic statistics on agriculture, 1972

Country	Estimated cultivated area ('000 ha.)	Irrigated land ('000 ha.)	Agricultural holdings (total in '000)	Share of agricultural population (%)	Share of gross agricultural product (%)	Index of per capita agricultural production (1961-65 = 100)		Share of investment allocations - plan targets - (%)	Agriculture as % of total trade	
						1961	1972		Exports	Imports
Algeria	6,700	270	-	56	9	91	86	18·0	12	11
Bahrain	2	-	-	6	1	-	-	-	-	16
Cyprus	432	102	1,642	35	16	91	163	-	53	16
Egypt	2,842	2,842	1,877	55	29	88	101	12·0	61	25
Iran	16,727	5,251	253	46	19	102	110	14·0	35	10
Iraq	10,163	3,675	-	47	18	101	133	24·0	4	19
Jordan	1,300	60	-	39	18	101	59	15·5	39	29
Kuwait	0·5	0·6	0·4	1	0·3	-	-	-	1	20
Lebanon	316	68	127	47	10	92	109	6·6	28	22
Libya	2,521	130	145	43	3	96	121	21·0	-	16
Mauritania	263	0·3	-	85	31	98	95	-	-	-
Morocco	6,015	594	1,106	61	31	85	113	46·0	56	21
Qatar	2	-	-	4	-	-	-	-	-	12
Oman	36	-	-	14	15	-	-	20·0	1	30
Saudi Arabia	809	131	188	60	4	99	101	-	-	32
Syria	5,899	495	1,064	49	22	81	98	31·5	58	25
Sudan	7,100	711	-	80	38	96	121	27·9	98	27
Tunisia	4,510	80	326	50	14	83	100	-	39	18
Turkey	27,614	15	-	66	31	99	109	12·0	75	21
United Arab Emirates	20	-	-	18	-	-	-	-	-	13
Yemen Arab Republic	1,500	105	-	90	66	103	84	14·5	97	48
Yemen Democratic Republic	252	-	-	62	24	98	97	22·3	9	21

Sources: FAO National Plans.

changed) will lead to shortages and high cost for essential items. The situation, socially, may therefore become highly explosive, especially in the densely populated areas of the non-oil-rich countries. And this despite government programmes to subsidise food imports.

The optimism about the world food situation and prospects which prevailed at the end of the sixties has now given way to widespread anxiety. Thus, according to FAO estimates, in the early eighties the cereals deficit for the developing countries might rise to around 100 million tons per year - three times their gross imports in 1969-71. Moreover, the main foreign suppliers (notably the United States for grain shipments) have resorted to export controls and a sudden curb on food aid. Tremendous steep rises in consumer prices are therefore to be expected whilst the regularity of food supplies could be impaired by eventual retaliatory campaigns against the Arab World, with the prospect of severe hardship for the poorest strata of the population.

Top priority, therefore, is to accelerate the expansion of agricultural production to attain greater self-sufficiency and better security of food supply, the more so since, at the regional level, calories fall short of average requirements and malnutrition among the poorer classes is widespread. (In particular, there is a lack of protein-rich food, vitamin deficiencies, anaemia, rickets and endemic goitres.)

5.2 The crucial inputs

The poor performance of agriculture in the past should by no means be regarded as indicative of a low potential for development in the future. Once the granary of the ancient world, the region could become in a matter of two or three decades a net exporter of grain,[4] as well as a major world meat producer[5] (given the large tracts of land for grazing in the arid and semi-arid areas and in the savannah plains of the Sudan). But first, crucial inputs and basic infrastructures must be adjusted to development requirements.

A major aspect limiting both crop and animal production is gross underutilisation of good farmland. The winter rainlands of Syria, Iraq, Iran, etc. are only half-cropped with cereals annually; fallows occupy more than half the area, sometimes even in zones of adequate rainfall of more than 350 mm. The summer rainlands of the Sudan are cropped continuously with sorghum and millet for around four years or more, then abandoned for about the same period before resumption of cropping.[6] Equally, the monoculture system of cereal production, without fertilisers, continues in several zones, despite repeated experimental evidence of the value of nitrogenous legumes in boosting grain yields, aside from their role as animal feeds. Increased attention needs also to be directed to more intensive use of existing resources, particularly of areas of fairly high or medium rainfall, and of irrigated lands whose yields are still low. Thus, in Syria and Iraq, wheat production can be raised from 250 kg. per feddan to 1,100 kg. under rainfall cultivation and to 2,500 kg. under permanent irrigation. Rice cultivation in Egypt can produce a yield of 3·5 tons per feddan instead of the actual 2·5 tons; cotton from 600 lb. per feddan to 1,000 lb. and sugar cane from 40 to 70 tons per feddan. Thus, at regional level – through intensified use of irrigated land – the harvested irrigated area is expected to be increased in the early eighties by 4·2 million hectares (a rise of 35 per cent over the 1962 situation). Further development is planned, by bringing around 2·9 million hectares of new land under irrigation by 1985, and by reconstructing about 800,000 hectares of irrigated land.[7] Additional advantages should be obtained by integrating cropland with animal husbandry, to achieve a more intensive and rational system of production.

Provided the appropriate animal hygiene, management and breeding can be achieved, the livestock industry has great potential for development in the region, given the rapidly increasing demand for meat, milk and other animal products, and the very promising future for intraregional trade. Since both marine and inland fishery resources have, in most cases, not yet been exploited, fish and fishery products can also play a major role in filling the animal protein gap. Again, there must be adequate usage and technical control.

However, in all countries under review, land and water resources remain a severe limiting factor on agricultural development. Thus, it is necessary to convey water from dams to farms, to search for underground water, build up large surface reservoirs and dams (such as the Euphrates in Syria, the Rahad project in the Sudan and the Lar project in Iran), and to desalt sea water (for which the use of nuclear power is envisaged). The situation also calls for: (a) the introduction of genetic strains requiring less water; (b) the scientific location of specific crops to ensure maximum efficiency of water; (c) improved irrigation methods, with emphasis on adequate drainage to check extreme salinity and waterlogging); (d) reallocation of water supply from irrigation projects, thus permitting intensification by growing short-duration autumn and spring crops and by providing supplementary irrigation to winter crops, especially wheat; (e) construction of water points so that livestock can move safely from the breeding and producing areas to the processing and consuming areas and to export points; (f) exploitation of the high-water potential of the Nile at its sources in the Sudan, much of which is being lost in marshes, or evaporated without being put to use; (g) conservation of natural resources (specifically by rational grazing of arid lands, by stopping the cultivation of marginal land and by afforestation, as well as by planting to afford shelter and sand-dune fixation and thus limit the encroachment of desert.

Further, other measures are needed to integrate the open grazing areas with dryland farming, with a view to securing an assured supply of feed through the critical months of the year. In fact most livestock production (outside Mauritania), now mostly under non-nomadic conditions, requires considerable feeding of the animals during the long dry summer and autumn. And, since animal feed crops cannot compete in the markets except as by-products (sugarbeet pulp, cottonseed meal, etc.) or provide more than a minor element in a rotation (trifoleum in Egypt), changes in existing cropping patterns are needed to emphasise cereal/legume rotation.

Egypt and Lebanon apart, much greater strides could also be made in rainfall areas with adequate soil moisture, by increasing the present use of fertilisers to raise yields of traditional seed. The goal of producing 10 tons of cereals per ton of fertilisers could be attained in several countries, since industry is establishing nitrogen-based plants and phosphorous units (in Morocco and Jordan) fed with natural gas. In addition, taking into account the requirements of the various crops, a more balanced use of fertilisers should be introduced.

Equally, the use of insecticides should be increased, to cover standing crops as well as produce in storage. Since (apart from the Nile valley) yields do not seem particularly outstanding, the use of improved, high-yielding varieties should be expanded more rapidly than in the past. The UNDP/FAO wheat and barley improvement and productive project has made a substantial contribution in raising the yield of these two crops throughout the region and is to be extended to other crops, including other cereals, legumes and oilseed. Except in Egypt and Lebanon, however, large-scale adoption of high-yielding varieties has not yet taken place; indeed none has as yet been developed for bread wheat or for barley grown in low rainfall areas, and very few for durum wheat. Research efforts must therefore be intensified in a bid for improved and disease-resistant varieties suited to dry conditions. Moreover, an accelerated programme of systematic production, certification and distribution of seed is essential to meet the annual requirements of farmers. The research efforts should also concentrate on the livestock sector where the Shami cattle (especially in Syria, Iraq, Jordan, Lebanon and Egypt) and Awassi sheep (in the larger part of the Middle East) are the highest yielders and most efficient feed converters.[8] In addition, study programmes should be intensified to breed resistance to rinderpest and foot and mouth, bovine pleuropneumonia and Brucellosis. Other measures are needed to prevent pollution (especially in the oil-producing countries) and to develop fishery resources.

Another major factor is the use of agricultural machinery, which in the last few years has increased rapidly (notably, the use of tractors in Iran, Egypt, Iraq, Syria, Libya, Cyprus, Tunisia, Morocco and Algeria; waterpumps in Lebanon, Saudi Arabia, Jordan, Iraq and Syria; combine harvesters in Iraq, Syria and North Africa). However, mechanisation needs adequate servicing and spare-part facilities, and satisfactory testing and adaptation to local conditions. Thus, in addition to assembly plants to be established in co-operation with the large international firms, action should be taken: (a) to develop the potential of existing small workshops (mostly repairing motor vehicles, tractors, combine harvesters and engines); (b) to create small and medium industrial units to provide common facilities and undertake research (to match machinery to the size of holdings, to the climatic conditions, etc.), and to manufacture locally (in the district of use) items such as the standard Arab chisel plough, cultivators, harrows, sprayers, sprinkler irrigation units, equipment for potatoes and beet, pumps, stone pickers, trailers, etc.); (c) to expand the scope of the farm machinery hire service, operating from a common pool (either co-operatively or through a public agency) – project implementation, machinery operation, etc. would be included, as well as practical training courses.

5.3 Changing farmers' attitudes and practices

Agricultural development requires transformation not only of production systems but also of the composition of the rural population itself. In many areas of the region a major problem is that the average share of arable land owned is only 1·3 hectares. But despite the large proportion of the working population engaged in agriculture, the increasing mobility of youth to urban areas – especially in the oil-rich states, but also Jordan, Lebanon and Syria – has resulted in labour shortages and labour problems, notably at harvest time.[9]

Action is therefore imperative to alleviate the poverty plaguing farming communities and to halt the drift from the land; also, to bring nomadism into the mainstream of economic and social growth. The best course would

Table 5.2

Trade in wheat and wheat flour, rice, sheep and lambs, cattle, cotton, dates, oranges and tangerines, tobacco, olive oil and sugar in 1962 and 1972

(quantity: 1,000 metric tons)

Trade	wheat and wheat flour(a)		rice		sheep and lambs(b)		cattle(c)		raw cotton		dates		oranges and tangerines		tobacco, unmanu-factured		olive oil		sugar	
	1962	1972	1962	1972	1962	1972	1962	1972	1962	1972	1962	1972	1962	1972	1962	1972	1962	1972	1962	1972
Imports																				
Algeria	507	814	1	16	3	20	10	10	9	6	-	-	-	-	4	4	-	-	313	255
Bahrain	14	19	6	20	-	60	-	5	-	-	-	-	-	6	-	-	-	-	9	2
Cyprus	60	42	4	3	-	-	-	-	-	-	-	-	-	-	-	1	-	-	18	18
Egypt	1,569	3,229d	-	-	1	1	24	-	-	-	8	4	-	-	12	15	-	-	189	11
Iran	161	2,500e	19	80	-	250	-	2	-	-	-	-	-	-	-	-	-	1	220	109
Iraq	-	90	69	30	-	2	-	-	-	-	-	-	-	-	-	-	-	-	351	277
Jordan	113	108	18	30	324	130	6	-	-	-	2	3	7	29	1	1	-	-	75	65
Kuwait	71	116	18	40	-	250	-	6	-	-	-	18	-	29	-	1	-	2	30	30
Lebanon	206	345	19	25	770	670	110	90	1	1	1	3	-	-	-	-	-	1	35	73
Libya	111	286	7	23	47	952	3	11	4	5	-	-	-	-	-	2	-	12	93	79
Mauritania	12	17	1	1	-	-	-	-	-	-	-	-	-	-	-	-	-	-	26	26
Morocco	394	396	-	-	-	-	-	1	6	7	-	-	-	-	4	6	-	-	300	250
Saudi Arabia	166	362	141	166	399	1,200	5	50	2	2	5	-	11	35	-	1	-	1	27	82
Syria	203	360	35	56	511	300	10	1	-	-	31	30	47	82	-	-	-	-	83	121
Sudan	88	213	4	9	-	-	-	-	-	-	4	9	-	-	-	-	-	-	82	145
Tunisia	272	278	3	2	26	100	-	17	4	5	-	-	-	-	1	3	-	-	91	121
Turkey	691	123	1	4	-	-	1	-	-	-	-	-	-	-	-	-	-	-	-	-
Yemen Arab Republic	-	83	3	5	-	-	-	-	-	-	-	6	-	-	-	-	-	-	50	54
Yemen Democratic Republic	74	67	26	25	316	300	2	-	-	-	-	11	1	1	3	2	-	-	40	44
Exports																				
Algeria	12	-	1	-	-	-	-	-	1	6	22	12	152	202	4	4	1	4	-	-
Cyprus	-	-	-	-	-	-	-	-	-	-	-	-	40	119	-	1	1	-	-	-
Egypt	6	-	143	456	6	50	1	-	250	295	-	-	8	82	-	-	-	-	12	20
Iran	-	4	-	-	-	50	-	10	47	90	26	34	-	-	-	-	-	-	-	-
Iraq	38	150	-	-	10	2	-	-	2	4	230	280	-	-	-	1	-	-	-	-
Lebanon	2	5	-	-	-	2	-	-	3	-	-	1	69	130	2	2	1	-	-	1
Mauritania	-	-	-	-	71	741	100	100	-	-	2	2	-	-	-	-	-	-	-	-
Morocco	74	-	2	-	2	-	-	-	10	4	-	-	49	64	4	6	2	3	3	9
Syria	214	150	-	-	260	219	16	54	113	116	-	-	-	1	1	4	1	-	-	-
Sudan	-	-	-	-	96	160	8	21	160	247	-	-	-	-	-	-	-	-	-	-
Tunisia	33	5	-	-	40	25	-	-	-	-	3	7	40	-	-	-	22	133	-	-
Turkey	-	1	-	-	363	389	47	20	223	252	-	-	24	59	92	124	12	3	82	133
Yemen Democratic Republic	27	8	18	3	6	-	-	-	5	4	2	1	-	2	2	-	-	-	5	2

Notes: (a) flour in wheat equivalent; (b) '000 head; (c) '000 head; (d) datum for 1973 obtained from export statistics of Australia, Canada and the United States; (e) datum for 1974 obtained from MEED, 25 October 1974, p.1285.
Source: *FAO Trade Yearbook*, Rome, 1973.

be to grant incentives to small farmers, invest more in improving living standards and in settlement, and to establish channels of communication, etc. rather than insist on structural changes, such as land tenure, related to ideologies and politics. Land reform has provided no panacea for the Middle East's employment and food problem. In Egypt, 5 to 10 per cent of the tenants and agricultural labourers working on expropriated estates received no land under the reform programme, and hence joined the growing number of landless unemployed, while the size of the units distributed proved to be too small, especially in view of the increase in the beneficiaries' families over the years. Nor have the reforms achieved all their political objectives, since many of the former landlords acquired urban real estate (and are now influential city figures), while the new military leaders in Iraq and Syria now possess estates in rural areas.[10]

However, if, in some areas, fragmentation of land is a serious obstacle to increase in agricultural production, this does not explain the lack of viable land in other large areas where fragmentation is unimportant. What is really lacking are: (a) appropriate incentives favouring small farmers, e.g. attractive guaranteed prices for major products and bonuses for high levels of production; a thorough review of the price structure to stimulate production of commodities giving a high return on production costs; subsidies in drought years; special subsidies, for the provision of seeds, fertilisers, machinery, water, fuel, etc; credit facilities; and co-operative marketing, etc. (b) knowledge as to management of rainfall, dry farming areas, the use of limited water supplies, the choice of cropping pattern, the interrelationship between livestock and crop husbandry, etc. (c) communication between the authorities and the farmers, since, as stated by Lamartine Yates – 'between the two there is an almost complete vacuum, even barriers of suspicion and mistrust'. [11] (d) reliable and timely information on production plans, prices, costs of production including transport, assessment of demand and supply of commodities. (e) effective investment in improvement of living standards, especially for backward rural villages with poor sanitary conditions, illiteracy, scanty supplies of drinking water and electricity, high infant mortality, etc; as also investment in settlement to help the growing number of landless and spontaneously reduce nomadism among the Bedouin population.[12] (f) rapid introduction of education and training facilities to meet the shortage of qualified people (especially veterinarians), to impart extension education and training to large numbers of small farmers so as to make agriculture productive. (g) radical revision of the structures of credit institutions and co-operatives. Finally, the serious deficiencies in research programmes, organisation and administration –

which hinder development and proper implementation - have to be challenged by reorganising the governmental machinery with emphasis on adequate co-ordination of the various departments and on active local participation. Procedures must not be so cumbersome as to discourage the farmer; adequate research facilities and a congenial research atmosphere must be provided, to halt the increasing outflow of technical staff; a veterinary drugs firm must be established, in view of the poor animal hygiene practised in the region; and the appropriate strategies must be developed to meet critical shortages of basic foodstuffs, e.g. a stockholding policy, limitation of the area used to produce export commodities, etc.

5.4 An integrated rural strategy

Both realistic targets and defined supporting policies are lacking in current development plans. And despite more emphasis on agriculture, the size of the investment programmes seems small in relation to the need. In particular, as regards implementation, an enormous gap persists between what appears officially and what actually happens on the farms. Additionally, in sharp contrast to the emphasis on the infrastructure of irrigation, drainage and land reclamation, relatively little attention is paid to investment in the broad agricultural subsectors: crops, livestock, forestry and fisheries. Agricultural projects often lack integration as part of a general programme. There is no assessment of long term prospects. And wide differences exist in the orientation of options for the various countries of the region.

A new approach is therefore needed to bring about more realistic development with improved implementation. Planning should be disaggregated into a reasonable number of subareas or zones (within an integrated whole), the potential of which should be determined on the basis of natural resources and adequate technical information. Well co-ordinated, short, medium and long-range plans for research extension and education, which meet the requirements for the development of the various zones, should be prepared. Field trials in the various zones are also necessary to obtain reliable and precise recommendations as to land-use patterns and use of inputs. Farm planning and management techniques should be taught to selected farmers in these zones to demonstrate, generally, the possibility of improving farm production and income through better management of existing resources and through addition of resources and inputs. Gradually, the extension should be

Table 5.3

Egypt: grain imports by country 1970–72 and 1973 estimate ('000 metric tons)

Commodity and country	1970	1971	1972	1973
Wheat:				
United States	–	–	–	426
Australia	–	1,082	1,805	625
Canada	–	421	–	–
USSR	109	244	–	–
France	336	–	565	405
West Germany	133	15	5	212
Italy	227	89	–	275
Rumania	–	–	–	–
Bulgaria	–	–	–	–
Spain	28	–	–	–
Sweden	–	15	–	–
Mexico	–	–	–	–
Greece	–	41	–	–
Turkey	–	10	140	–
Iran	–	–	–	–
Other	17	14	63	577
Total Wheat	850	1,931	2,578	2,520
Wheat flour:				
United States	–	–	–	54
Canada	11	–	30	–
Spain	152	58	60	–
Rumania	–	–	2	–
France	52	173	160	120
West Germany	–	–	–	30
Italy	51	113	125	106
East Germany	9	–	–	–
Other	–	–	183	200
Total Wheat Flour	275	344	560	510
Total wheat flour in wheat equivalent	382	478	778	709
Total wheat and wheat flour	1,232	2,409	3,356	3,229
Corn	73	39	92	230
Rice	–	–	5	–
Sorghum	–	–	–	–
Total grain and flour	1,305	2,448	3,453	3,459

Sources: Foreign Statistics of Arab Republic of Egypt 1971; Grain Bulletin from Commonwealth Economic Committee and export data from Australia, Canada, and the United States for the 1973 estimate.

Table 5.4
Saudi Arabia: estimated grain supply
('000 metric tons)

Crop	1971	1972	1973	1974
Wheat and flour:				
Production	72	150	150	175
Imports	325	370	420	530
Supply	397	520	570	705
From US	91	170	195	300
Rice:				
Production	3	4	4	5
Imports	220	167	158	250
Supply	223	171	162	255
From US	53	79	71	125
Coarse grains:				
Production	347	357	300	370
Imports	88	110	115	180
Supply	435	467	415	550
From US	17	7	1	20
Total cereals:				
Production	422	511	454	550
Imports	633	647	740	960
Supply	1,055	1,158	1,194	1,510
From US	161	256	267	445
	Per cent	*Per cent*	*Per cent*	*Per cent*
Share of grain supply imported	60·0	65·9	62·0	63·6
Share of grain supply imported from US	15·3	20·4	31·0	29·5

Source: US Department of Agriculture.

geared to stress a farm rather than a single enterprise approach. Thus, interzonal analysis would not only be helpful in the selection and relationship of projects, but also allow a more rational allocation of inputs along various zones, so that planners could adopt an integrated rural development approach to increase production, create employment opportunities, improve income distribution and build up the necessary institutions, etc.

The zonal strategy should be formulated so that full consideration is given to interrelationships between industrial and agricultural development and to the interdependence of agriculture and the food processing industry. In densely populated areas, especially, it is of the utmost importance for planners to achieve a balance between the industrial and agricultural sectors, and to foster the development of agro-industries which can stimulate progress in the whole agricultural field, giving farmers the possibility of moving into a market economy. In addition, to make the zonal approach viable, governments should encourage farmers to participate in agricultural planning through farm organisations and local authorities (village councils); this would lessen the risk of excessive government control and intervention, which inevitably leads to bureaucracy and decreases confidence.[13]

5.5 A more far-reaching price policy

A new approach is also needed for price policy. In some instances, farmers' incomes have been improved through the establishment of comprehensive agencies in Egypt, Iran, Syria, Iraq, Libya, Cyprus and North Africa, for products such as cotton, sugar beet, dates, citrus and potatoes[14] to facilitate purchase, storage and sale at minimum guaranteed prices (with a rising price scale for the best qualities); incentives such as the supply of inputs at comparatively low prices have also been adopted.

However, the integration of the production phase with input and marketing facilities under the aegis of state agencies managed, directly or indirectly, by government officials has resulted merely in 'red tape', operational efficiency being hampered and payments to farmers delayed. In addition, major areas such as the livestock sector and fisheries, which both have great potential for the region, have been neglected in instituting such schemes.

A more comprehensive strategy is therefore necessary to give small farmers' organisations a central role in the management of the state agencies. Equally, as in Bahrain, the State could take the initiative of establishing agricultural co-operatives to produce and market the goods of small farmers. In such a way, the co-operatives would contract supply commitments every year at a negotiated price, assuring quality levels and providing storage, packaging and transportation, while the government would supply farmer members of the co-operatives with technical expertise (for instance, by means of an efficient extension service) and special incentives (such as certified seeds, long and medium-term loans, adequate subsidies in case of drought, water and fertilisers at lower prices).

Moreover, with adequate rural representation, state agencies could play an important role in the establishment of priorities in homogeneous zones, with reference to needs, classes of products and areas to be developed.

Other priorities would include the sponsoring of quality control to develop a brand image; stabilisation of food prices and the means of production (through a managerial stockholding policy); establishment of nutrition programmes (for the more vulnerable groups); feasibility surveys to explore the investment opportunities of agro-industries (notably in the neglected areas, e.g. processing of hides and skins and other animal products) and of new food processing techniques (such as irradiation and the biosynthesis of proteins from normal paraffins and methanol).

5.6 Fostering joint operations and intraregional trade

Planning will be of limited use in advancing agricultural development if it does not promote joint operations, intraregional technical collaboration and intraregional trade.

Joint operations could be financed by the oil resources of the region with mutual benefit for both the capital-giving and capital-receiving countries. They could take the form of: (a) joint companies for the production of specific commodities (meat, poultry, fish, etc.); (b) joint organisations for marketing produce (e.g. fruit and vegetables) inside and outside the region; (c) joint endeavours to co-ordinate use of basic resources (e.g. surface and underground water common to two or more countries) and implement integrated plans (e.g. joint researches for subsoil waters). The Arab Organisation for Agricultural Development, with headquarters in Khartoum, could assist in identifying investment opportunities and prospects.

Technical collaboration would cover types of co-operation less than fully joint. An agreed programme would be needed for each purpose, carried out separately but in close consultation. Existing examples are the FAO-backed Near East wheat and barley improvement project, the Near East Animal Health Institute, the Mediterranean and Near East olive oil project, and the Fisheries Training Institute for the Gulf. Further regional centres are envisaged for plant breeding; for the multiplication and distribution of certified seed; for the development of the semi-arid zones; for the control of desert locusts; for range management; for horticultural produce; for agricultural mechanisation; and for marketing, research, training and exchange of information (on production plans, prices, costs of production, etc.).

Expanded intraregional commerce could also yield substantial gains. Diversity of natural resources and the practical impossibility for most countries of the region to attain broad agricultural self-sufficiency places a premium on co-operation in intraregional trade, favouring economies of scale; the widening of the market; reduced vulnerability to the uncertainty of world markets; and close agricultural links, through countries specialising in planned crop production, linked to agreed programmes of agricultural development. Thus, the crucial dilemma today facing several Middle East nations - whether to concentrate on production for export markets or, alternatively, to aim at increasing domestic production of food supplies, meeting pressing local needs and saving agricultural imports - could be overcome in the general interest of the whole region. Moreover, a country like the Sudan, in addition to achieving self-sufficiency in food (as almost everything needed for local consumption can be locally produced), could become the Arab World's granary and protein supplier. In fact, the Sudan already produces more meat, milk, hides and skins and has a larger area devoted to cereal cultivation, than any other Arab country.

Furthermore, the establishment of a wider and more stable commerce among the countries of the region would provide a basis for formulating co-ordinated agricultural policies to maximise use of available agricultural resources through emphasis on those products with the greatest potential for growth. Historically, when free trade agreements were in force in the twenties, a substantial part of the region's trade, especially in agricultural commodities, was intra-Arab trade. In 1930, the regional market was narrowed by the emergence of economic nationalism. In 1940, the British created the Middle East Supply Centre which, acting as a central planning authority, succeeded in reducing regional imports and raised intraregional trade for some products, notably wheat, rice and cotton.

After World War II, attempts to reconstruct intra-Arab trade failed. The Arab Common Market - based on a simple free trade area and ratified by only five countries (Kuwait, Egypt, Jordan, Iraq and Syria) - had little practical effect because of the numbers of important reserved items and the state trading procedures of the member countries, and because no preferences were given to stimulate trade between members. In addition, the lack of a multilateral payment agreement (to complement an effective customs union), and a series of bilateral agreements mostly affected by political factors, impeded any genuine effort towards economic integration. Thus, intraregional trade (concentrated on vegetables, fruit, eggs, poultry and livestock) has been increased only slowly in recent years, while numerous countries remain overwhelmingly dependent on agricultural commodities in their exports to industrial countries (cotton, rice, tobacco, oranges, dates, etc.).

New efforts to organise intercountry co-operation for agricultural trade are therefore needed. In particular, intraregional production and trade of as many as possible of the commodities currently imported (cereals, sugar, oilseeds and livestock products) could be fostered by: (a) large-scale joint commercial ventures to combine the resources, know-how and investment funds of two or more countries; (b) a marked preference for regional produce in the import programmes, through the machinery of intergovernmental co-operation and consultation. Thus, successful ventures already in operation, for instance in the poultry industry and fisheries enterprises, could be extended to other products (e.g. to meat production in the Sudan by developing feed-lot fattening of beef cattle in place of the current trade in live animals; to wheat and barley, which Syria and Iraq could regularly market within the region, once certain technical and administrative problems had been overcome; to rice, which Egypt, on successfully switching to long-grain varieties, could sell to Saudi Arabia and the Gulf states).

Steps could also be taken to start a common agricultural policy backed by a regional fund and aimed at gradually harmonising each country's objectives. Regional trade would enjoy preference through common import regulations and exchange allocations, adjustment of government interventions, priorities in transport, storage and refrigeration projects, etc.

5.7 Ample opportunities for Western countries

As part of a rapid expansion of agricultural production, there is tremendous scope for bilateral and tripartite collaboration among the industrial countries, the oil-rich states and those countries of the region disposing of great agricultural potential (e.g. the Sudan, which can supply massive quantities of grain, edible oils and meat, as well as fibres, if capital and technical assistance are provided). The resources to be harnessed are, on the one hand, Western technology, know-how, management and technical assistance, and on the other, oil funds, potential agricultural wealth and raw materials. Best option for mutual benefit is through establishment of joint ventures combining the physical and financial resources of the region with the skills and equipment of the enterprises of developed countries.

The type of joint-venture enterprise can vary considerably and should be adapted to specific cases. Thus, specialised consortia of Western companies can set up agricultural and food ventures in the region, in return for investment from the oil-rich countries in their respective fields. For example, Australia is helping Iran to set up a number of food ventures, while, in return, Iran is to invest in Australian industries which will meet the domestic requirements of both countries and export to third countries. Equally, Western companies that want to become part of the oil business can offer package deals aiming at greater self-sufficiency in food or at providing essential needs (e.g. supply and installation of water treatment plants). A formula of production sharing can also be agreed on (especially for fertilisers), with Western firms supplying the necessary manufacturing equipment, special skills and market outlets, in return for capital investment and part of the output. Furthermore, agricultural joint ventures can simply be financed by the oil-rich countries, and managed by Western companies. And oil-rich countries can buy cultivable land in the developing countries outside the region (or even in the developed countries), while Western firms take care of production and management.

Another possibility is for agricultural contracts to be awarded: (a) on a turnkey basis (for construction of silage units, processing plants, etc.) providing adequate technical assistance to train local manpower; (b) to carry out consultancy services (to formulate a water policy, prepare a national crop production plan, prepare feasibility studies, etc.); (c) to build up breeding centres (for cross-breeding low-yielding indigenous breeds with high-yielding Western breeds, e.g. Friesians), as well as supplying disease-resistant seeds of high yield and fast growth; (d) to create experimental and pilot schemes (especially desalination plants) and apply advanced experience in arid land agriculture, as well as model villages (to establish self-sustaining rural communities); (e) to assist in the selection and execution of suitable projects, and in the marketing of the products; (f) to participate in basic research on major regional crops and provide training facilities for local scientists.

To take advantage of the ample opportunities in the agricultural sector, Western enterprises must be prepared to deal with large-scale projects in the framework of integrated rural development. Thus, for example, in Iraq, the consortia for the Nahr Saad livestock project are expected to be made up of land reclamation and livestock consultants, land reclamation contractors, livestock equipment contractors, livestock suppliers, etc., capable of developing large-scale milk and meat production through intensive irrigation and drainage networks of 20,000 hectares; dealing with imports of large numbers of Holstein–Friesian cows; and undertaking infrastructure works, including roads, villages, electricity and drinking water systems.

Foremost among the region's numerous projects are those dealing with:

(a) *Arid land agriculture,* notably in the oil-rich states. Considerable areas rich in minerals might be turned into productive crop soil by use of water and watering techniques (such as watering the roots rather than the surface vegetation), or by using highly saline water for a range of crops of salt-resistant strains (a method devised by Israeli scientists at the Volcanic Research Centre, Beit Dagan).

In some cases, priority is given to: prospecting, development and use of groundwater resources; drilling of artesian wells; construction of water pumping stations or reservoirs; supply and installation of irrigators to be used in major agro-industrial developmental projects; establishment of arid land research centres to develop hydroponics (such as that run by Abu Dhabi on Sadiyat Island and, more recently, by Libya, under the supervision of the University of Arizona); the growing of trees in the desert (using a salt-water feed until the roots can reach the subsurface water table), and in this way to make it possible to grow other plants on the land there.

(b) *Land reclamation and conservation practices,* in particular, to build channels for rainwater drainage; for the improvement of existing irrigation networks; the breeding of drought-resistant crops in areas where irrigation is impossible; the promotion of proper soil and water practices; soil analysis; experiments with new drought-resistant crops for pasture improvement, and the introduction of new crop patterns; the sowing of more land by aeroplane; the building of dams and pilot farms; the supply of seed drills; for wind screens to protect cultivated areas, etc.

(c) *Manufacture of synthetic proteins* (for incorporation in animal feeds, a process which several Western companies are already able to advance on a commercial scale), *fertilisers,* and *pesticides.*

(d) *A wide range of food processing industries,* particularly fruit and vegetable canning and dehydration; production of fish protein, soft drinks, baby food, wheat flour, softwoods; the setting-up of slaughter houses; sugar refining (including use of the bagasse by-product for production of pulp and paper and particle board); cotton ginning; skin tanning; salt mining; grain silos; flour mills and feedstuff plants.

Since, for (c) and (d), economies of scale require the product to be sold on a large market, participation by large multinational companies (bringing both expertise and market outlets) is to be envisaged.

The assistance and initiative of the specialised international economic organisations for relating managerial skills, marketing know-how and technology to financial and physical resources can further promote co-operation between the countries of the region and the Western World.

Thus, the United Nations Industrial Development Organisation can pave the way to agreements between countries for an exchange of experience and other forms of co-operation in various aspects of the food processing industry. For example, meetings can be arranged between businessmen and industrialists to investigate partnership possibilities in projects from which both sides could benefit, and exhibitions can be staged, for processing and packing food for export, etc.

In co-operation with the Arab Organisation for Agricultural Development, the Food and Agriculture Organisation - which provides technical advice and assistance in project identification, appraisal, formulation implementation and assessment - could start pioneering efforts to link and co-ordinate the agricultural development plans of the Near East, as well as establishing an internationally supported research institute in the region, on the same lines as for other regions (CIMMYT in Mexico, IRRI in the Philippines, CIAT in Columbia, IIAT in Nigeria, ICRISAT in India, etc.). Moreover, the FAO Investment Centre - under the FAO/IBRD co-operative programme and the banking co-operative programme in collaboration with the African Development Bank and the Kuwait Fund for Arab Economic Development - promotes investment and identifies projects for agricultural development, while the FAO industry co-operative programme (ICP) provides a forum for objective dialogue between government officials and industrial executives, and a channel to establish new agro-industries with participation by major multinational firms.

Agricultural and irrigation projects (on an *ad hoc* basis and within the countries' overall development plans) are also established by the UNDP representatives for each country of the region. A Near East Institute for Agricultural Education in planned by UNESCO, while the UNCTAD/GATT International Trade Centre envisages the setting-up of a regional centre for training in trade promotion and export marketing, which will deal with the basic commodities of the region. In addition, the World Bank is helping to finance a number of agricultural projects, notably in the non-oil countries.

Within the Mediterranean region, the OECD-sponsored Centre International de Hautes Etudes Agronomiques Mediterranéennes is working through three institutes: in Bari (Italy), on irrigation techniques, land consolidation and drainage; in Montpellier (France), specialising in agricultural planning and rural economy; and in Zaragoza (Spain), for the livestock industry and animal husbandry. At national levels, important contributions can be expected from the research work carried out on arid agriculture in some American and Australian universities. In Europe, pioneer schemes are being carried out by Durham University (actual sites, in Oman at Al-Khabourah on the Batinah coast). Further work could be done by several other European centres (e.g. the Agronomic Institute of Florence, the Institut Français de Recherches Fruitières, the Institut National de la Recherche Agronomique, the Tropical Products Institute, etc.).

Notes

[1] ECWA, *Review and Appraisal of Progress in the Agricultural Sector of Selected Countries in the Middle East,* Beirut, April 1974.

[2] The Sudan, however, is by and large self-sufficient in its staple cereal (sorghum).

[3] FAO, *Agricultural Adjustment in the Middle East,* 7th session of the Near East Commission on Agricultural Planning, Beirut, April 1974, p.6.

[4] M. Clawson, H.H. Landsberg, L.T. Alexander, *The Agricultural Potential of the Middle East,* Elsevier Publishing Co., New York, 1971, p.4.

[5] 'Livestock Production in the Near East and North Africa', *The Arab Economist,* Beirut, May 1974.

[6] FAO, *Agricultural Research Priorities for the Near East Region,* Kuwait, 9–19 September 1972, p.3.

[7] FAO, *Land and Water Development,* 11th regional conference for the Near East, July 1972, pp.2–3.

[8] FAO, *Near East Regional Study on Animal Husbandry,* Cairo, 1972, pp.78–84.

[9] FAO, *Population, Land and Agricultural Labour in the Near East,* 7th session of the Near East Commission, Beirut, March 1974.

[10] Rodney J.A. Wilson, *Agricultural Development in the Middle East 1950–1970,* Centre for Middle Eastern and Islamic Studies, University of Durham, December 1972, p.11.

[11] J.P. Peroncel-Hugo, 'Deux visages de l'Egypte, le don des fellahs', *Le Monde,* 5 July 1974; G. Duprat, *Révolution et autogestion rurale en Algérie,* A. Colin, Paris, 1973; Tami Tidafi, *L'agriculture algérienne et ses perspectives de développement,* F. Maspero, Paris, 1969.

[12] A Bedouin settlement in the heat of the Jordan desert produces eleven alfalfa crops a year against only five in the Po Valley (J. Bonar, 'Turning the Desert into Farmland', *The Financial Times,* 26 September 1974.)

[13] FAO, *Integrated Rural Development,* 7th session of the Near East Commission on Agricultural Planning, Beirut, April 1974.
[14] FAO, *La commercialisation et son intégration avec la production et les institutions rurales connexes dans la région du Proche Orient,* Kuwait, September 1972.

6 The development of an integrated and more competitive industrial sector

6.1 General characteristics of industrial development in the region

The general characteristics of industrial development in the region can be grouped as follows:

(a) Despite the efforts exerted and the financial resources made available during the past decade, *the countries of the region are still at the start of the road to industrialisation.* In 1970, the share of the Arab industrial product was no more than 0·4 per cent of world industrial product and 4 per cent of the total industrial product of the developing countries. Average *per capita* share of industrial product in the Arab countries was 30·8 dollars per person, while industrial consumption was 52·1 dollars compared with 22·6 dollars in the countries of Latin America. On average, industry contributes 15·8 per cent of GDP in the Mediterranean area, 7·7 per cent in the Gulf area and 8·4 per cent in the Red Sea area, and only in a few cases (Turkey, Iran) does it contribute 20 per cent or more (notably Lebanon and Egypt). Data from the Industrial Development Centre for Arab States (IDCAS)[1] reveal that in the second half of the sixties the contribution of the industrial sector in GDP for eleven Arab countries taken as a group was less than 18 per cent, and was as low as 2–4 per cent in Libya and Kuwait, 8–10 per cent in Jordan, the Sudan, Iraq and Algeria, and 13–15 per cent in Lebanon, Tunisia, Morocco and Syria. Egypt was the only Arab state to achieve a rate of 18 per cent.[2]

(b) As a whole, the countries of the region have not yet started *to exploit their natural resources* on a sizeable scale. The oil-producing countries refine no more than 10 per cent of their production, while countries possessing iron ore export the larger part in primary form. To meet their requirements of petroleum by-products, steel products and agricultural foodstuffs, the countries of the region resort to imports from the outside world, while manufactures constitute a low percentage of total exports. In 1972, manufactured goods accounted for 0·2 per cent of the exports of Saudi Arabia, 0·3 per cent for Libya, 2·5 per cent for Iran, 7 per cent for Kuwait, 7·5 per cent for Democratic Yemen, 9·8 per cent for Algeria, 14·5 per cent respectively for Egypt and Morocco and 21·5 per cent for Turkey. Manufacturing industry is still confined to a limited number of industrial products, and there is heavy dependence on the developed countries as a source of equipment and other industrial goods. Thus, in 1972, industrial exports constituted some 7·7 per cent of the total exports of the Arab countries, and industrial imports about 47·6 per cent of total imports. In addition, more than 70 per cent of the exports and 60 per cent of the imports of the Arab countries were conducted with ten developed countries, while trade between the Arab countries themselves accounted for no more than 7·6 per cent.

(c) According to an IDCAS study, more than 70 per cent of the manufacturing industry is *concentrated* in four countries: Egypt, Lebanon, Morocco and Algeria. As to the main branches of manufacturing, the food industry (including beverages and tobacco) has its focus in Morocco and, to a lesser extent, Egypt, Algeria and Tunisia. The textile industry (including leather and leather products) is concentrated in Egypt and, to a lesser extent, Syria, Algeria and Morocco. The wood and furniture industry is mainly in Lebanon, then in Algeria, Morocco and Syria. The paper industry (including paper products, printing and publishing) is concentrated in Egypt and, to a lesser extent, Morocco, Tunisia and Iraq. Egypt, Kuwait, Morocco and Iraq are the centres for the chemical industry, including petroleum refining. The non-metals industry (including the cement industry and the construction group) is in Egypt, followed by Algeria, Lebanon, Iraq and Morocco. Algeria is the leading country for metal products and machinery, followed by Egypt and Morocco.

(d) *The major part of production is from light industry* (food, textiles, clothing, footwear, construction materials, etc.). On average, some 52·9 per cent of the output of the manufacturing industry, by value, consists of food and clothing products. Although, in some countries, industrial activities are gradually shifting to the manufacture of basic chemicals, fertilisers, acids, alkalis, etc., heavy industry (including mainly capital and intermediate goods) constitutes only a small fraction of the total (38·8 per cent according to IDCAS).

As to consumer goods, food, beverages and tobacco are the most important branch (accounting for 30·5 per cent of total manufacturing output against 10·7 per cent in industrialised countries). Relative importance of this branch, according to IDCAS, ranges from 20 per cent of output in Egypt to 63 per cent in Libya. Textiles (including leather and

Table 6.1

Concentration of manufacturing industry in selected Arab countries, totals and main sectors

Country	Total manufacturing industry	Main sectors of the manufacturing industry								
		Food, beverages and tobacco	Textiles, leather and leather products	Wood, furniture and fixtures	Paper, paper products, printing & publishing	Chemicals and petroleum products	Non-metal mineral products	Basic metal	Metal products and machinery	Other manufacturing
	%	%	%	%	%	%	%	%	%	%
Jordan	2·2	1·6	1·8	3·5	2·3	2·4	4·8	–	2·8	2·4
Tunisia	9·6	9·7	3·3	2·8	10·3	5·4	7·9	18·2	2·3	–
Algeria	13·3	10·8	12·4	23·8	–	7·0	16·9	–	27·5	–
Sudan	4·6	6·0	7·3	5·1	3·1	2·2	–	–	3·1	–
Syria	6·7	7·9	12·6	7·6	2·3	1·6	1·0	5·0	5·0	–
Iraq	9·7	7·1	5·3	1·8	8·1	15·2	14·8	– –	5·4	–
Kuwait	3·0	1·7	–	6·4	3·8	20·7	5·6	–	6·3	–
Lebanon	14·3	6·7	6·8	34·1	–[a]	–	16·2	–	7·3	40·4
Libya	1·7	3·5	0·4	0·8	2·3	1·3	1·4	–	0·8	1·8
Egypt	28·8	17·0	39·5	5·9	43·5	26·0	18·5	76·8	23·2	55·4
Morocco	14·0	28·0	10·6	8·2	24·3	18·2	12·5	–	16·3	–
Total Arab countries	100·0	100·0	100·0	100·0	100·0	100·0	100·0	100·0	100·0	100·0

Note: [a]Excluding oil refining.
Source: IDCAS, Cairo, 1974.

leather products) are the second largest group, with 22·5 per cent of the total manufacturing output (against 8·3 per cent in industrialised nations). However, the relative importance of this industry varies, from 5 per cent in Libya to 42 per cent in Syria. Tunisia and Morocco are attempting to double the relative importance of the sector, while Egypt aims to reduce it from 38 to 27 per cent. Wood and furniture are confined to only 49 per cent of manufacturing output. However, some countries (Egypt, Tunisia and Libya) aim almost to double this figure. Paper, paper products, printing and publishing contribute only 3 per cent of manufacturing output. But there is an attempt to increase the contribution of this sector in almost all Arab countries, bar Egypt.

Among intermediate and capital goods, chemicals, chemical products and petroleum products are the main group, with 17 per cent of manufacturing output (slightly lower than in the developed countries but higher than in the developing nations). These industries are particularly important in Kuwait and Iraq where output is respectively 62 and 32 per cent of manufactures, the percentage varying from 15–18 per cent in Egypt, Morocco and Jordan, through 13 per cent in Libya, 9 per cent in Algeria, to 4 per cent in Syria. Metals contribute 13·4 per cent of total Arab manufacturing output (18·6 per cent in developing countries and 38·5 per cent in industrialised countries). Relative importance of this intermediate and capital-goods industry varies from 5 per cent in Tunisia to 17 per cent in Jordan, amounting to 6 per cent in Libya, 10 per cent in the Sudan and Syria, and 12–13 per cent in Egypt, Morocco and Lebanon. Non-metal mineral products account for only 7 per cent of the Arab manufacturing output (5·7 per cent in developing countries and 4·2 per cent in industrialised countries), and the sector varies from 1 per cent output in Syria to 9 per cent in Tunisia; it is most important in Jordan and Iraq where it reaches 15 and 13 per cent respectively. Basic metal industries are the least important of the intermediate and capital-goods industries, their share of total manufacturing output being 1·4 per cent only (4 per cent in Egypt).

(e) Most large-scale industries of the region suffer from *under-utilisation of productive capacity*. There is also a scarcity of skilled labour and advanced management techniques, technology is backward, and marketing problems and – in some cases – duplication of industrial projects have arisen. The inevitable result has been that productivity is low, from both the capital and labour standpoints. The small size of the internal market itself limits development. Indeed, for the five Gulf states, with a population of less than 1 million, there is no alternative to industrialisation via export markets. Even for Iraq, with a population of

Table 6.2

Structure of the manufacturing industry in selected Arab countries (present and planned percentage distribution of the manufacturing sectors)

Country		Basic sectors of the manufacturing industry										Classification according to economic use		
		Total manufacturing industry	Food, beverages and tobacco	Textiles, leather and leather products	Wood, furniture and fixtures	Paper, paper products, printing and publishing	Chemicals and petroleum products	Non-metal mineral products	Basic metal	Metal products	Other manufacturing industry	Consumption goods(c)	Intermediate and capital goods(d)	Total
Jordan	actual[a]	100	21	18	7	3	18	15	-	17	1	50	50	100
	projected[b]	-	-	-	-	-	-	-	-	-	-	-	-	-
Tunisia	actual	100	48	12	2	5	15	9	4	5	-	67	33	100
	projected	100	27·9	27·8	3·8	8·8	12	7·1	-	13·3	-	67·7	32·5	100
Algeria	actual	100	25	21	8	-	9	9	-	28	-	54	46	100
	projected	100	19	21·1	-	-	12·1	8·1	7·3	14·4	17·7	58	42	100
Sudan	actual	100	46	36	5	2	8[e]	-	-	9	-	83	17	100
	projected	-	-	-	-	-	-	-	-	-	-	-	-	-
Syria[f]	actual	100	36	42	5	1	4(6)	1	1	10	-	84	16	100
	projected	-	-	-	-	-	-	-	-	-	-	-	-	-
Iraq	actual	100	27	15	1	3	32	13	-	9	-	46	54	100
	projected	-	-	-	-	-	-	-	-	-	-	-	-	-
Kuwait	actual	100	9	-	5	2	62	7	-	15	-	16	48	100
	projected	-	-	-	-	-	-	-	-	-	-	-	-	-
Lebanon	actual	100	27	20	20[g]	-	-	15	-	13	5	72	28	100
	projected	-	-	-	-	-	-	-	-	-	-	-	-	-
Libya[f]	actual	100	63	5	2	4	13(6)	6	-	6	1	75	25	100
	projected	100	32·5	5·7	4·8	-	31·2	11·9	12·3	-	1·6	45	55	100
Egypt	actual	100	20	34	1	5	17	5	4	12	2	62	38	100
	projected	100	16·8	27·3	2·8	3·7	16·5	3·9	9·9	17·5	-	51	49	100
Morocco	actual	100	47	13	2	4	17	5	-	12	-	66	34	100
	projected	100	33	25	3	5·2	9·9	6	0·5	17·4	-	66	34	100
Total	actual	100	30·5	22·4	4·4	3·0	17·0	7·0	1·4	13·4	0·9	61·2	38·8	100
	projected	-	-	-	-	-	-	-	-	-	-	-	-	-

Notes: [a]Represents the average relative importance of the branch in 1969. [b]Projected relative importance after the execution of the plans. [c]Includes food, textile, wood, paper and other industries. [d]Includes chemical, non-metal mineral, basic mineral and metal product industries. [e]Includes non-metal products. [f]Excluding oil refineries. [g]Includes paper, printing and publishing.
Source: IDCAS, Cairo, 1974.

10·2 million and a *per capita* GNP of $US 490, industrialisation for the domestic market would be insufficient unless based on efficient import substitution, with spillover to external markets.

(f) While development plans generally project a rate of industrial growth appreciably higher than the overall growth of GNP, industrial development plans in many cases fail to constitute *an integral part of the overall plan of economic development.* This means that not only is a higher growth rate sacrificed, but bottlenecks and unforeseen pressures on the balance of payments often cannot be avoided. Moreover, in countries where the public sector is dominant in industrial development, no clear-cut boundaries are indicated for activities to be undertaken by the private sector. Here again, potential for further industrial development is sacrificed, the more so since no effort is made to involve representatives of the private sector in the process of planning. Further, plans fail to include details even of large-scale projects, or of policies and measures to be initiated to ensure the movement of the private sector in planned directions. In addition, the formulation and evaluation of industrial projects leaves much to be desired. In some cases, reference is made to projects only by title, and there are no serious preinvestment or feasibility studies. And rates of implementation of industrial plans often fall behind schedule, undermining growth targets and creating serious bottlenecks where complementarity was taken into account in the construction of plans, whether for the industrial sector or for the economy at large. In many cases, delays have been due to drawn-out procedures and bureaucracy in the commissioning of projects, or underestimation of the capital needs of the projects.

(g) Where shortage of capital is a constraint on industrial development, notably in non-oil-producing countries, no *financial planning* is undertaken to delineate the relative importance of various sources of finance or to ensure the flow of investment funds in the desired direction. Such financial planning is of the utmost importance, not only to avoid inflation, but to ensure maximum use of a country's potential for growth. Furthermore, while several countries have established specialised financial institutions in the form of industrial or development banks, the resources at the disposal of these institutions are far too limited to afford them an important role in financing industrial development. In some countries, this is in sharp contrast to the high liquidity levels of the commercial banking system. Moreover, these institutions are often passive in their role of moneylender and do little to promote new industrial activity. Further, the credit needs of small industries do not receive much attention whether from specialised institutions or from the commercial banking system.

(h) By and large, no serious thought has been given to the interrelationship between *environment and development,* particularly industrial development. Problems of pollution and waste management have as yet had no visible impact on plans and policies.

6.2 Towards an outward-looking industrialisation strategy

Industrialisation in the countries considered is based on the policy of import substitution within the framework of local markets and concentrating on consumer industries. The result has been that productive capacities are not fully employed, due to the limited size of markets, the rise in the cost of production, and a decrease in quality because of strict customs protection which favours products newly produced in an economy which as yet provides no incentive to improve quality and performance; there is also increasing dependence on the outside world both to build new production capacities and to maintain existing capacity. Thus the share of Arab imports of industrial consumer products, as compared with total industrial products, has fallen from nearly 38 per cent in 1967 to less than 35 per cent in 1970, while the rate of industrial investment imports increased from nearly 28 per cent to about 37 per cent for the same period.[3]

In addition to widening the gap which separates the developed countries from the countries of the region, the international trend towards trade liberalisation and the growing strength of economic blocs between the advanced countries indicates that a policy of import substitution established in a closed economy cannot, by itself, solve the problem of the industrial development of the Middle East area. It has therefore become necessary to consider an outward-looking industrialisation strategy, with particular emphasis on export industries and Arab industrial co-operation.

Such a policy implies that domestic industry is linked permanently with international industrial development in respect of production technology, management techniques and higher efficiency. In this way, the comparative advantage, specialisation and adequate development of the industrial structure and its technologies would facilitate production of goods whose quality and cost is broadly equal to similar products in the advanced countries, whether such goods are produced for export or for import substitution. Moreover, outward-looking industrialisation would allow import substitution to develop so as to avoid the pitfalls mentioned above, at the same time permitting the establishment of many basic industries (e.g. chemicals, metals, capital goods and consumer durables) which have a major effect in guiding the economic structure towards equilibrium. Such industries would by their very nature be large-scale, capital-intensive and technologically advanced, thus assuring that greater attention is given to effective intraregional co-operation to overcome the limitations imposed by the smallness of domestic markets. In addition, an outward-looking policy would require due consideration for export industries with the aim of improving the balance of payments, for some countries, and decreasing the dependence on export of a single commodity, for others. To ensure that such industries are established on the basis of large units, with substantial capital resources, and meet modern international industrial standards, greater intraregional industrial co-operation is necessary.

The development of many basic industries is characterised by powerful 'downstream' effects in the economy, as well as by important investment multiplier results likely to have rapid and widespread impact. It must therefore be viewed in the light of a global and integrated economic development policy. Thus, the major industrialisation operation should be within the context of a comprehensive economic plan in concert with the exploitation of agricultural resources, the promotion of intraregional exchanges, and the provision of the necessary material and social infrastructure.

Since economic growth cannot be achieved by increasing export revenues alone, and excessive dependence on world markets is a risky business, it is vitally important to foster the integration of economic activities (e.g. linking oil production and refining to petrochemicals and other energy-intensive industries) and to develop local markets (by increasing national consumption and, above all, reducing disparity of income). Therefore, the expansion of basic industries should be paralleled by a diversification of the industrial base through development of the engineering industries, which, in addition to favouring indigenous technology, are of paramount importance in the interrelations between the different branches of industrial production; similarly, there must be modernisation of light industry (mainly catering for the domestic market), establishment of subsidiary industries (in the wake of large-scale plants) and development of alternatives to oil as a source of energy (nuclear and solar power, especially). All this should be accompanied by the establishment of scientific research centres and universities (to adapt imported technology to local production factors as a step to creating a technology which suits the region). Likewise, there must be a suitable investment climate; manufactured goods must comply with world standards; production costs must be reduced; experience and technical know-how acquired and manpower trained to improve skills and productivity, so that locally manufactured goods can enter export markets successfully in the face of international competition.[4]

6.3 The establishment of basic industries

Implementation of outward-looking industrialisation is based on the establishment of dynamic large-scale enterprises, which would reduce dependence on external factors, raise the rate of capital formation and of export trade - and generally act as a base for rapid development of the economy. Given the necessity for accelerated economic growth, the countries of the region are conscious of the urgency of establishing integrated plants centred on heavy basic capital goods, notably on processing hydrocarbons into semi-finished products at the place of production, and on more advanced processing of other indigenous raw materials such as phosphates, copper and cotton.[5]

A spectacular development in the industrialisation of natural resources is therefore expected. Thus, within the decade, the Arabs and Iranians envisage meeting 25 per cent of the international demand for petroleum products by building around 24 new refineries (each with a capacity of at least 20 million tons a year). In addition, in the eighties this programme will be expanded, with the construction of 95 giant refineries, in order to cover half the world requirements for petroleum products. Already the total new capacity planned throughout the region is well over 200 million tons a year, Algeria deciding to increase refining capacity by 25 million tons a year, Egypt by 35 million, Iran by 75 million, Abu Dhabi by 30 million, while Libya and Saudi Arabia are planning to double their refinery outputs within a decade.[6]

Furthermore, the countries of the region (in particular Algeria, Iran and the other Gulf states) intend to exploit their enormous reserves of natural gas (9,000 billion m^3 in the Arab countries alone), which have, up to now, flared to waste in the oilfields. Huge liquefied natural gas factories are to be built (as, for example, at Arzew, western Algeria, where 15·5 billion m^3 of liquefied natural gas will be produced annually, becoming the most important LNG plant of its kind in the world). International trade in natural gas is in fact expected to attain 300 billion

Table 6.3

Crude oil production of Arab countries, 1968 and 1974
('000 metric tons)

Countries	1968		1974	
	'000 tons	% of Middle East	'000 tons	% of Middle East
Saudi Arabia	140,998	19·0	408,000	33·3
Kuwait	122,085	16·5	110,000	9·0
Libya	124,524	16·8	77,000	6·3
Iraq	73,848	9·9	93,000	7·6
Abu Dhabi	24,006	3·2	70,000	5·7
Algeria	42,145	5·7	48,000	3·9
Neutral zone[a]	22,827	3·1	29,000	2·4
Qatar	16,363	2·2	24,500	2·0
Egypt	10,995	1·5	12,000	1·0
of which: Sinai	2,000	0·3	4,500	0·4
Oman	12,068	1·6	14,500	1·2
Dubai	–	–	12,000	1·0
Syria	1,000	0·1	6,000	0·5
Tunisia	3,137	0·4	4,500	0·4
Bahrain	3,768	0·5	3,380	0·3
Sharjah	–	–	1,300	0·1
Total Arab countries	597,764	80·5	917,680	75·0
Iran	141,791	19·1	302,000	24·7
Turkey	3,103	0·4	3,500	0·3
Total Middle East and North Africa	742,658	100·0	1,223,180	100·0
Total world output	1,975,315	–	2,867,940	–
Share of Middle East and North Africa in world output (%)	37·6		42·6	
Share of Arab countries in world output (%)	30·3		32·0	

Notes: [a]Production divided between Saudi Arabia and Kuwait.
Source: *Petroleum Intelligence Weekly.*

m^3 by 1980. Correspondingly, world LNG traffic is expected to increase from 50,000 m^3 per year in 1980, to between 100,000 million and 150,000 million in 1990, thus requiring the construction of 70 LNG carriers of 125,000 m^3 capacity. In addition, locally available natural gas will boost the region's production of synthetic protein (of considerable importance to the agricultural and livestock industries) and provide a source of power to expand the electrometallurgic industry (especially aluminium production on the pattern of the ALBA venture in Bahrain), and also the electrochemical industry.

A rapid and massive build-up is, then, expected for petrochemicals dependent either on natural gas or on naphtha. In particular, the biggest investments are planned in 'first stage' petrochemicals such as ammonia-based fertilisers, methanol and ethylene. Additionally, the oil-producing nations will begin production and export of a variety of chemicals (such as benzene, PVC, polystyrene, vinyl chloride, etc.) and other intermediary or finished products (detergents, solvents, pharmaceutical products, synthetic rubber and fibres, etc.). Thus, with some $US 6,500 million worth of chemical projects in the oil-producing states said to be certain or fairly certain to proceed, and with another $US 24,000 worth under study, petrochemicals produced in the Middle East and North Africa could capture around 30 per cent of the world market by 1985.[7]

Prodigious steps are also being taken to set up iron and steel industries. In fact, the steel mills enjoy a high priority in the development plans because of the dynamic effect of steel development on the rest of the economy. Thus, Iran aims to produce, by 1983, about 15 million tons a year (600,000 tons in 1973). Mauritania, in association with a Kuwaiti company, is building an iron and steel complex at Nouadhibou, with an annual capacity of 1 million tons. Morocco is on the way to completing an integrated plant with an annual capacity of 300,000 tons. And Iraq has signed an agreement with a French consortium for the installation of a plant with an annual capacity of 400,000 tons. Kuwait has started to build a 380,000 tons per year plant. Saudi Arabia – which could become the world's lowest-cost steel producer – is erecting an iron and steel complex with annual capacity of 3 million tons in its early stages, rising to 10 million tons per year. Algeria is planning to expand its steel production and product mix in three phases from 0·4 million to 2 million tons in 1978 and is also studying the feasibility of increasing production capacity to 10 million tons yearly. Egypt – the first Arab state to establish an integrated iron and steel industry, at Helwan – is expanding its integrated and semi-integrated plant up to about 2 million tons in 1976 and is studying the establishment of a foam-iron plant with an annual capacity of

2 million tons in its final stages. Tunisia intends to increase the capacity of its single plant up to 300,000 tons per year and has agreed with a group of Japanese and German companies to install a foam-iron plant with an annual capacity of 1 million tons. Turkey, whose yearly production, over 1·1 million tons, is now the largest in the Middle East, is building a third integrated plant at Iskenderum with an initial capacity of 1 million tons a year, though agreement has already been reached with the USSR to expand this, first to 2 million tons and later to 4 million tons a year. In addition, according to the Turkish Planning Bureau, two more integrated plants are projected, though only one has reached the stage of a feasibility study.

A target of 200 million tons by the year 2000 is therefore not only realistic, but well within the Arab World's capabilities. In fact, the countries of the region are well placed in respect of major raw materials like iron and manganese ores, limestone and dolomite. Only in respect of coking coal are the Arab countries deficient, but this is more than amply compensated by their large natural gas reserves which favour the adoption of gaseous direct-reduction process to produce sponge iron (for conversion to steel in electric-arc furnaces). Thus, most of the iron and steel projects of the region (notably the Gulf area) are based on direct-reduction processes. Although at present steel production based on direct reduction is accountable for less than 1 per cent of world output, and the technique is still largely at an experimental stage, the production of sponge iron is the logical way to proceed, given the abundance of natural gas and iron ore combined with the possibility of producing electric energy at low price. A considerable number of mini-steelworks (with a capacity of 400,000 to 600,000 tons per year) will therefore be built up in the region, although this will not exclude the more traditional technology of the oxygen converter.[8]

The engineering industry – which is less capital-intensive than, for example, chemical industries, but more capital-intensive than light industries – is also a focal point, receiving major priority in the industrial development of the region, parallel with the development of ancillary plants such as foundries and forges. In fact, engineering contributes substantially to gross capital formation in the production of metal products, machinery and transport equipment, and has done more than any other industry towards establishing an indigenous technology and a diversified industrial base, thus significantly influencing technical training and labour management.[9]

In the initial stages, the type of engineering product to be manufactured locally should be simple. For the production of high-quality machines, it may be better to obtain designs and technical know-how from industrialised countries, through either licensing or partnership arrangements. Oil-rich countries find themselves in a specially advantageous position with regard to those production units with a fairly high initial capital investment and for which automated production is sufficiently advanced to require a minimum of skilled manpower. The products of the metal-working industries (e.g. non-ferrous and ferrous castings, high grade alloy steel forgings, anti-friction precision bearings, high-tensile screws and bolts, electric controls and motors, cutting tools) are an essential prerequisite to production of heavy general-purpose machine tools (earth-moving machinery, drilling machines, hydraulic presses, sheet-metal working machines, etc). In addition to fostering relationships between the various branches of production, such output lends itself to intense specialisation and to production of a wide range of products, thereby facilitating active participation in world markets. Although machinery can be bought from developed countries, it is only when it has achieved the ability to produce some of the necessary machinery locally that a country can fully control its industrial development and move its economy to the take-off stage.

Another point of attraction is the production of consumer durables such as refrigerators, air conditioners and television sets (importing compressors, electric motors and other components) and the development of the automotive industry based on the production of commercial and passenger service vehicles and on assembly of passenger cars and tractors. Thus Saudi Arabia, Lebanon, Egypt and Tunisia have decided to install the French SECAM colour television system, while several countries have placed contracts with foreign partners to manufacture air conditioning, tanks for storage, tankers for land transport, etc.

In the automotive sector the most ambitious project is being carried out by the Iran National Manufacturing Co. – the largest car manufacturer in Iran – which, under an agreement with Chrysler of the US, plans to raise production from 50,000 units in 1974 to 500,000 passenger cars in 1980. Iranian businessmen, in agreement with General Motors, have also decided to set up a joint subsidiary (Iran General Motors Co.) which, towards 1980, will produce 160,000 lorries of a wide range (including 25-ton trucks), 15,000 utility vehicles of the 'Jeep' type and 160,000 private cars. Of considerable importance are the projects of General Motors in Morocco with 'Société Africaine pour l'Industrie Automobile' (SAIDA), Star-Auto (for the manufacture, assembly and marketing of GM trucks and buses), and Saudi Arabia – the major importer of commercial vehicles in the Middle East – for setting up a joint venture to assemble Chevrolet passenger cars and GMC commercial vehicles (8,000 vehicles per year from 1975); also the projects of Nissan Motors, which will assemble light commercial vehicles in Saudi Arabia; the Nissan Diesel Motor Co. which is establishing a truck assembly plant in Saudi Arabia aiming to serve the whole of the Middle East; Volvo, which seems interested in setting up a joint venture to assemble 34,000 trucks a year in Algeria; Berliet, which is setting up a factory in Morocco to manufacture spare parts for commercial vehicles, as well as a heavy-vehicle assembly plant in Algeria, for which more than two-thirds of parts will be produced locally; Massey–Ferguson of Britain, which is forming a joint venture in Iran to produce 5,000 tractors per year, rising to 20,000 units a year by 1980; Scania of Sweden, which is assembling Scania trucks in Iraq; Pirelli of Italy, which is setting up a tyre plant expected to produce 300,000 tyres a year by 1977; and British Leyland, which, in 1975, started to produce 10,000 Land Rovers a year in a vehicle assembly plant in Egypt and will eventually expand production to include Minis, trucks and commercial vehicles. The importance of these projects in the motor industry is increased by the emphasis given in the development plans to expanding the manufacture of parts and components, including gear boxes, differentials, transmission systems, back axles, electrical parts, etc. – all products which promote the establishment of a host of auxiliary industries.[10]

Major attractive projects concentrate also on the exploitation of sulphur, phosphorus and phosphates (to produce phosphoric and sulphuric acid and phosphate fertilisers, especially in Morocco, Tunisia and Jordan); copper deposits (Morocco, for example, is establishing a copper treatment plant worked by a consortium consisting of Ominium Nord Afrique and Mitsui of Japan in association with the state mining agency); bituminous shale deposits (especially in Morocco and Lebanon); rock salt (along with other raw materials of the oil refineries, to produce chemicals for use in the local production of PVC products, paper and soap); cellulose and paper (especially in Turkey where three new paper plants began operation in 1974); and cotton ginning (especially in Egypt, Syria and the Sudan). The cement industry is another relatively simple capital-intensive industry which is of considerable importance to the development of the region.[11]

In fact, fairly dramatic increases in productive capacity are planned in most countries owing to the ever-increasing demands of industrial, commercial, residential and infrastructure projects (*per capita* consumption of cement in the Gulf area is currently generally recognised as the highest in the world) because of the plentiful local supply of raw materials (limestone, clay, gypsum). Another factor encouraging the production of cement and cement-based products is that comparatively little technical knowledge and skill is required for their manufacture. Therefore, almost all countries of the region give top priority to the further expansion of their own cement plants. Thus, for example, the Qatar Cement Co. has drawn up plans to double production, and larger plants are envisaged, with the 500,000 tons per year Dubai cement works becoming the biggest in the Gulf.

Substantial opportunities for tourism also exist. Apart from the basic requirements of sun, sea and sand, the region can offer splendid archaeological sites and a wide variety of landscapes and exotic views. In fact, the well-established holiday areas of Cyprus, Lebanon, Jordan, Egypt, Tunisia, Morocco and Algeria are being expanded, and the micro-states of the Gulf - Iran, Iraq, the Yemen Arab Republic, Democratic Yemen, the Sudan and Libya - are keen to develop tourist projects, including a chain of hotels with associated facilities, transport and communications. So, in June 1975, the fourth conference of the Arab Hotels Federation decided to create an Arab hotel investment and management company, with a capital of £100,000, and an institute of higher education for the training of tourist guides.

Finally, since the rapid growth of the basic industries requires parallel accelerated development of the basic material and social infrastructure, there are tremendous possibilities for the construction and building industries.[12]

It is indeed vital for the countries under review to increase the capacity and productivity of these industries, because of the essential contribution they make to the implementation of development plans, and the indirect effect on many other industries, e.g. those involved in production of furniture, textiles, domestic appliances. However, lack of adequate equipment and trained personnel makes it necessary to depend on foreign help for supervision and on contractors for execution of the work.

Also of interest in the region is the possibility of developing alternatives to oil as a source of energy, most notably in those countries which will run out of oil in perhaps twenty to fifty years, and in countries with scarce water resources. Of particular relevance is the use of nuclear power, both to generate electricity and for related applications in industry, agriculture, medicine, and water desalination.

Thus, Turkey's first nuclear power station is due to come into operation in 1978. In addition, the US and the USSR have each agreed in principle to supply Egypt with a nuclear reactor for peaceful purposes, while Libya, Kuwait, Iraq, Saudi Arabia and Algeria have expressed determination to set up nuclear power plants. The most spectacular development is, however, taking place in Iran, where the Atomic Energy Agency has already decided to buy 8 nuclear power stations from the United States, 5 from France and 2 from the German Federal Republic. Western countries, on the other hand, are committed to exploiting enriched uranium and providing proper training for Iranian technicians and scientists. To combat serious water shortages, most countries of the region are investing heavily in power stations combined with desalination plants (Bahrain being the most outstanding example, since the Sitra power station under construction will be able to meet the demand both for power and for distilled water from the sea); also, in hydro-electric resources (mainly through impressive dam-building programmes such as the massive Euphrates Dam and the suggested 55-mile-long dam which would trap the Gulf's waters in an area of 6,000 km^2). Underground water location is also being undertaken. Research is being carried out, too, on the establishment of solar power stations to harness this so far neglected energy source.

6.4 The role of small enterprises

Small enterprises remain the predominant form of industrial organisation in most of the countries under review, particularly in the densely populated areas. In some industries, like footwear, food, wood, plastics, furniture, soft drinks, dairy products, clothing, textiles, printing and publishing, leather, and vehicle repair, more than 90 per cent of the workers are employed in small firms. Underlying this is a variety of factors: market conditions, raw material sources, transport availability, diversity of demand, type of technology, nature of the capital market, etc. These small firms - which act as a 'seedbed' of managerial supply for the larger enterprises - have established close relationships with distributors and customers, and know their tastes and needs. They are meeting the demands of the masses for basic processed foodstuffs, clothing, household utensils, tools and equipment. The common denominator between them is a lack of specialisation in management, because such undertakings are either family concerns or small units using simple machinery, while the small mechanised factories may have up to 100 workers.[13]

Small businesses are well suited to the needs and circumstances of the Middle East and North Africa, because they secure widespread economic benefits (avoiding undue social conflicts during the process of change), ensure a high level of deployment (by undertaking subcontracted work and through the relative ease of servicing and repair), use relatively labour-intensive techniques, contribute to a more balanced rural and regional development (encouraging co-operation between farm and factory, particularly when periods of activity in industry do not coincide with those in agriculture) and foster mobilisation of the dynamic forces of the private sector (to which the small firms belong).

Not only are the small enterprises frequently in the forefront of technological innovation (notably in the light industry sector), but industrialisation is no longer thought of in terms of new Pittsburgh or Birmingham[14], but rather as a process in which small businesses have important roles to play. Therefore, given the major role of small firms in the Middle East and North Africa, the aim of an enlightened economic policy is to foster the efficiency of viable small factory enterprises by helping them surmount obstacles hindering their development. In particular, the Industrial Development Centre for Arab States recommends: (a) the establishment of industrial zones, including the provision of common-facility centres (quality control, etc.); (b) the granting of loans and other credit facilities on reasonable terms; (c) training workers, technicians, accountants and managers as befits the type of small-scale industry; (d) offering the necessary technical advisory services and assistance in applying technical specification and maintaining financial registers and accounts; (e) securing the basic materials needed and promoting marketing of products. Finally, IDCAS recommends that the Arab states take account of small-scale industry when preparing industrial programmes, and aim to establish rules and bases for co-ordinating and integrating them with large-scale industry.[15] In this respect, it is interesting to cite Iran, which has set up a government agency – the Organisation of Small-Scale Industries and Industrial Regions – in order to provide assistance and consultancy services for private investors interested in establishing small firms. In particular, this organisation will provide loans on easy terms, through separate offices to be set up within specialised banks, and assistance will also be given in marketing, and recruitment and training of staff. Additionally, regional centres will be established to help provide infrastructure facilities.

6.5 The construction of an Arab fleet

Another major result of the oil crisis is the construction of an Arab fleet of oil tankers, oil-product carriers and dry-cargo ships to transport crude and refined products to the consumption centres and to expand trade relations within the region, as well as with the industrial nations. Thus the last two years have seen rapid growth in Arab contracting for ships, and much more is expected in the near future.

The most significant development so far has been the establishment of the Arab Maritime Petroleum Transportation Company (AMPTC), a $US 500 million consortium set up by the governments of Abu Dhabi, Algeria, Bahrain, Kuwait, Libya, Qatar, Iraq and Saudi Arabia. The company has already ordered four ultralarge crude carriers from French and West German yards. And since it is planning to spend some $US 2 billion over the next three to five years, more orders are on the way, involving around 50 smaller crude carriers of 80,000 to 150,000 dwt and product carriers in the range of 40,000 dwt to 70,000 dwt. Quite significant, also, is the establishment of the Gulf Navigation Company with participation by the governments of the United Arab Emirates, Qatar, Bahrain and Oman. In addition, individual countries are establishing or extending their own shipping services so that, according to some estimates, the Arab countries might attain a tonnage of around 7 million tons by 1978 (1·5 million tons in 1974).

Although several tanker owners have cancelled orders for giant tankers, and several of the major shipping companies are converting their tanker fleets (into more sophisticated product tankers, LNG vessels and specialised ships for the transport of iron, coal and other minerals), Western and Japanese shipping industries can conclude mutually advantageous joint ventures with the Arabs. Thus, for example, a joint Saudi Arabian/US shipping company (Samarco) – believed to aggregate between 650,000 and 800,000 dwt – has been set up in Jeddah, and a joint Egyptian/US maritime transport company (Egyptian Overseas Shipping Company) has been established in Cairo to handle the main Egyptian imports of petroleum products, oil, coal and wheat. Substantial opportunities also exist in the construction of shipyards and major harbour projects (including new ports, additional deep-water berths, naval stations, fisheries, etc., as well as the expansion of existing ports) since the building of modern ship-repair facilities and the relief of port congestion are of outstanding importance for the expansion of the economies of the Middle East and their trade ties with Western countries. Not only is there as yet very little shipbuilding in the Middle East, but port congestion is threatening to impair trade and development because vessels operating in the Mediterranean and the Gulf have to sustain heavy additional costs due to the many days needed to discharge.

Thus, for example, the Bahrain dock (built for OAPEC, which holds 60 per cent of the project) will be operated jointly by Lisnave of Portugal and

Kawasaki of Japan. Associated Marine Consultants of the Netherlands is assisting the Kuwait Shipbuilding and Repair Yard Co. which is building a yard for use in 1977. And the German enterprise, Blohm und Voss, is to draw up plans for the biggest shipyard in Iran on behalf of the Persian Gulf Shipbuilding Co.

Middle East countries may also participate in Western shipping companies and shipbuilding enterprises. Thus, in addition to the French shipyard at La Ciotat, controlled by the Beirut-based Intra Investment Company (largely owned by the governments of Kuwait, Lebanon and Qatar), the United Arab Emirates is envisaging an investment of $US 200 million in the German shipbuilding industry.

Furthermore, the reopening of the Suez Canal will greatly benefit world commerce by: (a) eliminating economic dislocations (estimated by UNCTAD at $US 7 billion for the period mid-1967 to 1971 and continuing at an annual rate of $US 1·7 billion); (b) reducing the cost of carrying oil from the Persian/Arab Gulf to Europe, particularly Mediterranean ports; and (c) adding impetus to economic activity, notably in the Mediterranean, the Red Sea, the Gulf and the Indian Ocean. In particular, the recommencement of trade flows in the Mediterranean will offer a unique opportunity for shifting to the south the transit of goods now shipped through Dutch and German ports. Thus, for example, the activity of ports such as Trieste, Genoa and Marseilles – which suffered heavily from the closure of the Canal in 1967 – will bring about new prosperity for the Mediterranean countries (notably for Italy and France, but also for countries such as Greece, Cyprus, Malta and Spain), thus fostering trade relations with the Middle East, East Africa, South-East Asia, the Far East and Australia. Indeed, the Mediterranean should again become a kingpin for the economic prosperity of the entire world.

6.6 A constructive international co-operation

The Middle East build-up of refineries, gas-chemical plants, aluminium smelters, petrochemical industries, steel and iron mills, etc. is favoured by abundant and secure supplies of cheap energy, huge financial resources and the geographic location itself – at the crossroads of three continents whose economic and demographic resources are largely complementary. Thus shipping costs to major projected markets should be at a minimum and there is a great potential regional market (about 300 million inhabitants at the end of the eighties), with cheap labour easily available. Furthermore, the countries of the region can make the conclusion of new oil agreements with foreign groups conditional on the establishment of energy-based projects on their territories.

However, if they are to achieve the target of developing their basic integrated industries in the next fifteen to twenty years the countries of the region must, firstly, depend on the advanced technological know-how of the industrial countries; secondly, import the necessary equipment; thirdly, ease the drastic shortage of skills; and fourthly, achieve economies of scale, obtaining outlets on world markets for exports of manufactured products, as well as achieving efficient commercialisation. There must therefore be constructive co-operation with the industrial countries, through (a) joint industrial ventures; (b) the supply of complete plants or production lines on a turnkey basis; (c) co-operation and specialisation; (d) licensing and technical know-how agreements (with payment for resultant products); (e) subcontracting (to supplement the production capacity of the Western partner); (f) the provision of technical assistance, including training programmes and various forms of management assistance; (g) the supply of other services such as the preparation of detailed project reports, provision of basic and detailed engineering data relating to the choice of production methods, equipment and machinery specifications, plant design and factory layout, etc.; also, help in selection of machinery, plant construction, machinery erection and installation, etc.

The joint industrial venture would seem to offer by far the best opportunities,[16] the active presence of a foreign partner being likely to: guarantee a more even flow and speedier transfer of technology; assure a higher-calibre management than would be possible with locally managed organisations run by public officials; ensure more serious participation in the concern than under a management contract; and add stability to the development of economic relations (a particular advantage at times of inflation, since a fairly stable price structure is built into many enterprise-to-enterprise contracts).

These ventures involve, to varying degrees, production, marketing and R and D, usually based on co-management, co-ownership of capital, barter agreements, and sharing of profits and risks. Thus, for instance, the construction of two giant oil refineries in Iran with a German and a Japanese group respectively, on a 50:50 basis, is linked with the delivery of oil products. Since the countries of the region desire economic independence, a majority holding is frequently reserved for them. In fact, partial foreign ownership is sufficient to reduce the risk incurred in building and operating large-scale plants. For distributing and selling on world markets, however, the majority interest can be left to the foreign partner. Thus, for example, the petrochemicals plant set up at Umm Said (which in 1978 will produce annually 200,000 tons of ethylene and 100,000 tons of polyethylene using ethane gas from existing oilfields) is owned by a joint venture, with 80 per cent of equity controlled by the government of Qatar and 20 per cent by the French group CDF-Chimie. But, while the joint transport company set up at the same time is also under minority control (40 per cent) of the foreign partner, the French concern Gazocean

Table 6.4

Production and consumption of commercial fertilisers, Near East countries, 1972

Country	Nitrogenous Fertilisers		Phosphate Fertilisers	
	PDN '000 ton	Cons. '000 ton	PDN '000 ton	Cons. '000 ton
Algeria	40	85	15	95
Bahrain	–	–	–	–
Cyprus	–	15·5	–	9·5
Egypt	150	400	78	55
Iran	80	115	40	78
Iraq	29	15	–	6·5
Jordan	–	1·5	–	3
Kuwait	800[a]	–	–	–
Lebanon	–	40	50	20
Libya	–	9	–	9
Mauritania	–	–	–	0·8
Morocco	18	50	155	50
Oman	–	–	–	–
Qatar	–	–	–	–
Saudi Arabia	50	1·8	–	5
Sudan	–	60	–	9
Syria	5	55	25	20
Tunisia	1	25	–	–
United Arab Emirates	–	–	–	–
Yemen Arab Republic	–	7	–	2
Yemen Democratic Republic	–	–	–	–

[a]Mostly rock phosphate.
Source: FAO.

has a 75 per cent interest in a similar joint distribution and marketing venture.

In any event, though individual cases differ, sufficient confidence should be built up within the venture to avoid the risk of abuse, such as political leverage and espionage (the main reasons why the Iraqi Government turns down all joint ventures). Moreover, Western industries must be prepared to consider joint ventures in the framework of wide-ranging government-to-government agreements, extending their field of action to other areas of the economy. Thus, for example, within the co-operation schemes agreed by Iran and Italy, in addition to the establishment of a joint steel mill (by the National Iranian Steel Co., NISCO and the IRI Group) and a range of steel-related industries, infrastructure facilities, such as the creation of a satellite town for some 80,000 people, construction of highways, a desalination plant and a 500 MW thermal power plant, must be envisaged. Conglomerates offering package deals therefore enjoy special privileges in dealing with the Arabs and Iranians.

Major deals may also involve exchange of oil supplies for weapons, as well as the establishment of national arms industries. Thus, Northrop and Lockheed and Hawker Siddeley hope under a licensing agreement to assist the Turkish Government to set up a national aviation industry (for military purposes). Similarly the Westland Aircraft Co. plans to manufacture Lynx helicopters in Egypt on the basis of an agreement extending into the eighties. Besides the Arab–Israeli conflict, various other causes explain the arms build-up, for example, the penetration of the Popular Front of Oman and the Arabian Gulf (PFLOAG), which aims to overthrow all the rulers of Arab littoral states in the Gulf area except Iraq; the long-standing rivalry of Syria and Iraq, and that of Iraq and Kuwait; the need for strong internal security against takeover attempts, etc.

Western companies interested in establishing joint ventures in the Middle East area should also be prepared to: (a) open up new markets outside the region fostering geographical diversification of exports (thus, for instance, NIOC - National Iranian Oil Co. - and the Shell group envisage an association agreement which would give NIOC a 50 per cent holding in Shell's distribution network in the United States; in exchange, NIOC would commit itself to assuming 75 per cent of the costs of building an oil refinery on the Gulf; half of the production capacity of 500,000 barrels of refined products a day would be purchased by Shell); (b) help identify business opportunities, since the main problem of many oil-exporting countries is a lack of experience and a shortage of qualified manpower; and (c) offer on-the-job training, the formula being: 'no more plants on a turnkey basis, but joint ventures in which the foreign partner also provides the necessary training until the factory can work with local manpower at all levels and its output conforms to the negotiated rules.'[17]

In their turn, Middle East countries must face the difficulty of acquiring technology and of the acute shortage of trained labour (notably specialised workers, semi-skilled staff and maintenance personnel) by: (a) obtaining direct access to the technological resources and skills of industrial countries, for example, on the pattern established by Iran and Kuwait (which took a stake in the equity capital of Krupp, Daimler-Benz and Lonrho); (b) having recourse also to the intermediate technology of the highly specialised small and medium-size multinationals of the industrial countries in order to help spread technology and diffuse industrial facilities to broad segments of the economy; (c) with assistance and guidance from foreign partners, building the necessary infrastructure in the form of research and development units which should be able to absorb imported technology, modify and improve it to suit domestic conditions, and provide the ability to create indigenous technologies more suited to specific needs (e.g. through financial incentives aimed at encouraging appropriately sized industrial enterprises to undertake R and D activities): thus the degree of technological dependence will be reduced[18]; (d) exercising control over the transfer of technology (with the aim of acquiring a suitable form of technology, from countries which own production licences, at a reasonable cost and on reasonable terms and conditions in keeping with the overall interests of the national economy); there should thus, for example, be adequate information about alternative sources of technology and methods of licensing in various sectors, or adequate follow-up in respect of the implementation of existing technology agreements so that a co-ordinated policy approach can be adopted for purposes of acquiring such technology; (e) determining the training requirements, and organising - in conjunction with the developed countries - comprehensive and suitable training programmes and facilities (with emphasis on certain types of engineering skills, for which the demand is great), as well as repair and maintenance centres, seminars, exchange of information, etc.; (f) sending governmental missions to various countries in search of skilled manpower (it would seem that Cyprus, India and Pakistan can supply a substantial number of specialised workers and skilled staff to overcome, for instance, the shortage of medical and teaching personnel); (g) undertaking specific agreement with the training centres of the industrial countries (including

Table 6.5
Car and commercial vehicle sales in 1973 to Arab states and Iran by country of origin

	Egypt[a]		Iran		Iraq		Kuwait		Lebanon		Libya		Saudi Arabia		
	Cars	CVs	Cars	CVs	Cars	CVs	Cars	CVs	Cars	CVs	Cars	CVs	Cars	CVs	Total
UK	96	106	42,900	1,230	75	55	290	104	1,320	325	615	575	80	60	47,831
USA	20	51	445	325	-	40	6,800	1,680	2,612	990	54	130	3,410	4,155	20,712
France	754	10	8,070	36	790	660	1,875	40	4,745	160	8,620	4,035	1,210	35	31,040
Italy	3,298	24	120	210	-	-	895	-	3,050	30	2,810	2,645	1,183	95	14,360
W. Germany	356	340	3,250	955	60	-	1,510	1,085	3,185	390	4,190	1,585	1,100	1,830	19,836
Japan	2	52	560	6,030	-	345	7,630	3,410	4,015	1,330	5,916	4,580	9,730	24,510	68,110
TOTAL	4,526	583	55,345	8,785	925	1,100	19,000	6,319	18,927	3,225	22,205	13,550	16,713	30,685	

[a]The Egyptians have bought a large number of Eastern European trucks which do not show in these figures.
Source: *The Financial Times*.

the universities), offering to pay all the expenses of students going there to study (in subjects considered technically or socially useful) and guarantee jobs on their return (on condition that an undertaking is given to return to the country); (h) strengthening co-operation with international organisations such as UNIDO, ILO, FAO and the World Bank; and (i) attracting home (through secure, well-paid jobs offering real prospects) qualified personnel at present abroad.

Additionally, to promote further growth of industrial co-operation between the countries of the region and the Western nations, other urgent steps are necessary at international level. A primary requirement is more widespread and accurate knowledge of opportunities for negotiating and concluding industrial co-operation contracts, and of the institutional framework to which such contracts must necessarily be adapted. In order to accomplish such a task, OECD and IDCAS, in co-operation with other international organisations (UNIDO, the FAO industry co-operative programme, etc.) would seem to be specially qualified under the suggested framework of the diplomacy of resources, as would some private organisations such as Patindex - a computerised data bank service for the world wide dissemination of new patents, products and processes covering 21 industry segments and over 260 major product categories.

Furthermore, preferential treatment - in respect of tariff and non-tariff barriers - for goods covered by industrial co-operation contracts could undoubtedly contribute greatly to the growth of co-operation in the region. Although the problem is a complex one, raising issues which go beyond industrial co-operation, the principle of special tariff treatment for such goods, as generally accepted in East-West economic relations, could be extended to the Middle East and North Africa. Initially, preference could be given to certain volumes of specific products (according to a gradual time scale) and could also take the form of special arrangements for simplifying customs procedures. Another urgent matter is to ensure a sounder legal framework for industrial co-operation contracts, through international conventions or codes of practice, since the present lack of international norms - particularly for clauses referring to the impact of inflation - seems to act as a major constraint on the development of full industrial co-operation.

6.7 Regional co-operation

The adoption of an outward-looking industrial strategy necessitates reappraisal of regional co-operation, the basic question being that of adopting the quickest route to more effective regional co-operation, rather than establishing a kind of unified superstructure. In particular, *sectoral co-operation* would seem to be the best way to speed up industrial development in the region, achieve a more balanced regional collaboration serving all parties and helping to establish new industries, or to expand existing industries, in order to reach an optimum size in line with the criteria for industrial specialisation within the region.

This form of co-operation – which is favoured by greater willingness to accept limited commitments – is considered by the Industrial Development Centre for Arab States from two aspects. The first deals with the achievement of co-operation as between existing industries, the second with co-operation as between industries yet to be established. Perhaps the most viable form of co-operation and co-ordination as between existing industries is the establishment of *federations,* comprising existing productive units and similar to the Arab Iron and Steel Federation, operating successfully since 1972. Such federations could co-ordinate purchases of raw materials, plant and machinery, product marketing, training of technicians and skilled labour, extension of productive services and product diversification. The IDCAS Conference held in Tripoli in 1974 has, in particular, recommended the encouragement of efforts to promote establishment of federations in the fertiliser, textile and foodstuffs industries. As regards regional co-operation in establishing new industrial enterprises, this may be realised through two or more countries setting up joint enterprises or by agreeing among themselves as to the location of some enterprises, so that a basic enterprise is established in a certain country, while other 'satellite' firms, being as it were intermediate links, are established in other countries.

Joint projects may take the form of major basic enterprises, which will act as a base for industrial development and the foundation for many other industries, that should be deemed as national or at least regional. However, this does not imply establishment of a single enterprise at the national level; rather, several enterprises could be set up and co-ordination effected between them in respect of production and marketing. The clearest examples are the petrochemicals and iron and steel industries. Co-operation between the parent company offering the licence and the licensee can be initiated at great advantage to both. The parent company can entrust to the licensee the production of certain parts (or certain 'first stage' products), making use of the relatively cheap labour and stable conditions in its factories. The licensee gains the advantage of large-scale production, thus reducing production costs. Thus, for example, Kuwait has built a chemical fertiliser plant in Turkey, near to consuming markets and enjoying cheap labour. Other examples are the joint projects to exploit minerals such as phosphate, iron and phosphorus; these projects were advanced by the Second Arab Mineral Wealth Conference held in Jeddah in 1974, and involve two or more neighbouring countries with similar geological characteristics. And there is also Project Arcomsat (Arab communication satellite system) which aims to foster telecommunications in the Arab World.

Joint enterprises may be established within a certain area or – as recommended by IDCAS – by virtue of an agreement between two or more countries in the field of consumer industries (e.g. spinning and weaving, foodstuffs, paper and wood); also in respect of industries that are in large measure complementary (e.g. tractors, engines, electric generators, agricultural and workshop machinery) and in import-substitution industries (e.g. special steel and electric and electronic equipment). This form of co-operation can also take the form of barter, for parts and components, one country specialising to cover the needs of others besides itself.

The most spectacular inter-Arab enterprises have been promoted by the Organisation for Arab Petroleum Exporting Countries. Thus the Arab Maritime Company for Petroleum Transportation has, since the beginning of 1973, undertaken all maritime transport of hydrocarbons and all activities that help facilitate operations such as purchase and sale of real estate and the undertaking of commercial and financial deals and transactions. The Arab Shipbuilding and Repair Company commenced activity by constructing, in Bahrain, the largest dry dock of the Gulf area to service tankers and ships. The Arab Oil Services Company (established 1974) provides Arab states with oil exploration and other services previously handled by foreign companies. The Arab Petroleum Investment Company (endowed with about $US 1 billion) invests oil revenues in oil refineries, petrochemical complexes and other basic industries. In addition, Egypt, Saudi Arabia, the Emirates and Qatar have agreed to create a joint arms industry (with an initial fund of about $US 1·04 billion), establish a Pan-Arab airline, and develop an integrated transport system (linking the East Mediterranean with the Gulf, and the Turkish border with the Arab peninsula) and thousands of miles of railways.

These sectoral forms of economic integration seem to offer better prospects than have past efforts, because a new *investment climate* is encouraged. In fact, a new open door policy prevails in Arab capital-importing countries, providing incentives to reduce the investment risk, for creation of industrial zones (especially along the Suez Canal),

Table 6.6

Cumulative growth in the estimated number of small, medium and large computer installations in the Arab countries, 1970–73

Country	1970	1971	1972	1973
Egypt	26	30	32	36
Lebanon	19	31	34	35
Iraq	3	6	10	10
Kuwait	5	7	9	10
Saudi Arabia	7	7	9	9
Libya	9	9	9	9
Sudan	3	3	3	4
Jordan	–	2	4	4
Syria	1	2	2	2
Abu Dhabi	2	2	2	2
Bahrain	2	2	2	2
Oman	1	1	1	1
Yemen Arab Republic	1	1	1	1
Total	79	103	118	125

Source: *The Arab Economist,* 'Computers in Lebanon and the Arab World', vol. VI, no. 66, July 1974.

guarantees against non-commercial risks such as nationalisation, the transfer of some profits abroad, etc. Thus the surplus states can deploy their capital resources more systematically in promoting Pan-Arab co-operation. For example, Kuwait has concluded several agreements with other Arab states (Iraq, Sudan, Tunisia, Egypt, Syria) which provide substantial treatment of Kuwaiti investments. Moreover, twelve Arab countries have approved the establishment of an Arab Investment Guarantee Corporation and of an Arab Centre for the Settlement of Investment Disputes[19], while the governments of states party to the Agreement of Arab Economic Unity (Jordan, Sudan, Syria, Kuwait, Egypt, the Arab Republic of Yemen) have defined an agreement concerning investment and free movement of Arab capital among Arab countries. In addition, the Kuwait Fund and the Abu Dhabi Fund have prepared an Inter-Arab Investment Code whereby the host countries determine the fields in which Arab capital can be invested and, at the same time, declare that capital invested in these sectors will not be nationalised or seized. The great importance attached to establishing a suitable investment climate is apparent, at the political level, in the visits to Cairo of the late King Faisal and of Sheikh Sabbath of Kuwait and, on the economic front, in the co-operation between Egypt and Iran, Egypt and Iraq, Syria and Iraq, the Democratic Yemen and the Arab Republic of Yemen, regardless of their political differences.

This is a long-overdue shift in the Arab approach to regional co-operation, which, if it persists, augurs well for the future of Arab economic unity. In addition, other effective instruments for regional development are already at work, notably in the financial and institutional sectors.

In the *financial sector,* the channelling of Arab funds into Pan-Arab investments has been pioneered since 1962 by the Kuwait Fund for Arab Economic Development (which, with $US 3·4 billion capital, has a loan potential of more than $US 10 billion and offers technical assistance, promotion of local development banks, and acts as an intermediary in the negotiations of trade agreements between Arab states); since 1971 by the Abu Dhabi Fund for Arab Economic Development (which, with a capital raised to $US 625 million, mainly favours closer co-operation within the Federation of Arab Emirates, of which Abu Dhabi is a constituent part); and by the Arab Fund for Economic and Social Co-operation (which, sponsored by the Arab League and with a capital of $US 1·5 billion, seeks productive investments for capital surpluses in the Arab World, the formulation of an Arab monetary policy and hopes to attract the numerous Arab experts who live abroad).

In the field of co-operation between Arab capital-importing countries such as Egypt and sources of finance in surplus countries, a pioneering role is also played by the Arab International Bank for Trade and Development (formerly the Egyptian International Bank for Foreign Trade and Development), which enjoys almost unique privileges. (Since deposits with the bank are not divulged, deposits and shareholders' equity cannot be nationalised, the bank's funds and profits are exempt from all taxes and duties, and the bank is not subject to Egyptian laws controlling companies, banking, credit and exchange control.)

Other ventures financing inter-Arab trade include the Beirut Riyadh Bank (Lebanese/Saudi-owned), the Audi Bank (Lebanese/Kuwaiti), the Bank Misr Liban (Lebanese/Egyptian), the Banque du Liban et d'Outre-Mer (Saudi/Lebanese), the Libyan Tunisian Bank (Libyan/Tunisian) and the Arab African Bank (Egyptian/Kuwaiti).

Arab/foreign joint ventures have also been established in European capitals (e.g. UBAF, Union des Banques Arabes Françaises) which afford the opportunity for investment of surplus funds in some countries of the region, finance specific projects, offer advisory services to Arab institutions and governments, and contribute to the creation of local capital markets. And because Arab/foreign joint ventures do not satisfy the need for long-term large-volume financing of local enterprises, multinational investment institutions between Arab and foreign shareholders have also been created. Examples are: Arab Finance Corporation (with American, Japanese, French and four different Arab shareholders), Banque d'Investissement et de Finance, Finance Bank, Union Bank, SNA Bank, American Express Development Co., Iran International Investment Bank, Darias Bank, etc.[20]

Another company type currently being established in the Arab World comprises inter-Arab investment companies aiming at investing their subscribed capital in one or more of the Arab countries and taking an equity position in specific projects. Thus there is the $US 255 million Arab Investment Company set up in Riyadh by Saudi Arabia, Kuwait, Egypt, Sudan, Qatar, Abu Dhabi and Bahrain and later joined by Syria, Iraq and Jordan which, ultimately, aims to invest in projects in Egypt, Sudan and Somalia in relation to wheat, cattle and shipping matters. In this respect, it is worth noting that inter-Arab investments also enhance the possibility of co-operation with the industrial countries, in particular between – on the money side – the Arabs and Iranians as partners, lenders, mediators or co-ordinators and – on the other side – multinational companies whose technology and management is essential for major projects to be implemented. An example of this type is the $US 400 million venture to construct a pipeline from Suez to the Mediterranean (SUMED project).

More recently, some agencies and consulting offices have also emerged; these are capable of identifying specific projects which have suitable markets and are appropriate to the economic development needs of the country concerned. Examples are the Investment Promotion Group, created in Beirut in 1972, and International Financial Advisers, created in Kuwait in 1974 (whereby also three Western banks – Worms Bank of Paris, R. Fleming and Co. of London and W. Kent and Co. of New York – participate with a 15 per cent share each). Furthermore, the public agencies in charge of industrialisation in Arab capital-importing countries have begun to realise the importance of reaching external sources of finance in the Arab World, and are contacting these sources and encouraging them to invest in their projects.

In the *institutional sector,* a progressive step along the path of inter-Arab economic co-operation is the establishment of several sectoral organisations associated in varying degrees with the machinery and activities of the Arab League. Thus, in addition to the establishment of the active Industrial Development Centre for Arab States, to foster industrial co-ordination and research, an Arab Standards and Measurements Organisation has been set up, on the basis of the recommendations of the international agencies (ISO and DEVCO) and is working to standardise within the Arab states technical terms, methods of testing, analysis and measurements, and to co-ordinate and unify specifications whenever possible. Of great importance, also, is the Economic Commission for West Africa, ECWA (which, in addition to performing a multidisciplinary role with international organisations, favours Arab co-operation in the form of sectoral surveys, expert group meetings, preparation of specific projects, dissemination of data and information, advisory services and the sponsoring of useful regional ventures). Also operating are the Federation of Chambers of Commerce, Industry and Agriculture for Arab states, various economic associations, trade unions and professional associations, etc.

Thus a rapid process of co-ordination is taking place which could evolve (with a minimum of political effort) into a unified superstructure, provided that the main limitations are overcome, in part by further steps to attract and channel investment into specific industrial projects. The limitations here include the absence of a regional financial market; the excessive emphasis which the specialised institutions for industrial financing give to security, rather than considering the profitability and earning potential of an enterprise; the conservative approach the commercial banks follow in their lending policy; a lack of adequate managerial and entrepreneurial skills; and the small size of the markets.

Moves to attract investment to the various projects could be made through establishment of a regional promotion centre and a regional industrial development bank. And, again, the fostering of financial institutions, development corporations and industrial banks (to exchange knowledge, co-ordinate policies and efforts, and undertake joint ventures) would help to limit the bars to co-ordination. So would a planned R and D effort (setting up a technology fund, as suggested by IDCAS), industrial management and training (creating industrial departments in the universities and a regional centre), a monetary union (linked to the value of oil) and a money market (to support the enterprises of the region in financing their investments).

Consequently, it would be possible to pursue more ambitious projects, such as the revival of the Arab Common Market (to eliminate barriers impeding the trade exchange of industrial goods)[21], the formation of an economic unity among the Gulf states (as advocated, for example, by the Prime Minister of Bahrain, Bin Sulman) and of an Asian Economic

Community (including, as suggested by the Shah, all the northern states bordering the Indian Ocean).

Notes

[1] IDCAS, 'L'industrie de transformation dans certains pays arabes', paper submitted to the 3rd Conference on Industrial Development for Arab States, Tripoli, 7–14 April 1974.

[2] UNESOB, *Review and Appraisal of Progress in the Implementation of the International Development Strategy for the Second Development Decade,* Beirut, 1 October 1973, pp. 71–89.

[3] IDCAS, 'Conception des grandes lignes pour une stratégie du développement industriel arabe compte tenu des évolutions récentes et analyse des résultats et objectifs des plans du développement industriel dans les pays arabes', paper submitted to the 3rd Conference on Industrial Development for Arab States, Tripoli, 7–14 April, 1974.

[4] UNESOB, *Some Objectives of Industrial Policy and the Measures or Instruments Used to Achieve them,* Beirut, October 1970.

[5] M.L. Boudjemeline, 'Suggestion pour une nouvelle stratégie générale d'industrialisation des pays arabes', paper submitted to the 3rd Conference on Industrial Development for Arab States, Tripoli, 7–14 April 1974.

[6] Office Arabe de Presse et de Documentation, 'Pétrole Arabe', *Syrie et Monde Arabe,* no. 245, June 1974, pp. 1–31.

[7] Z.B. Terzian, 'La coopération pétrochimique italo-arabe', paper submitted to the international meeting on economic co-operation between Italian industry and the Arab countries, Cetraro (Italy), 12–14 July 1974; R.B. Stobaugh, 'The Economics of Energy Versus Non-Energy Uses of Petroleum: The Case of Petrochemicals', *Arab Oil and Gas,* vol. 3, no. 66, 16 June 1974; S. Bluff, 'Mixed Prospects for a Middle East Petrochemical Industry', *Middle East Economic Digest,* 5 April 1974.

[8] O. Grine, 'Possibilities of Industrial Cooperation between Italy and the Arab Countries; The Case of the Steel Industry', paper presented at the international meeting held in Cetraro (Italy), 12–14 July 1974; 'The Third Technical and Commercial Conference of the Arab Iron and Steel Union', *Arab Steel,* vol. 2, no. 16, Algiers, May 1974; S.Y. Ezz, *Establishment of Iron and Steel Industries in the Arab Countries,* UNIDO, October 1973.

[9] UNIDO, 'Regional Seminar on Machine Tools in Developing Countries of Europe and the Middle East', Varna, Bulgaria, 18–27

October 1971.

[10] 'Prospects for the Middle East Motor Industry', *Middle East Economic Digest* Special Report, London, 29 November 1974; 'Some Aspects of the Establishment of the Automobile Industry in Developing Countries with Special Emphasis on African Countries', a survey by Dr. A. Gazarin, Chairman, El Nasr Automotive Manufacturing Co., Arab Republic of Egypt (unpublished).

[11] UNESOB, *The Cement Industry in Arab Countries of the Middle East,* Beirut, August 1973.

[12] 'Construction and Building in the Gulf', *Middle East Economic Digest,* 8 March 1974; UNESOB, *Review and Appraisal of Progress in Housing, Building and Urban Planning,* October 1973.

[13] ILO, 'The Role of Small Enterprises in the Industrialisation of the Arab Countries', a paper prepared for the conference on industrialisation in Arab countries, Kuwait, 1-10 March 1966.

[14] B. Hoselitz, *The Entrepreneurial Element in Economic Development,* UN Conference on the Application of Science and Technology, New York, 1962.

[15] E. Asfour, *Situation, Problèmes et Perspectives de la petite industrie dans six pays arabes du Moyen Orient,* a report by UNIDO; New York, 1972; United Nations, *Industrial Development, Arab Countries,* report by the Kuwait Symposium, New York, 1967.

[16] Case studies of joint ventures already established with East European countries (notably Rumania, Hungary and Yugoslavia) are extremely useful. See *Prospects of East-West Joint Ventures,* Hobbema, Brussels, 1974; Economic Commission for Europe, *Analytical Report on Industrial Cooperation among ECE Countries,* Geneva, 1973.

[17] 'Une nouvelle charte de la coopération industrielle', *Le Monde,* 30 November 1974.

[18] 'Transfer, Adaptation and Development of Technology to Arab Countries', paper presented to the 3rd Conference on Industrial Development for Arab States, Tripoli, 7-14 April 1974.

[19] This regional institution has now been implemented. I. Shinata, *The Arab Investment Guarantee Corporation,* Kuwait Fund for Arab Economic Development, Kuwait, January 1974.

[20] Sabbah Al Hay, 'Investment Channels in the Arab World', paper presented at the international meeting held in Cetraro (Italy), 12-14 July 1974.

[21] IDCAS, *Financing Arab Industrial Development,* 3rd Conference on Industrial Development for Arab States, Tripoli, 7-14 April; R. Hajjar, *Elements for a Regional Plan for the Application of Science and*

Technology to the Development of Selected Countries in the Middle East, ECWA, Beirut, 1973.

7 Progress towards control of financial resources

7.1 The petrodollars flow into the Western credit market

Most of what Arab countries earn on the oil front is immediately lost for the financial plan because the largest part of the oil revenues go on flowing into the Western credit market (mainly in the form of bank deposits, treasury bonds, shares, loans, etc.).[1] 'Thus, Wall Street and the City of London remain the privileged centres of Arab surplus funds', Mr. Abushabi, chairman of Union de Banques Arabes et Françaises (UBAF), points out.[2]

The West's money markets, in particular, are the first circuit into which the oil-producing countries' swelling currency reserves are injected. In the case of Saudi Arabia, the essential payments are made to accounts held with the big American banks, notably Morgan Guaranty – of which one American director is also a member of the Saudi Arabia Monetary Agency, SAMA, defined by international bankers as 'an ultra-conservative pension fund' – the Chase Manhattan Bank, the First National City Bank and the United States Trust. As for the Gulf countries, payments of oil revenues are made in London either directly to the Bank of England or to large merchant banks operating the Eurodollar system. The recycling of these funds is handled by the monetary authorities of the oil-producing countries, advised, as in the case of Saudi Arabia, by European and American banking experts, or through their own investment boards (e.g. the Kuwait Investment Board, the Abu Dhabi Investment Board) located in London and managed with the assistance of highly qualified Western financiers. In addition, Kuwait and Saudi Arabia have respectively established an investment office in London to follow day to day operations on the London market. Thus, only a small part of these capitals is invested directly in real estate and stock portfolios. The largest part goes to the Eurobanks (notably the British banks and, to a lesser extent, the Swiss banks) as short-term liquid deposits, returning in the consuming nations through Euro-issues and Eurocredits. It is, then, the Western banks which assume the responsibility of recycling the surplus funds, with all the risks involved.

More recently some parts of Arab–Iranian oil revenues have been placed in less liquid form. A few spectacular operations have drawn attention, such as the 25 per cent stake of Iran in Krupp Huttenwerke; the 13 per cent shareholding of Iran in Pan Am; the 25 per cent purchase of Iran in Deutsche Babcock and Wilcox; an indirect 10 per cent held by Iran in the capital of Eurodif; the Abu Dhabi majority shareholding in London's Park Tower Hotel; the 20·7 per cent stake in the British contractors, Richard Costain, of the Ambassador of the United Arab Emirates, Al Tajer; the 40 per cent holding of preference shares of the Bank of the Commonwealth, Detroit, and the 7½ per cent stake in Occidental Oil by Saudi Arabian interests, represented by Chaith Paraon, the son of a Saudi diplomat; the Kuwaiti purchase of St Martin's Property Corporation and of the 'Tour Manhattan' skyscraper in Paris, as well as the 14 per cent Kuwaiti stake in Daimler–Benz, the 22 per cent in the financial and industrial group, Lonrho, and the 5 million shares in Nippon Steel Corp., Japan's largest industrial concern and the world's leading steel maker, the 25 per cent participation of an Arab consortium in the banking concern Edward Bates.

So far, however, the oil producers of the Middle East have spent little on direct investment and have been careful to avoid going for complete control. In fact, for large land deals, rumoured to have occurred in the United States (particularly in South Carolina and Georgia by the Kuwait Investment Co.), American firms take full care of the management.

A second, significant, circuit by which petrodollars are reinvested in the West, and one which is expected to become more and more important – with increasing oil revenues accruing *directly* to governments – is direct government-to-government loans (e.g. Saudi Arabia's to Japan, Iran's to the UK and France), as well as the purchase of government bonds in oil-using countries (e.g. in the US, UK, Japan). In this category as well comes the IMF oil facility and the financial help granted to Western official and semi-official agencies (e.g. Iranian help to finance Eurodif). In effect, by lending to the governments of the world and their agencies, rather than foreign private borrowers, the oil producers are asking official monetary agencies to become their bankers.

A third circuit is for revenues to make their way back to the Middle East to finance the budgetary needs of the oil-producing countries. But, here again, a considerable portion is rapidly recycled into the West, namely the budgetary expenditure mainly utilised for infrastructure and investment programmes which boost imports of industrial goods and equipment. Another part of budgetary receipts is designated for international economic and financial aid, either directly (as gifts or subsidies to the poorer Arab countries) or indirectly by participation in intragovernmental financial and investment institutions (e.g. the Arab Fund, the Arab Bank for Industrial and Agricultural Development in Africa and the Islamic Development Bank). A further part is used to finance regional economic aid through national financial institutions (e.g. the Kuwait Fund for Arab Economic Development). As a rule these funds (totally established with public capital) operate according to the principles of an international development bank (financing specific projects at reduced rates of interest following the pattern of the World Bank).

So far as private capital is concerned, Arab sources seem irresistibly attracted to the West, especially by investment of direct shares in European and American companies. Thus, for example, Intra Bank (refloated since its collapse) owns an 82 per cent share of France's third largest shipbuilders, Chantiers Navales de la Ciotat. Two of Kuwait's banks have gained control of the Spanish motorway construction company, Autopista Concesionaria Espanola, and Kuwaiti businessmen have financed the construction of Holiday Inns in Lebanon.

Until Intra Bank's notorious crash, Beirut was the most important financial centre through which the investments of the Arab bourgeoisie were channelled. Since then, an increasing proportion of private funds has been channelled through Kuwait, notably through two very active semi-public investment companies (the Kuwait Investment Company, KIC, of which the State owns 50 per cent of the capital, and the Kuwait Foreign Trading Contracting and Investment Company, KFTCIC, of which the State has 75 per cent). KIC has a branch in London, works together with Western financial institutions such as American Express, and plays an important role in placing Middle East private funds in secure Western countries. The Arab Bank, with headquarters in Amman, is another less known but also quite active financial institution channelling private funds to the West. It has a branch in Zürich, which allows cautious movement of funds between the Arab centres, and numbered accounts with the big Swiss banks. KFTCIC's assets are also deployed in Europe and America, but the company has two other interregional offshoots in Africa - the Sudan-Kuwait Investment Company, in which KFTCIC has 50 per cent, and the Afro-Arab Company for Investment and International Trade (AFARCO), which was formed in July 1972 to invest only in African states south of the Sahara. KFTCIC is also used as an agent for placing Kuwaiti government loans.

7.2 An independent capital market

The way the Arab financial surplus has been used until now does not serve Arab interests, since oil revenues are deposited in leading international banks, with comparatively small amounts being recycled to the Arab World. Thus the leading institutions of the oil-producing countries of the Middle East - as well as less rich states such as Egypt and Sudan - continue to seek funds in the Eurodollar market despite the massive growth of oil revenues.

The position is summed up by Abdul Malek Teman, chairman of the National Bank of Algeria: 'We are still dependent upon international financial decisions which are always far from helping us resolve our problems. We still lack sufficient proper institutions to make our voice heard, like OPEC and OAPEC. We do not act for our own interest, but directly *against* or *in favour of* foreign interests'.[3] And again, C. Akhras, chairman of the Arab Finance Corporation, stresses: 'We are faced with the challenge of channelling our financial resources towards investments which could serve Arab interest both at home and abroad'.[4]

The attraction of Western credit markets for Arab capital in fact reflects three important factors:

1 A lack of adequate investment outlets in the oil countries themselves.

2 The relatively low risk associated with foreign financial investment.

3 The weakness of local financial infrastructures, the Arab banking structure being characterised by fragmentation, absence of co-operation, inadequacy of specialised institutions, overwhelmingly short-term credit facilities, lack of intermediaries to ensure the smooth transformation of short-term funds into medium and long-term credit, and a trend towards foreign control.[5]

These disadvantages are now, however, receiving drastic attention.

First, by realising that oil is a wasting asset, the Arabs, as discussed earlier, envisage a massive expansion of their own absorptive capacity on a scale that should permit the investment of a large part of this capital within both the oil-exporting and other, less fortunate, countries of the region. 'The most urgent objective of the Arab leaders is to use our wealth for the development of our countries and of the Arab World as a whole', says Ablatif Y. Al-Hamad, Director-General of the Kuwait Fund.[6]

Second, foreign financial investments have become risky because of consecutive devaluations, hyperinflation and the strong opposition of Western nations to industrial direct investments. 'Western governments could turn the tables and nationalise Arab assets for political reasons', Arab oil expert, Abdellah Al-Tariki, points out.

Third, there is a strong desire to replace what the Kuwaiti Finance Minister, Abdel-Rahman Atiqi, calls 'unsatisfactory relationships which make us a mere source of finance for economies stronger than our own' by, as Dr Akhras describes it, 'a financial system that can safeguard the capital surpluses accruing to Arab countries (by investing and utilising them profitably rather than merely accumulating foreign assets liable to inflation and devaluation) as well as Arab financial institutions having a strong international audience'.

Thus, in addition to new national and interregional institutions (e.g. the Kuwait Industrial Development Bank, the Kuwait Real Estate Bank, the UAE National Development and Investment Bank, and the Arab Bank for Investment and Foreign Trade set up by the United Arab Emirates, Libya and Algeria), efforts are under way to create an Arab financial market with a regional and international role, rather than one which is a mere appendage to Western financial centres. In particular, a new type of Arab institution has been set up, providing long and medium-term lending (usually in association with the big names of Western finance), namely: (1) Banque d'Investissement et de Financement, set up in Beirut by Banque Audi (Lebanon), which holds 35 per cent with Hambros Bank, the Caisse Centrale des Banques Populaires de France, Namura Securities and 25 per cent of private Arab interest; (2) Arab Finance Corporation, with 46 per cent capital owned by non-Arab interest (Manufactures Hanover, Banque de l'Union Européene, Bank of Tokyo) and with major Lebanese and Kuwaiti interests; (3) International Financial Advisers Company, established in Kuwait by Robert Fleming, William Kent, and Banque Worms plus private Kuwaiti interest; (4) Oryx Investments, a merchant banking operation in Dubai in which Arbuthnot has 20 per cent, the Standard and Chartered Bank 20 per cent, and seven families (from Saudi Arabia, Abu Dhabi, Bahrain, Dubai, Kuwait and Qatar) the rest, the aim being a service institution to mount medium-scale projects and help guide Western companies to the right area; (5) Arbuthnot, along with four other international banks (Banque de Suez and Banque de l'Indochine, the American Philadelphia National Bank and the Japanese Taiyo Kobe Bank), is also a major partner in Arab Financial Consultants, another merchant bank owned by leading figures in Kuwait and non-Kuwaiti Arab shareholders which provides a full range of financial services and operates in the area of major project finance; (6) the Kuwait Finance Centre set up by Kuwaiti businessmen with a foreign partner, the International Bank of Washington, holding a 21·4 per cent share in the company, whose object is to finance import and export operations, act as broker between those extending and those receiving credits, provide consultancy services, both financial and technical, and trade in foreign exchange markets and in the market for precious metals in Kuwait and abroad; (7) the Hispano-Arab Investment Bank, 40 per cent of which belongs to Spanish interests (banks and state holding company, INI) and the remainder to the Foreign Trade Contracting and Investment Corporation (Kuwait) and the Libyan Arab Foreign Bank; (8) the Kuwait International Investment Company, established in 1974 by a group of wealthy Kuwaiti merchant families; (9) the Saudi International Bank, where a 55 per cent majority of Saudi interests shares with the American bank Morgan Guaranty Trust (which holds 20 per cent of the capital) and four European banks (Banque Nationale de Paris, Deutsche Bank, National Westminster Bank and Union Bank of Switzerland) and a Japanese bank (Bank of Tokyo), which each have 5 per cent; (10) the International Bank of Iran, where the Chase Manhattan Bank and the Iranian bank Etebarate Canati each hold 35 per cent of the capital. These institutions complete the already existing network of Euro-Arab joint banking ventures: Unions de Banques Arabes et Françaises, set up in Paris in 1970 on the initiative of Crédit Lyonnais (which now has a 32 per cent stake), Banque Française du Commerce Extérieur (with an 8 per cent stake) and 24 Arab shareholders from 19 countries. UBAF extended its regional representation to London in 1972, with the Midland Bank and the state-owned Libyan-Arab Foreign Bank each holding 25 per cent and UBAF (Paris) the other 50 per cent. A similar formula - local banks, Arab banks and UBAF (Paris) - has been adopted in Frankfurt (UBAE), Rome (UBAE Rome), and in its new Japanese associate established in Hong Kong (UBAN); as well as in New York with four American banks (Bankers Trust, First National Bank of California, Security Pacific Bank, Texas Commerce Bankshares), which control 20 per cent of the capital; also in the FRAB Bank International, established in Paris in 1969 by Société Générale (which now has a 36 per cent stake), Société Générale de Banque, Swiss Bank Corporation, Banco Urquijo, and Kuwaiti interests, which hold 36 per cent. In February 1974, it was also announced that the Industrial Bank of Japan, the Amsterdam-Rotterdam Bank and the National Bank of Greece would acquire a holding in the bank, together with an important group of Saudi Arabian companies and semi-public Moroccan and Algerian shareholders; European Arab Holding Company, set up in Luxembourg in 1972 by European Banks International Company with two operating banks in Brussels and Frankfurt. EBIC members directly hold more than 40 per cent of the bank and there are 17 Arab shareholders; and the Banque Arabe et International d'Investissement, created in 1973, owned 50:50 by a consortium of Arab shareholders and a group of 13 European banks. Similarly, the Iran Overseas Investment Bank was set up in London in 1973 with the participation of Bank Melli (the largest commercial bank in Iran, which is state-controlled), the government-sponsored Industrial and Mining Development Bank of Iran and eight international banks (from the UK, Europe, the US and Japan). Another important step towards the development of an independent capital market has been the floating of several bond issues (in local currencies but also in dollars as in the case of a ten-year $US 25 million bond issue for Brazil) *solely underwritten and managed by Arab financial institutions* to meet medium-term investment, not only in the industrialised world, but in the Middle East (to finance national and regional enterprises as, for instance, in the case of Uniceramics, a factory in the Bekaa in Lebanon) and in the rest of the Third World. Another breakthrough has been the floating of World Bank bonds in Kuwait, which makes the country the world's fourth largest participant in World Bank issues.

Other likely steps towards the creation of an independent Arab capital market are the establishment of exclusively Arab multinational banks and of Arab money brokers. Thus, just as the national Arab oil companies are now controlling their oil production, Arab financial institutions will emphasise control of their own financial resources. Petrodollars, therefore, should be seen as an interim problem - huge, but relatively short-lived. For the Middle East countries are going to be big spenders, lenders and investors for many years - until relatively cheap new oil sources are found, or until oil itself is superseded.

7.3 Institutional deficiencies

In at least three Arab cities, Beirut, Kuwait and Cairo, there are strong possibilities for building up a financial market that can absorb and deal with oil funds surpluses. These three might be considered complementary to each other. Beirut, now disrupted by civil war, could have been by far the most advanced of the three in terms of banking facilities, communications, mass media and human resources; Cairo - in pursuing an open economy and by providing guarantees against nationalisation, confiscation and sequestration, as well as establishing a stock-exchange market for foreign securities and cancelling routine administrative procedures - has a wider scope for investment; while Kuwait, although having a feeble base to support a financial centre, is nearest to the sources of funds.

Table 7.1
Lebanon's 16 leading banks (£Leb million) (1972)

	Nationality[a]	Assets	% of total assets	Deposits	% of total deposits	Loans	% of total loans
Arab Bank	F	569	6·3	529	8·5	97	2·3
British Bank of the Middle East	F	402	4·5	338	5·4	206	4·9
Banco di Roma	F	354	3·9	328	5·3	134	3·2
Banque Nationale de Paris (Intercontinentale)	F	379	4·2	317	5·1	270	6·5
Société Nouvelle de la Banque de Syrie et du Liban	LF	386	4·3	316	5·1	183	4·4
Banque Libano – Française	LF	362	4·0	274	4·4	167	4·0
Banque Libanaise pour le Commerce	L	315	3·5	244	3·9	176	4·2
Banque G. Trad (Crédit Lyonnais)	LF	248	2·8	228	3·7	140	3·4
Banque Française pour le Moyen-Orient	LF	241	2·7	216	3·5	123	2·9
Banque du Liban et d'Outremer	L	258	2·9	197	3·2	130	3·1
Banque Misr-Liban	LF	311	3·4	194	3·1	88	2·1
Bank of America	F	263	2·9	192	3·1	90	2·2
Société Générale Libano-Europóene de Banque	LF	342	3·8	177	2·8	125	3·0
First National City Bank	F	249	2·8	169	2·7	90	2·2
Arab African Bank	F	236	2·6	111	1·8	146	3·5
Moscow Narodny Bank	F	439	4·9	40	0·6	152	3·6
Total 16 banks		5,354	59·4	370	62·1	2,317	55·6
TOTAL ALL BANKS		9,014	100·0	635	100·0	4,171	100·0

L = Lebanese-owned, F = Foreign-owned, LF = Lebanese–Foreign venture.
Source: *Middle East Economic Digest*.

But the necessary elements for a unified Arab financial market, with Arab financial institutions able to control their own wealth, have largely still to be evolved.[7] In particular, solutions have yet to be devised for two types of deficiency: the absence of an effective institutional mechanism for channelling Arab capital; and the lack of an economic climate conducive to attraction of investment funds. In effect, financial institutions in the Middle East must be more than intermediaries. They should be initiators and entrepreneurial, especially in the fields of investment and merchant banking. They should also perform a more complete role and offer a more complete package than similar institutions in Europe or the United States, because of the relative underdevelopment of the countries of the region. In particular 'they must identify projects and see them right through appraisal and structuring; getting together interested parties - local and foreign - and arranging the finance if need be,' says A.M. Asselly, Managing Director of Henry Schroder (Beirut).[8]

In a national framework, the contribution of *commercial banks* to industrial development - the most effective mechanism for mobilising savings - has been mainly confined to financing established industries in the form of short-term credits for working capital. This tendency has been strengthened by a lack of sufficient support from the central banks, which, with a few exceptions, have not used preferential rediscount rates and have rediscounted only papers valid for less than one year. A number of measures, therefore, should be taken to induce the commercial banks to undertake term lending. In particular, loans to industry should be facilitated by central bank action in permitting preferential discount rates, longer periods and larger volume quotas for the industrial papers of the commercial banks than for papers relating to commercial and other purposes. Central bank incentives might also take the form of lower reserve requirements for industrial loans, or, alternatively, the imposition of a higher reserve requirement as a penalty for an inadequate industrial portfolio. Moreover, a government guarantee system would allow the banks to liberalise the required credit standards for industrial borrowers, extend the type of risk involved, extend term loans and widen the range of industries served. In addition, measures should be taken to increase co-operation between the commercial banks and existing, or newly established, industrial development banks.

The simplest form of such co-operation is the exchange of credit information regarding industrial borrowers. More important, however, would be to channel funds from commercial to industrial banks through low-interest loans. Alternatively, both types of financing institutions could participate jointly in granting industrial loans, with the commercial banks concentrating on medium-term tranche and the industrial banks on longer-term tranche.

Policy changes should also affect existing specialised institutions which, so far, place too much emphasis on security and too little on the profitability and earning potential of an enterprise. In particular, the financial resources of such institutions could be strengthened, firstly, by calling on the whole of the authorised capital, and, secondly, by providing a way for the private sector to join in financing the expansion of the bank's resources. This could be done by issuing bank shares or bonds, making them available both to institutional and individual investors. It would be particularly desirable to establish closer links between the specialised institutions and the normal channels of saving, so that the distributing mechanism would become increasingly capable of autonomous growth. And, to attract private capital, governments could provide appropriate incentives such as a guarantee of minimum dividends, or tax-free dividends.

A shift in concern from security to potential earning power would naturally lead to more effective support of local industrial firms by participating in their equity capital rather than extending loans to them. This approach could foster the development of Arab private industrial and agricultural sectors and hence allow small companies to grow with bank participation. And since access to managerial advice and modern techniques is sometimes more important to small and medium-size enterprises than access to financial resources is, adequate research and technical divisions should be created in the various specialised institutions, and where they do exist they should be strengthened. Further, industrial banks should be more active in identifying feasible projects, rather than merely waiting for applicants to submit such projects. This is of particular importance, given the lack of entrepreneurial talent and the shortage of qualified personnel.[9]

In a regional framework the adoption of some measures could expand the investment capability of the Arab World. Development funds already operating could co-ordinate their activities, consult each other and widen their objectives by including the process of identifying and planning of projects in co-operation with national governments. Moreover, given the capital resources of the Arab World and the present stage of underdevelopment of the area, it could be more appropriate to use less stringent criteria than hitherto in evaluating projects to be financed, with a lower rate of opportunity cost for capital used by the funds. In addition, following a suggestion put forward by Abdul Malek Teman, an association of Arab banks could be set up to study and discuss the main financial problems. Moreover, the Arab bank for Development in Africa could expand its activity to cater also for Asian and Latin American developing countries.

With respect to a *proper climate* for efficient growth of the above-mentioned institutions, on a national level a serious effort should be made by each government to increase the output of projects studied and planned; to allow the emergence of an economic climate more conducive to capital movements through greater liberalisation of economic policies; to give inducements for investment companies to merge (through legislation), rationalise and simplify procedures and formalities. On the bilateral level, closer economic relationships should be worked out between the various countries of the region to regularise their special economies of scale. On the multinational level, the obstacles to the free circulation of capital funds, investments and labour between the various Arab countries should be removed. Of paramount importance here is the scheme promoted by the Kuwait Fund for an Inter-Arab Investment Guarantee Corporation (which will insure private Arab citizens and companies against non-commercial risks in their investments in other Arab states), and also significant would be the emergence of a formal stock exchange in either Beirut or Kuwait (where there is already a very active trade in a few stocks), since a fundamental barrier to the trade of local securities is the present secretive style of dealing; also desirable is an Arab information centre for investment, to publish facts about the investment climate in each country and about specific projects.[10]

7.4 The role of the dinar

Simultaneously with the creation of an Arab capital market, Arab experts have suggested the creation of an Arab dinar to replace foreign currencies which, under present international economic conditions, are subject to monetary instability and inflation, thus eroding the value of Arab assets. In particular, the barrel of oil could be the measuring unit of the Arab dinar which, in preliminary stages, could be used not so much among Arab countries themselves, since inter-Arab trade is still very weak, but rather as a unit of expressing a stable value for oil in international trade. According to Abdul Malek Teman, 'the aim is to prevent oil - expressed in different currencies - from generating revenues which fluctuate depending upon the degree of change in the value of these currencies on the international money markets. In effect the Arab dinar would always be equal to the value of a barrel of oil whatever its price; therefore, the number of foreign currencies adjusted to the unit would have to be modified daily as a function of the respective value of each of these currencies on the foreign exchange market: this daily quotation would help to fix, day by day, the adjustment and the number of currencies that would enter into the determination of the unit. This quotation would also establish the value of the unit expressed in each currency, so that the buyer could pay in whatever currency he chose, while the seller was sure that the value of the settlement would not be diminished by any erosive tendencies operating on that particular currency.'[11]

The Arab dinar would also act in all essential ways as an international currency.[12] In effect, with oil having jumped from 8 per cent of the value of international trade during 1973 to an estimated 25 per cent of the 1974 value, a good enough justification for the creation of an international currency to be issued by the oil-exporting countries indeed exists. Thus, guaranteeing a sizeable demand for their Arab dinars, the Arab oil producers could proceed to make this monetary unit a real reserve currency and acquire dinar-denominated assets, the value of which would be under the control of the investing countries rather than the control of investment countries.

The Arab dinar could be issued by a body representing the Arab oil producers, namely the Inter-Arab Monetary Fund (set up in February 1975 and endowed with $US 750 million capital), whose main tasks, apart from the provision of medium and long-range loans, would be to:

- create an Arab strategy concerning international currency co-operation;
- support the Arab dinar and the fixing of exchange rates;
- finance deficits in balance of payments;
- foster trade exchange and facilitate the movement of capital among Arab states;
- attempt to remove all obstacles and controls on trade;
- help Arab states in their endeavour to achieve economic integration.

Of significance also is Iran's decision to peg its currency to the IMF's special drawing rights, thus changing the rial–dollar rate whenever the dollar–SDR value shifts.

7.5 Monetary co-operation

Western countries will need to be prepared to meet the forthcoming financial challenge of the Arabs by proposing to the oil-producing nations new and imaginative forms of monetary co-operation. Although uncontrolled expansion of foreign interests in the region would be harmful to both parties in the long run, financial autarky is certainly no solution for the Arabs. To build up international financial centres, the banking system must be thrown open to the outside world. Thus, Arab banks abroad and the Arab multinational banks located in the international financial centres of Europe can play a leading role in linking the new Arab financial centres with international capital markets. In particular, the consortia are well placed to assume a prominent role in the management of official Middle Eastern funds. A consortium operation would, in effect, offer links with established and well-known international banks, and the opportunity to draw on their wider experience of international financial markets.

In any event, a formula will have to be worked out to allow foreign banks and enterprises to operate within a framework ensuring mutual benefits. This could be expressed in terms of regulations issued by the various governments of the area, taking into account prospective local development and conditions. Moreover, to overcome the fragmentation of holdings among a large number of shareholders, the interests of existing Eurobanks could be harmonised and co-ordinated by establishing a far-reaching financial institution in which the oil producers could deposit a part of their capitals.

Similarly, Western nations will need to develop a mutually beneficial programme for investment of Arab oil money in the West. In particular, the West should take the initiative towards providing a 'safe area of investment' for Arab money, thus avoiding a public outcry every time the Arabs bid for an equity in a major industrial or commercial firm. A good example is the Association for the Promotion of Foreign Investment in the Walloon area of Belgium, whose aim is the promotion of selected industrial projects and in which, for instance, Kuwait has already taken a substantial stake. In fact, the opposition is likely to be much less where investments form part of a co-operative arrangement with Western companies or state agencies designated to promote industrial development in the less developed areas of the industrialised countries, as well as in the less fortunate nations of the Middle East and of the Third World.

An alternative would be to trade-off self-imposed limitations on the active management of Arab investment portfolios in the West against partial exchange guarantees, the burden of which would be shared among Western subscribers to the scheme. There is also a need to establish a Euro-Arab economic intelligence unit (to be staffed by economists, analysts and information specialists), with the aim of counselling and keeping Arab investors, public and private, abreast of investment opportunities and investment prospects, and of offering on-the-job

Table 7.2

Arab World financial structure, 1974

Country	Central Banks Public Agencies	Commercial Banks	Development Banks	Medium and Long-Term Banks	Representing Offices	Investment Trade Institutes	Other Specialised Banks
Lebanon	1	73	2	3	2	48	3
Kuwait	1	5	2	–	3	–	3
Saudi Arabia	1	11	2	–	2	–	–
United Arab Emirates	1	26	1	–	–	–	–
Libya	1	5	2	–	–	–	1
Iraq	1	2	3	–	–	–	3
Syria	1	1	–	–	–	–	4
Jordan	1	9	–	–	–	–	3
Egypt	1	5	–	–	–	1	1

Source: Sabbah Al Haj, *'Investment Channels in the Arab World'*, a paper submitted to the Seminar on Economic Co-operation between Italian Industry and the Arab Countries at Cetraro, Italy, 11–14 July 1974.

training for Arab college graduates, so that Arab professionals will become available to share adequately in the management of Arab funds. Moreover, to overcome misconception about the Arabs, their religion, history and economic and social life, an institution should be set up to organise frequent and regular cultural exchanges, meetings, debates, etc.

Another measure would be to promote greater participation of the oil producers in the management of the international monetary system. In this respect, the Arabs - to protect their interests - seek a greater share in both the special drawing rights and the policy making of the IMF, in which the present distribution of shares and rights is a representation of past world monetary conditions (the US holding 22 per cent of shares and the UK 9 per cent, Arab countries having less than 5 per cent). Moreover, the Arabs seek removal of controls on the formation of currency reserves and abstention from measures against the oil producers to correct their balance of payments. The justification for this is that Arab currency reserves do not represent added value to capital created by industrial development and economic growth, but the results of a changing status from raw materials to revenues in currencies liable to losses in value.

So far as the stability of oil revenues is concerned, the issue by Hambros Bank (Britain) of the ARCRU (a unit of account based on the currencies of Arab countries) is quite helpful in providing loans to some Western companies. The value of the ARCRU is based on the movement of twelve Arab currencies against the US dollar, with one ARCRU being equal to $1 on 28 June 1974. Subsequent value is based on the average dollar parity of eight currencies after ruling out the two which have most appreciated and the two which have most depreciated against the dollar. The currencies involved are those of Algeria, Libya, Egypt, Sudan, Syria, Iraq, Lebanon, Saudi Arabia, Kuwait, Oman, Qatar and the United Arab Emirates. Although the ARCRU functions as a unit of account rather than a currency unit, it expresses a useful attempt at compromise between the interests of the investors and the debtors. In addition, it has the advantage of representing both a unit of account based on oil and the financial, economic and political situation of the region.

Notes

[1] G. Corm, 'Le défaut de structures financières pour recycler l'argent du pétrole', *Commerce du Levant,* supplement no. 161, April/June 1974, p. 97.

[2] 'Arab Countries will Invest Funds in Stocks, Banker Says', *International Herald Tribune,* 12 June 1974.

[3] A.M. Teman, 'Les pays arabes en face des problèmes monétaires internationaux', *Banque,* July/August 1974.

[4] Charles Akhras, 'Arab Banking: Development and Prospects, Banking in the Arab World', *The Arab Economist,* August 1973, p. 7.

[5] In fact, 42 of the 75 banks chartered in Lebanon are controlled or owned by foreign interests. Y. El Bitar, 'Le système bancaire arabe', *Banque,* June 1974; Talfa Yaffi, 'Puissance financière et évolution des structures du monde arabe', *Banque,* November 1973.

[6] 'Arab Investment: Prospects for the Future', *Bulletin of the American Arab Association,* March 1974.

[7] E. Collard, 'The Middle East in World Finance', *Middle East Economic Digest,* 27 September 1974.

[8] 'The Middle East in World Finance', *The Arab Economist,* October 1974, p. 33.

[9] ECWA, 'Financing of Industrial Development in Various Countries of the Middle East', paper submitted to the 3rd Conference on Industrial Development for Arab States, Tripoli, 7–14 April 1974.

[10] N. Azhari, 'Les perspectives pour les marchés financiers moyen-orientaux', *Commerce du Levant,* 28 September 1974; Y.T. El-Zein, 'The Arab Challenge', *The Arab Economist,* May 1974, p. 26.

[11] A.M. Teman, 'An Arab Oil-Based Monetary Unit', *The Arab Economist,* February 1974.

[12] The idea of the Arab dinar is different from that of the Arab dollar. The Arab dinar is projected as an original and independent Arab currency, the Arab dollar as following the pattern of the Eurodollar market. 'Arabische Länder auf der Such nach einem Erdöl-Dollar', *Neue Zürcher Zeitung,* 12 September 1973.

8 The pattern of Middle East trade and development co-operation with the industrialised countries

8.1 Heavy dependence on foreign trade

The Middle East countries as a whole enjoy a substantial *export surplus* which is rising considerably because of the change in international terms of trade for the principal export commodities, notably petroleum and phosphates. The Middle East economies, however, continue to rely heavily on foreign trade. In particular, external demand plays a great role as a generator of income in the oil economies. Thus in 1972 exports of goods and services compared to GNP represented 130·2 per cent in Saudi Arabia, 108·7 per cent in Qatar, 87·2 per cent in Kuwait, 84·3 per cent in Libya, 57·2 per cent in the United Arab Emirates and 37·2 per cent in Iraq. The corresponding ratios in the non-oil-rich economies were: 7·7 per cent in Jordan, 19·3 per cent in Tunisia, 22·6 per cent in Lebanon, 13 per cent in Syria, 7·3 per cent in Turkey and 5·5 per cent in Egypt, while in the least developed countries the ratios were: 130 per cent in Oman, 46·5 per cent in Democratic Yemen, 22·2 per cent in Sudan and only 2·2 per cent in the Yemen Arab Republic. With the exception of Bahrain, the highest import/GNP ratios are a feature of diversified economies and of the least developed countries of the region rather than of the oil-rich economies. Thus, imports of goods and services represented in 1972 over 70 per cent in Democratic Yemen, 68·4 per cent in Oman, 57·3 per cent in Lebanon, 43·7 per cent in Jordan, while the import shares of Iran and Saudi Arabia only represented 19·9 per cent and 32 per cent respectively.

The composition and direction of trade give further evidence of the high reliance on foreign trade. In fact, while the bulk of export earnings consist of a few traditional commodities, of which petroleum accounts for over 90 per cent of the total in the oil-rich economies, the entire region is dependent for its daily needs, and to furnish its development schemes, on a wide range of imports (from basic foodstuffs to industrial machinery, building materials, chemicals, textiles, etc.) which account for a relatively small fraction of the goods sold by the industrialised nations.

The trade links with the West are absolutely dominant moreover (around 77 per cent of the total imports of the region and 80 per cent of total exports), while the share of intraregional trade represents only about 7 per cent of imports and 5 per cent of exports in 1972.[1]

Thus, thc EEC – led by France and followed by the German Federal Republic, Italy, the Benelux countries and the UK – is Algeria's most important trading partner (66·6 per cent of imports and 68·2 per cent of exports in 1972) while the USSR's share of the overall Algerian foreign trade is only around 8·5 per cent. A similar situation exists for Morocco (in 1973, 54 per cent of imports came from the EEC and 63 per cent of exports was sold to the Common Market), Mauritania (60 per cent of imports and 71·3 per cent of exports in 1972) and Tunisia (72·9 per cent of imports and 54·9 per cent of exports in 1973). In addition, while the trade links of the Maghreb nations with the United States are becoming increasingly important, intra-Maghreb exchanges (even including Libya) amount to little more than 4 per cent of Moroccan and Algerian exports and 7 per cent of Tunisian overall trade.

Equally, it is the West and Japan that benefit most from the trade boom of the oil-rich nations of the region. Thus, Saudi Arabia's trade with Western Europe in 1973 represented 41 per cent of total exports and 33 per cent of total imports, while both Japan and the United States (which, in 1973, represented respectively 17 and 11 per cent of Saudi imports) are registering an impressive performance.

The EEC is also the biggest of Iran's trading partners (33·8 per cent of imports in 1973–74). In particular, Iran's major suppliers are the German Federal Republic (by far the most important single trading partner), Japan, the US, the USSR, France, Italy, the Benelux countries, Switzerland, Sweden, Australia and Austria. Japan, on the other hand, is the overall leading trading partner of most of the micro-states of the Gulf area (notably of Kuwait and the United Arab Emirates), although the trade links of the small sheikhdoms with the UK (much the biggest trading partner of Abu Dhabi, Qatar and Bahrain), the US, the German Federal Republic, Italy and Australia are expanding rapidly. Italy, in turn, is Libya's major trading partner (26 per cent of Libyan imports and 19·9 per cent of exports in 1973) while the share of the German Federal Republic, France and Japan is growing considerably. Western Europe is also the main supplier of Iraq (41·1 per cent of imports in 1972), Egypt (32·7 per cent of imports in 1971–72), Syria (41·4 per cent), Lebanon (over 50 per cent, with the EEC supplying 32·5 per cent in 1972) and Jordan (about 30 per cent in 1972, with the EEC supplying 32·5 per cent). Moreover, the European markets – which account for most of Turkey's international trade (70 per cent of exports and 64 per cent of imports in 1973) and of the Sudan's (39 per cent of exports and 41 per cent of imports in 1973) – are of increasing importance for Syria (38·7 per cent of exports in 1972), Lebanon (16·5 per cent) and Egypt (15 per cent of exports in 1971–72).

The relative expansion (from 1·9 per cent in 1965 to 4 per cent in 1969) in *intra-trade* among the four Arab Common Market countries was mainly accounted for by the shipment of crude oil from Iraq to Syria. Thus, despite Egypt's leadership in the Arab Common Market, the share of Egyptian trade with other Arab countries remained at about 8 per cent only of overall trade in 1971–72. Moreover, the commodity structure of intra-Arab trade, taken as a whole, has not changed significantly, though half of the increment between 1965 and 1969 in the value of intra-Arab trade was accounted for by manufactured goods, followed by agricultural products (for household use), crude oil and refined petroleum products.[2] The major part of Jordan's, Iraq's, Kuwait's and Lebanon's exports (respectively 68·2, 67·2, 58·6 and 58·1 per cent of exports in 1973) went to Arab countries (with Saudi Arabia the leading customer), and, though representing the emergence of new patterns of trade in the region, these percentages are inflated by the transit of goods mainly originating from the industrialised world.

8.2 A changing trade scenario: imports

Until the oil crisis of October 1973, Middle East markets did not loom large in the total flow of world trade; their share of aggregate exports and imports amounted in 1972 to about 6 and 4 per cent respectively of the world total. The current, immense boost in buying power of the Arabs and Iranians is, however, transforming the trade scenario of the region out of all recognition, making the Middle East, in its unique location, the trade crossroads of the world.

In the short and medium term, it is imports which will be subject to the biggest changes.[3] The large income derived from the hydrocarbon sector – which will increase when natural gas sales deals become operative, and when an increasing volume of profits is repatriated from investments abroad – means that the Middle East is becoming an enormous market for foreign suppliers. Thus, in 1974, all major industrialised nations not only increased their sales of goods and services to the region, but entered into a substantial number of bilateral contracts which, in the next few years, will increase their exports spectacularly. The already high dependency on the West and Japan of Arab and Iranian trade will therefore increase even more in the next decade. And it is not unrealistic to think that in the late eighties the region as a whole might have a current account deficit, given the tendency of the developed countries to diversify their energy sources and reduce consumption of oil.

With priority given to industrial development, the import bill will still be made up largely of capital equipment and machinery (mostly through large, single contracts with builders and engineers) for construction of roads, docks, airports, generators, communications systems, refineries, petrochemical plants, steel and iron complexes, fertiliser plants, aluminium smelters, etc. Similarly, defence contracts (including the provision of know-how, maintenance and other services) will also remain of cardinal importance in the pattern of trade of Middle East countries. However, the region's needs will gradually change and it is expected that other opportunities will emerge for foreign suppliers, notably in the fields of shipping, agriculture, foodstuffs, smaller manufactured goods and advanced industries. At the same time there are increasing indications that a substantial market for consumer goods (especially the sophisticated durables such as cars and household goods) will materialise, favouring the sale of a wide range of articles, to the advantage of Western nations especially.

Nevertheless, foreign suppliers face intense competition in the Middle East. To gain an effective share of the markets, it will be essential for them to pursue a vigorous *investment policy.*[4] In this respect, three key problems must be faced by the Western nations: (1) the construction of large industrial units requiring the establishment of well-organised consortia incorporating the most technologically advanced firms (in fact the authorities in the countries of the region would prefer each exporting country to nominate a single company or consortium to compete for each project); (2) the provision of massive facilities for training local manpower, since both the authorities and businessmen want to achieve effective management of their industrial units in the shortest possible time; (3) attracting qualified expatriate technicians and managers (granting them material incentives as well as better terms for retirement, insurance and social security), since it is no longer possible to build up a plant in a developing country, then leave. Industrial complexes have in fact to be kept operational while staff are being trained. In most cases, moreover, a part of the output has also to be bought or commercialised.

Furthermore, in supplying goods and services, foreign suppliers have to comply with *import regulations.*[5] In particular, in the countries which act as entrepôts and middlemen for the Middle East area (Lebanon, Jordan, Kuwait, Bahrain, the Emirates) the rates of customs tariffs are low. Thus, in Dubai, most products are subject to only 2 per cent duty; goods in transit pay 1 per cent duty; and gold, silver, fruit, vegetables, livestock and reading material are imported duty free. Similarly, in Kuwait, most products pay 5 per cent duty only, while the exports to the Beirut free zone find their way to many countries in the area. Moreover, in accordance with economic liberalisation measures, a substantial reduction of import tariffs on a wide range of products has been enforced by Iran, Tunisia and Saudi Arabia. Even in Egypt – where the average level of nominal tariffs is about 36 per cent – imports of machinery and industrial raw materials have *ad valorem* duties not exceeding 5 per cent and 2 per cent respectively. Luxury items, however, are subject to higher duties and are forbidden in some states (Iran, Algeria, Iraq, Syria).

In the countries which adhere to a basically liberal system (Lebanon, Jordan, the micro-states of the Gulf, Saudi Arabia), licences are in most cases required only for a small number of items or are even unnecessary (as in the Emirates and Saudi Arabia); also, payments are not subject to exchange control. In contrast, where imports are mainly made by specialised state organisations, through which buyers must carry on their imports – as in Iraq, Syria, Egypt, Algeria, Sudan – all imports are tied up to licensing and subject to exchange control. But even in these 'socialist countries', a series of recent measures has relaxed exchange controls (notably on hard currencies). Similarly, Iran has reduced or abolished the commercial benefit tax, while licensing is now allowed even for goods previously banned (consumer durables such as refrigerators, gas cookers, radio and television sets). In Tunisia and Morocco, tariffs provide special incentives for the domestic assembly of cars, trucks and certain household appliances.

As far as non-tariff barriers are concerned, imports from Israel, Rhodesia and South Africa are prohibited – regardless of origin. Imports of a few items (alcoholic beverages, drugs and narcotics, dangerous chemicals, arms and munitions, etc.) are barred (because of religious, health and security reasons) or reserved for state monopoly (as in the case of sugar, salt, cigarettes, etc.). Special permission is needed from the Ministry of Health of the individual countries to import certain products (e.g. canned foods in Lebanon, veterinary supplies in Iran, and plants and seeds in Saudi Arabia).

Markings must conform with the shipping documents and the certificates of origin. It is advisable to use Arabic letters, especially for markings such as 'Glass', 'Handle with care', 'Up' and 'Down'. And all goods should bear a sign showing the country of origin. At least five copies of the commercial invoices are needed: three must be certified by a Chamber of Commerce, and two of these must also be endorsed by a consular official. Certificates of origin, in most cases, must be in quintuplicate and legalised by the national Chambers of Commerce and by the Embassies. In addition, certificates of origin must state that the goods will not be shipped on Israeli facilities and are not blacklisted. A certificate from the shipping company must also be presented (stating that the carrying vessel is not of Israeli origin and will not stop at Israeli ports) as well as a manufacturer's declaration affirming his identity. The term 'Persian Gulf' on shipping documents is not allowed to be used in Arab countries; 'Arabian Gulf' should be included instead; vice versa for goods sent to Iran.

Most countries (Saudi Arabia, Sudan, Tunisia, Morocco, Jordan, etc.) also offer attractive terms to promote foreign investment, e.g. exemption from customs duties and profits tax, transfer of profits abroad, early repatriation of capital, guarantees against nationalisation, etc.

With regard to *commercial practices,* payments offer no difficulty, the oil-rich countries in fact paying cash. Most payments are made through letters of credit or cash against documents. Where 'cash on delivery' applies, it is important to make sure that the import licence - if requested - is provided. Delivery dates are important also, and failure to respect delivery terms can seriously undermine the competitive position. At the negotiation stage, it must be realised that patience and careful attention to personal contacts in the local governments and business communities are often essential for successful conduct of business. More than any other peoples, the Arabs attach an element of permanency to relationships, jobs and the useful service of a machine or product, and nothing registers worse than a fast deal. The older and better established businesses in the region - German, British and American - have learnt this lesson very well. Foreign suppliers should, therefore, avoid excessive reliance on local agents, though these are quite useful because of the language barrier and the local legislation (which in most cases only allows local citizens to represent foreign firms). In particular, contacts with middlemen whose tactics are to make it look as if 'anything can be fixed in the Arab World' for an adequate commission must be restrained, since honesty and straightforward relations are assets highly cherished in the Arab nations.[6] On the other hand, the Arab boycott rules (applied by the Arab Boycott Office with headquarters in Damascus) are quite flexible and do not proscribe ordinary commercial trading with Israel. In fact, according to the General Union of Arab Chambers of Commerce, the objection is to the maintenance in Israel of main or branch factories or of assembly plants, even if such assembly is carried out by the Israeli agents of the foreign company; maintenance in Israel of either general agencies or main offices for the foreign company's Middle East operations; and the granting by a foreign company of the right to use its name or the giving of licences to Israeli companies, provision of consultative services or of a technical experience or share holdings in Israeli companies. Other points which are regarded as grounds for blacklisting are membership in joint foreign-Israeli Chambers of Commerce: prospecting for natural resources in Israel; construction of ships for Israeli shipping lines; and also refusal to answer questionnaires requesting information on the foreign company's relations with Israel.[7]

The legal framework for business activities differs from country to country. In some (Lebanon, Turkey, Iran) the influence of the European codes is strong. In others, legal concepts are derived from the Koran, thus raising uncertainty when problems such as the settlement of disputes are not covered by specific codified provisions. In addition to the joint commissions established in the framework of the bilateral agreements, Arab-Iranian Chambers of Commerce (e.g. the UK-Arab Chamber of Commerce, the US-Arab Chamber of Commerce) can play a significant role in overcoming business difficulties, notably in the private sector. Apart from issuing all certificates of origin and endorsing other necessary official documents, these bodies - in co-operation with the Arab Federation of Chambers of Commerce (headquarters in Beirut) - should help to render more flexible and underwrite the terms of agreed contracts, by providing adequate machinery for friendly settlement of disputes and by defining special clauses on currency conversion risks, the impact of inflation, etc. (They also already disseminate trade information, publish monthly bulletins, organise national trade fairs, trade missions and economic conferences.) Similarly, joint co-operative enterprises (e.g. Abelar-Belgo-Arab Economic Expansion Association, with capital subscribed on an equal basis by seven firms and the Saudi lawyer Faez Al Aijaz) should be set up to prospect the markets of the region, as well as promote Western trade and industry. Moreover, the countries of the area - in addition to safeguarding non-payment, commercial and political risks - should consider authorising (under appropriate tax havens) ownership or operation of plants by foreign firms producing exclusively for the export markets; also, permitting the establishment of a substantial number of foreign commercial and financial institutions.

Table 8.1

Direction of Middle East trade,[a] volume and percentage distribution ($US)

Country	1968 Exports Million $	%	1968 Imports Million $	%	1968 Balance	1972 Exports Million $	%	1972 Imports Million $	%	1972 Balance
Industrial countries:										
US	394,828	3·2	1,052,103	12·4	— 657,275	968,110	4·4	2,012,221	12·9	—1,044,111
Canada	55,470	0·4	29,570	0·3	+ 25,900	263,337	1·2	137,344	0·9	+ 125,993
Australia	124,684	1·0	70,282	0·8	+ 54,402	158,144	0·7	398,451	2·5	— 340,307
Japan	1,449,556	11·8	474,621	5·6	+ 974,035	2,894,577	13·2	1,154,692	7·4	+1,739,885
EEC	6,500,326	52·8	3,844,077	45·3	+2,656,249	11,674,305	53·3	7,283,693	46·5	+4,390,612
Other Western Europe	660,664	5·4	418,937	5·0	+ 241,727	1,527,212	7·0	1,025,007	6·5	+ 502,205
Sub-total	9,185,528	74·6	5,889,590	69·4	+3,295,938	17,485,685	79·8	12,011,408	76·7	+5,474,277
Intraregional trade	786,724	6·4	820,700	9·7	— 33,976	1,111,626	5·1	1,153,822	7·4	— 42,196
Developing countries:										
Latin America	109,710	0·9	65,250	0·8	+ 44,460	362,272	1·6	154,700	1·0	+ 207,572
Africa	139,882	1·1	69,583	0·8	+ 70,299	263,746	1·2	118,196	0·8	+ 145,550
Other Asia	674,955	5·5	411,348	4·8	+ 263,607	1,246,128	5·7	583,265	4·4	+ 562,863
Subtotal	924,547	7·5	546,181	6·4	+ 378,366	1,872,146	8·5	956,161	6·2	+ 915,985
Socialist countries:										
USSR	318,545	2·6	330,690	3·9	— 12,145	219,934	1·0	468,738	3·0	— 248,804
Yugoslavia	51,590	0·4	70,110	0·8	— 18,520	92,210	0·4	84,507	0·5	+ 7,703
Eastern Europe	366,075	3·0	566,518	6·7	— 200,443	391,350	1·8	600,649	3·8	— 209,299
China	63,910	0·5	140,745	1·7	— 76,835	103,472	0·5	134,979	0·9	— 31,507
Subtotal	800,120	6·5	1,108,063	13·1	— 307,943	806,966	3·7	1,288,873	8·2	— 481,907
Others	618,436	5·0	118,631	1·4	+ 449,805	635,625	2·9	240,938	1·5	+ 394,687
Total	12,315,355	100·0	8,483,165	100·0	+3,832,190	21,912,048	100·0	15,651,202	100·0	+6,260,846
World totals	212,435		225,355			370,761		390,601		
Middle East % of World	5·8		3·4			5·9		3·9		

[a]Note: Middle East trade refers to the 22 countries under consideration in this study. The table summarises two large matrices showing the volume and direction of Middle East trade for 1968 and 1972. These two years were selected because they bracket the most extensive recent period. Although available, 1973 data were omitted because the conditions of supply in 1972 were more normal and corresponded with the usual trade flows.
Source: IMF/International Bank for Reconstruction and Development, *Direction of Trade Annual 1968–72,* Washington DC, 1973.

8.3 A changing trade scenario: exports

In the medium and long term, important changes will affect exports also. Despite the dramatic acceleration of oil exports in 1974, the development and modernisation of the economic base of the region will help *to diversify* the main export components and to open up new markets. It is expected that, in addition to remaining a major source of crude oil (as well as of phosphates, raw cotton, certain minerals and some agricultural products) the region will become an important source of petroleum products and many other goods. In effect, such tendency is already noticeable in some countries (Bahraïn, Kuwait, Algeria), where exports of chemical fertilisers and machines, aluminium, manufactures, etc. are increasing year by year.

Despite its predominant economic leadership, the industrialised world will therefore have to rely on the area for vital commodities other than oil, thus fostering mutually beneficial co-operation, given economic complementarity with the region.[8]

However, modification of the economic base of the countries of the region is by itself insufficient to penetrate the markets of the developed world. Further specific action is therefore required. In particular, in addition to seeking modification of the US Trade Bill, which deprives petroleum-producing countries of benefit from the most favoured nation clause, Middle East nations should:

1 Play an active and co-ordinated role in *multilateral trade negotiations* organised by GATT in Geneva, at which GATT non-members such as the oil-rich nations of the region can also participate, aiming at: (a) liberalising import barriers which affect their exports (in particular, the levies and excise duties on mineral oil; the discretionary licensing on distillate fuels and lubricating oil; quotas on pig and cast iron; on phosphoric acid and superphosphates; all duties on cotton textiles on an MFN (Most Favoured Nation) basis or, alternatively, the concession of duty free entry under national GSP (generalised system of preference) schemes for developing countries; all remaining quantitative restrictions on imports of raw cotton and cotton yarn; restrictive business practices especially associated with patent licensing; duties and levies on certain agricultural products); (b) revising GATT regulation and procedures so that its decision making process more nearly reflects the economic interests of suppliers of raw materials; (c) resisting pressures for control of access to scarce supplies (for which raw material export commitments should be conditional on supply commitments for essential commodities –

wheat, for example – by the industrialised nations).

2 Request that under national GSP schemes whereby imports of manufactures and semi-manufactures from the developing countries (including the states of the region) are admitted duty free or at concessional rates by nineteen developed market economies and six socialist countries of Eastern Europe; improved market access is given also to other primary and processed agricultural products of special interest to the Middle East (e.g. dates, raw hides and skins, livestock (sheep and cattle), foods, tomato, apple and pear juices, prepared fish, dried and dehydrated vegetables, dried grapes and figs, etc.); some manufactures for which duty free entry is not yet provided should be covered also. Moreover, in compliance with the notification requirement, a further simplification of administrative procedures should be requested, together with the relaxation of origin requirements (notably by adopting a system of cumulative origin for the whole region on the pattern followed by the EFTA countries).

3 Because of the suitability of its geographical location *vis-à-vis* the Arab World, contract with the EEC specific agreements for the entire region, extending duty free and trade preference access, as well as developing intra-Mediterranean co-operation with the other countries of the Mediterranean (Greece, Albania, Yugoslavia, Italy, France, Spain, Portugal, Malta).

On the other hand, it is essential to build up effective competition by the Arab states, by ensuring that quality control is a priority; by developing a system of trade information, arranging training courses on the marketing techniques and the planning of foreign trade; setting up joint marketing groups (to share promotional and running costs in export markets); establishing direct relations with import promotion organisations and other agencies in the developed nations (e.g. trading companies, industrial federations, large department stores, Chambers of Commerce); widening participation in international fairs and exhibitions; consolidating the network of commercial attachés abroad, and opening new offices; devising a market strategy to exploit export potential systematically (a task in which the help of IDCAS, UNIDO and the international trade centre UNCTAD–GATT – which is to establish in Cairo a subregional research and training unit for trade promotion and export marketing – would be very useful). Prerequisites for successful exporting also depend on: the application and efficient administration of incentives such as

Table 8.2

Leading import commodity groups of the Middle East countries

Importing countries	Year of reference	Leading commodity groups – % of total			
		First	Second	Third	Fourth
Algeria	1971	Iron and steel products (12·7)	Agricultural Products (11·0) wheat: 4·5; sugar: 2·8	Motor vehicles and parts (5·7)	Electrical machinery (5·6) Textiles (5·5)
Bahrain	1970	Machinery, transport and construction goods (29·5)	Consumer goods (24·0) household goods: 8·8; clothing: 4·7	Foodstuffs (15·9) rice: 3·3; fruit and vegetables: 2·1	Manure (6·0)
Cyprus	1970	Machinery and motor vehicles	Fuel		
Egypt	1971/72	Intermediate goods (41·3) animal fats: 6·9; chemicals: 5·7	Capital goods (21·0)	Raw materials (15·9) wheat: 10·2	Consumer goods (16·4)
Iran	1973/74	Machinery and mechanical appliances (28·9)	Base metals (22·2)	Foodstuffs (10·6)	Chemicals (7·9) Textiles (8·2)
Iraq	1973	Machines and transport equipment (33·7)	Manufactured goods (30·3)	Foodstuffs (16·3) sugar: 12·6	Chemical products (9·7)
Jordan	1973	Food and live animals (30·5) wheat and flour: 6·5	Manufactured goods (21·4)	Machinery and transport equipment (15·9)	Fuels (3·8)
Kuwait	1972/73	Machinery and transport equipment (32·6)	Manufactured goods (21·5)	Foodstuffs (20·1)	Chemicals (4·8)
Lebanon	1973	Machinery and equipment (13·6)	Textile materials (12·1)	Precious stones and metals (8·9)	Chemicals and pharmaceutical products (8·2); Vegetable products (8·4)
Libya	1972	Manufactured goods (23·7) iron and steel: 6·2; textiles: 5·2	Machinery and transport equipment (34·3)	Foodstuffs and tobacco (15·9)	Chemicals (4·8)
Mauritania	1972	Machinery and electrical goods (20·1)	Transport equipment (19·5)	Iron and steel products (11·6)	Petroleum Products (6·4) Cereals (5·0)
Morocco	1973	Semi-finished products (25·1) metal products: 6·8; chemicals: 3·1; cotton yarn: 3·0	Foodstuffs (23·1) wheat: 10·0; sugar: 5·7	Finished equipment (18·1)	Consumer goods (11·8) Crude oil (4·8)
Oman	1972	Foodstuffs (29·7)	Building materials (10·8)	Cars and parts (12·2) Machinery and parts (9·6)	Textiles (7·5)
Qatar	1973	Industrial machinery (14·6)	Foodstuffs (14·1)	Electrical and machinery (10·7); Steel (6·4)	Cars and parts (10·4) Building materials (4·9)
Saudi Arabia	1973	Machinery, electric appliances and transport equipment (44·2)	Foodstuffs (20·6)	Building materials (8·9)	Textiles (8·6) chemicals (4·2)
Sudan	1973	Machinery and transport equipment (24·9)	Foodstuffs (23·5) sugar: 8·7	Textiles (14·4)	Chemicals (12·1) pharmaceutical products: 3·9
Tunisia	1973	Industrial equipment (45·8) mechanical machinery: 14·4	Foodstuffs (18·7) wheat: 4·7; sugar: 3·1	Yarn and fibres (3·7)	Pharmaceutical products (2·5)
Turkey	1973	Industrial equipment (44·1)	Raw materials (38·8) fertilisers: 6·3; chemicals: 7·6		
United Arab Emirates a) Dubai	1973	Machinery (17·1)	Household goods (14·7)	Building materials (13·9)	Foodstuffs (12·1) Oilfield equipment (11·6)
b) Abu Dhabi		Oilfield equipment (18·0)	Machinery (11·6)	Foodstuffs (10·4)	
Yemen Arab Republic	1972/73	Foodstuffs (46·3)	Manufactured (18·8)	Machinery and transport equipment (13·8)	Fuel (4·5)
Yemen Democratic Republic	1971	Fuels (40·9)	Foodstuffs (20·8)	Consumer goods (11·4) textiles: 9·1	Machinery and transport equipment (5·5)

Sources: National Statistics.

export subsidies, the encouragement of the temporary entry system, the expansion of loans and credit facilities to promote industrial exports, the reduction of insurance costs relative to exports, and the reduction of the price of some inputs, e.g. power supply and water; the streamlining of complex export procedures, with the aim of reducing documentation to a minimum and evolving a system which rewards the exporter almost automatically; the provision of services and adequate assistance, to tackle all problems that may arise during the various stages from conception to marketing and consumption, by means of specialised technical agencies which would supervise the formulation of export promotion programmes and co-ordinate the efforts of all parties concerned with exporting; the provision of storage facilities, particularly for perishable products, and of adequate handling capacities of ports; regularity of supply, a serious problem with products such as cotton, which depend on factors such as the weather, or, as with phosphates, transit difficulties for Jordan, etc.

A vital role is also to be fulfilled by creation of new free zones and ports (Lebanon has two free zones in Beirut and Tripoli and two more are in the planning stage for Sidon and Riyak in the Bekaa; Syria has four new free zones under construction at Damascus airport, Aleppo, Latakia and Tartou; Jordan has a free zone at Aqaba; Morocco has Tangiers; and Egypt will have several free zones along the Suez Canal). These zones will promote export industry establishment on account of the financial and administrative facilities offered to productive units and the tendency towards the liberalisation of the economic policies of the Arab socialist régimes.

8.4 Expanding intra-regional trade

The potential for expanding intraregional trade is considerable. Export possibilities exist for foodstuffs (e.g. live animals, meat and dairy products, vegetables, fruits, cereals, oilseeds and tobacco), industrial raw materials (cement, iron ore, phosphates, oil by-products) and for locally manufactured goods which enjoy either a natural price advantage because of lower transport costs or a preferential margin in some Arab countries over similar goods from the rest of the world. And besides the co-operation in intraregional development which is likely to result from the mutual interest of the countries involved, no major obstacle to increase of exports should arise through the imposition of import duties. A number of the countries either belong to the Arab Common Market, enjoying preferential access to markets of other member countries as a

Table 8.3
Leading export commodity groups of the Middle East countries (percentages)

Exporting countries	Year of Reference	Leading commodity groups (% of total)			
		First	Second	Third	Fourth
Algeria	1971	Crude oil (70·6)	Agricultural products (12·5) (wine: 7·1; citrus fruit: 2·2)	Gas (3·1)	Minerals (2·9) (iron ore: 1·7)
Cyprus	1970	Agricultural products, wine and tobacco (50·0)	Minerals (pyrite of iron and copper) (32·0)		
Egypt	1971/72	Raw cotton (45·4)	Cotton yarn (11·9) Cotton textiles (5·1)	Rice (6·5)	Fuels (5·6) Oranges (2·7)
Iran	1973/74	Crude oil (88·1)	Carpets (2·6)	Cotton (2·3)	Nuts (1·9)
Iraq	1973	Crude oil (90·0)	Dates (4·0)	Hides and skins (2·0)	Cement (2·0); wool (1·0)
Jordan	1973	Food products (33·2) (vegetables: 17·6; fruit and nuts: 12·3)	Phosphates (28·7)	Cement (9·3)	Batteries (2·9)
Kuwait	1972/73	Crude oil (90·0)	Machinery and transport equipment (2·9)	Chemicals (2·5)	
Lebanon	1972	Vegetable products (11·7)	Transport equipment (10·6) Electrical goods (10·6)	Textiles (10·5)	Chemicals and pharmaceutical products (7·7)
Libya	1972	Crude oil (98·4)	Gas (1·3)		
Mauritania	1972	Iron ore (74·2)	Fish products (10·6)	Copper ore (10·2)	Arabic gum (2·5)
Morocco	1973	Food products (48·8) (citrus fruit: 13·2; tomatoes: 6·1; olive oil: 2·7; tinned fish: 5·0; pulses: 4·8; wine: 2·4)	Phosphates (22·0)	Tinned fruit and juices (3·0)	Carpets (2·1)
Oman	1972	Crude oil (99·2)	Agricultural products (0·8)		
Saudi Arabia	1973	Crude oil (99·7)	Animal products (0·3)		
Syria	1972	Raw cotton (34·0)	Other agricultural products and livestock (25·0)	Crude oil (19·0)	Textiles (11·1)
Sudan	1973	Raw cotton (52·9)	Groundnuts (9·0)	Sesame (8·6)	Arabic gum (7·1)
Tunisia	1973	Agricultural products (37·3) (olive oil: 15·3; wine 5·4; almonds: 2·3; dates 1·4)	Crude oil (30·9)	Phosphates (16·9)	Carpets (1·6)
Turkey	1973	Agricultural products (63·1) (cotton 23·2; tobacco: 10·1; hazel nuts: 9·2; dried fruit: 6·3)	Manufactured goods (22·3) (textiles and clothing 8·0)	Processed food (11·3)	Mineral ores (3·2) (chrome 1·0)
Yemen Arabic Republic	1972/73	Raw cotton (42·7)	Coffee (21·6)	Hides and skins (13·2)	Khat (1·0)
Yemen Democratic Republic	1971	Petroleum products (87·9)	Raw cotton (4·5)	Fish products (3·4)	Hides and skins (1·5)

Sources: National statistics of the relevant countries.

result of tariff liberalisation, or have bilateral agreements with other Arab states.

Nevertheless, new ways of expanding trade must be envisaged, since expansion continues to be held back by quota restrictions and exchange allocations; administrative restrictions of various sorts; lack of export credit and export credit insurance; inadequate transport and storage facilities; lack of uniformity in transit formalities and documentation; lack of market information; institutional problems between countries practising state-trading and those where external trade is in the hands of a private sector.

The problem is not so much a need for complete liberalisation of trade as for *regional co-ordination of industry.* [9] Intraregional co-operation should therefore concentrate on establishing a multinational plan which – in addition to serving as a guide to planning industrialisation at national levels – would bring out and develop the region's balance of structure and resources. Other significant steps would be the establishment of joint-stock export companies and specialised export federations responsible for marketing and sales promotion – these would encompass some existing industries in all or some countries of the region – and the definition of special payments arrangements such as a multinational clearing system. In addition, it would be useful to: encourage the simplification and standardisation of customs documentation, transit and port formalities; co-ordinate marketing by small-scale and handicrafts industries; and hold exhibitions of local goods in major consumption centres of the region.

Finally, attempts at co-operation between the Arab countries and Iran should not be neglected. Iran, in effect, is already the major receiver of goods exported and re-exported from the United Arab Emirates (Dubai in particular) and is expected to participate in some development schemes in the Arab World (notably in Egypt). Moreover the Shah, who has pointedly recognised the Palestine Liberation Organisation (PLO) and called for Israeli withdrawal from occupied territories, is urging both military co-operation – notably with Saudi Arabia to buttress the security of the Gulf area – and economic co-operation to establish a Common Market embracing all countries of the region, including Pakistan.

8.5 Economic co-operation with the US, Canada and Australia

The United States is the leading world power in the Middle East. American investment, trade and other financial transactions with the countries of the region – the bulk of which arises from repatriation of American oil companies' profits and from purchases of US goods and services by the oil-producing countries – provide a large net inflow of funds into the United States. In addition, the big American banks manage and utilise a large part of the Arab surplus funds to finance the investment requirements of the US economy and promote the expansion of US exports. The United States also has the dual benefit of being at the same time the biggest supplier of arms to both Israel and most Arab countries, not to mention its impressive sales of sophisticated weaponry to Iran. Further, the US has developed a substantial number of cultural centres, foundations and non-profit-making cultural organisations both in the Middle East (the American University of Beirut, the American University in Cairo, Robert College near Istanbul, the Jesuit University in Baghdad, the Aleppo College in Syria, etc.) and in America (American Friends of the Middle East, the Franklin Books Program, the Near East Foundation, the Near East Emergency Foundation, the Rockefeller Foundation, the Ford Foundation, the Middle East university centres at Berkeley, Georgetown, Charlottesville, Boulder, UCLA, Utah, Texas, Michigan, Pennsylvania) which, even if they do produce a minority of left-wing revolutionaries (Habache and Hawameth were educated at AUB), create a highly qualified élite educated with an American viewpoint.

The US political and military commitments are also of the utmost importance. In the first place, such involvement in the region aims, while avoiding a clash, to prevent the Soviet Union from gaining domination over the Middle East and Eastern Mediterranean, an area of overriding capital importance both strategically (linking Europe, the Balkans, south-western Asia and Africa) and commercially (containing a vast portion of the energy by which Western industrial progress is fuelled). In fact, the control of the region by Moscow would cut American and Western defence links with southern Asia and the Far East. And Russian influence on the flow of Arab oil would dramatically shift the world's strategic balance in favour of the Communist. Thus, the United States has established multilateral alliances (NATO, in the Eastern Mediterranean involving Turkey and Greece; and CENTO, a regional defence and co-operation pact grouping Turkey, Iran, Pakistan, the UK and US as non-signatory active participants); bilateral security arrangements (notably with Turkey, Iran and Pakistan) and military bases, installations, advisory missions, etc. in Greece, Turkey, Iran, Pakistan, Bahrain and Saudi Arabia. The United States has also requested from Oman the use of the island of Masirah. The presence of the Sixth Fleet, the Marines and other highly mobile units can also be strengthened rapidly in the region.[10]

Secondly, because of the important Jewish lobby pressure in domestic politics, the United States ensures Israel's survival, although since the October War the US has paid more attention to the views and interests of moderate Arab leaders and is prepared to persuade Israel to make some concessions. Thirdly, to curb revolutionary movements, the United States has developed a system of delegating influence to 'subpowers' economically or politically linked to America, whose autonomy it acknowledges. In particular, 'subpower' status has been assigned to Iran and Saudi Arabia.[11] Finally, on the economic front, America's goal is to consolidate its economic interests by promoting the export of US goods and services, to offset the growing cost of oil imports, and by establishing several industrial and financial ventures, notably with the oil-rich nations.

Despite the soaring cost of oil and gas imports, US trade in the area – which showed a surplus of $US 1,224 million in 1973 – maintained a substantial balance in 1974. In that year US exports to the Middle East (excluding Israel) were worth $US 5,638 million, while US imports were worth $US 5,732 million.

The United States has a negative balance of trade position with Saudi Arabia ($US 835 million), Algeria ($US 775 million), Iran ($US 397 million), the United Arab Emirates ($US 135 million) and Qatar ($US 45 million). The US trade surplus, on the other hand, is considerable with Egypt ($US 387 million), Turkey ($US 323 million), Iraq ($US 285 million), Lebanon ($US 259 million), Kuwait ($US 198 million), Morocco ($US 165 million), Libya ($US 139 million), Jordan ($US 105 million) and Tunisia ($US 68 million). It is also large with Sudan, Syria, Bahrain, Oman, Democratic Yemen and the Yemen Arab Republic. Total US trade, in addition, represents only about 5·7 per cent of both total American exports and imports. The Israeli market – which, in 1973, represented the biggest single outlet for American goods in the region – has now been bypassed by the Iranian and Arab markets.

Iran is the biggest single outlet. In 1974 it represented 30·7 per cent of total US exports in the area (excluding Israel) and 37·2 per cent of US total imports. The Iranian market is of special importance to the US for the sale of heavy industrial goods, transport equipment, armaments and the supply of cereals. US–Iranian economic ties also involve several joint ventures to build oil refineries and petrochemicals complexes, and to market petrol and other fuels in the United States; also, to develop agriculture, construct new infrastructure facilities and supply enriched uranium. To promote US–Iranian economic co-operation a joint committee was established in 1974. Early in 1975, the United States and

Iran signed an agreement involving $US 15 billion in non-oil trade between the two countries over the following five years. Of this amount, Iran will spend about $US 12 billion, with the United States, to set up eight large nuclear plants (total output, 8,000 MW), 20 prefabricated housing factories; 100,000 apartments and other housing units; five hospitals, with a total of 3,000 beds; an integrated electronics industry; a major port for handling agricultural commodities; joint ventures to produce fertilisers, pesticides, farm machinery and processed foods. At the same time, a technical co-operation agreement (in fields such as agriculture, manpower, science and higher education, and health services) was also concluded.

Saudi Arabia is the second most important market for the United States. In 1974, Saudi Arabia represented 14·8 per cent of total US exports to the area (excluding Israel) and 29·1 per cent of US total imports. The economic relations between the two countries have been considerably strengthened by a wide-ranging agreement concluded in 1974 and held up by Washington as a prototype for American co-operation with other Arab states. In particular, in terms of the special relationship thus created with the world's largest oil exporter, the US is to help Saudi Arabia to develop industrially and train and build up its armed forces. Thus, two joint commissions have been created: one to study economic co-operation, with emphasis on the utilisation of the oilfield gas, at present flared off, for expanding the production of fertilisers, and the development of advanced industrial projects, notably for petrochemical and steel products, the training of Saudi technicians, desalination operations, the use of solar energy and the development of desert agriculture; the other to modernise and train the Saudi armed forces equipped by the US during the past twenty years.

Among the other Gulf states the US retains a position of rapidly growing importance with the *United Arab Emirates* (mainly providing oilfield materials and armaments), *Kuwait* (mainly providing saloon and estate cars, spare parts, cigarettes, oil-well drilling equipment, air-conditioning units, food, mechanical equipment, clothing, pipes and fittings, as well as consulting and engineering services), *Iraq* (where the pragmatic push from Vice-President S. Hussein is gradually opening up economic advantages for both sides) and *Jordan.*

Algeria has rapidly become the most important US trade partner in the Mediterranean area (except for Israel, of course). In 1974 Algeria resumed diplomatic relations with the US and views the American market as its main outlet for natural gas and, in the near future, perhaps also for wine. *Turkey,* which represented 23·1 per cent of American total exports to the

Mediterranean area, purchased machinery and industrial equipment to a total value of $US 463 million and sold the United States fruit, oil-seed-tobacco, mineral ores and other agricultural products to a value of $US 140 million. A rapid rise in the dollar value of US exports (mainly cereals and industrial equipment) has also occurred in trade with *Egypt*. In fact, as a result of the improved relations between the two countries (Egypt being seen in Washington as pivotal to relations with Arabs just as ties with Saudi Arabia and Iran are seen as vital to oil diplomacy and Gulf security), in 1974 US exports to Egypt reached $US 455 million, thus restoring a traditional pattern of trade (prior to the 1967 War half of Egypt's agricultural products were imported from America).

The political, economic and cultural agreements concluded in 1974 commit the US to promote bilateral trade; to participate in the reconstruction and development of the Suez Canal; to establish joint ventures such as exploiting the phosphate mines of Abu Tartul and building up petrochemical and fertiliser industries; to help to increase agricultural production by use of the latest technology; and to develop medical, scientific and research co-operation.

Moreover, the two countries have also agreed to reduce obstacles to trade and investment and to stimulate a greater flow of private investment capital in car production and other engineering industries, and in electrical and electronic equipment. Thus, there has been agreement both to eliminate double taxation and guarantee the safety of US investments. Egypt, furthermore, has granted permission to several US financial institutions to open offices in Cairo (the Chase Manhattan Bank, First National City Bank, the Bank of America and American Express). Another significant area of co-operation would have been an agreement by which the United States would sell nuclear reactors and fuel, making it possible for Egypt to generate a substantial additional quantity of electric power by the early eighties. The deal, however, foundered over Egyptian insistence that stringent US-imposed safeguards be applied not only to their reactor, but also to Israel's existing nuclear plant at Dimona. Washington has also promised financial aid (to finance the purchase of cereals and the reconstruction of towns along the Canal) as well as limited military assistance, but Congress is reluctant to ratify such a commitment.

Remarkable also is the expansion of US trade with *Lebanon,* considered by American firms to be a focal point for trade in the Levant and hinterland (notably for US sales of animal fats, vegetable oils, soya beans, aircraft engines and parts supplied to the MEA airline, cars and trucks, computers, and food processing machinery); with *Morocco* (notably for US sales of wheat and industrial equipment) where US investment is active in oil prospecting and a number of industrial projects; *Libya* (which needs US technology); and *Tunisia.*

The outlook for expansion of US economic co-operation in the Middle East is very promising, in view of growing US imports of Arab and Iranian oil.[12] US imports from Iran increased nearly 70 per cent from summer 1973 to summer 1974, then comprising more than 10 per cent of America's foreign oil from all sources. US imports of natural gas are also increasing sharply. Algeria, in particular, will export to the United States about 30 milliard m^3 per year in the next five or six years. Thus, since the Arabs and the Iranians are likely to export heavily to the US in the foreseeable future and thereby amass huge surpluses, US exports to the Middle East are bound to increase considerably. In fact, according to the US Secretary of Commerce, US exports to the oil-producing countries of the Middle East should reach between $US 7 billion and 10 billion by 1980, and it is already significant that US food exports to the region are expected to exceed $US 2 billion in the fiscal year 1975–76, compared with $US 521 million in 1972. The largest US export gains are projected for Saudi Arabia, Iran and the other major oil-producing countries of the Gulf area, although US exports to non-oil-rich nations (e.g. Egypt, Lebanon and Turkey) are also likely to become increasingly important. The emphasis will be on the supply of capital goods (aircraft, oilfield equipment, construction machinery, agricultural machinery, feed processing equipment, etc.) food (notably wheat, rice and feedstuffs), consumer durables, as well as on the establishment of economic ventures (from petrochemicals to banking), with the oil-rich nations providing the bulk of the capital and manpower.

American presence in the region is greatly favoured by Arab eagerness for help in building a modern industrial economy. In effect, the United States has a dual attraction for the Arab World. Economically, because America symbolises free enterprise, abundance of foodstuffs, the consumer society, and modern technology, by which it will be possible to face issues such as the shortage of water and the development of desert agriculture.[13] Politically, because the United States has stood - and stands - alone as the one country with the power to persuade Israel to accept an honourable peace settlement without territorial acquisition. American influence in the region has proved itself effective, for example, in the US resumption of diplomatic relations with the Arab nations (except for Iraq and Democratic Yemen), the extraordinary friendship and admiration for the Jewish-German-born Kissinger, architect of US policy in the Arab Sadat, and in the aftermath of the October War, by more favourable treatment during the oil embargo, when, in contrast, two

EEC member states, the Netherlands and Denmark, were discriminated until the end.

Any new hostilities in the area would have a drastic impact on America's interests, however. It follows that peace is essential if the United States wants to maintain economic leadership and become a political fixture in the region. Thus, the time has now come for America to reassess policy *vis-à-vis* Israel. In particular, it is high time that Washington concentrated on a new political programme integrating Israel – whatever its size or form – into the geographical area it inhabits.[14] In view of the establishment, after World War II, of a special relationship between France and the German Federal Republic and between the US and Japan, it does not seem unrealistic to consider the forging of mutually beneficial co-operation between Israel and neighbouring Arab countries, on the basis of economic complementarity and a new security concept.[15] After all, the *de facto* economic co-operation between Israel and the West Bank of Jordan is already an accomplishment. 'Once the Arabs were afraid of Israeli economic and technological domination. But now we feel that we have the means for achieving a take-off and there is a complete change of attitude', an *Al Ahram* spokesman has said.

Moreover, it is clear that a more determined policy is needed by the United States in the Gulf area, the success of US policy currently depending on how far King Khalid and the Shah can be persuaded to co-operate in asserting their influence in the region.

Canada's economic presence in the Middle East is still only minor. In 1974 Canadian exports (mainly to Iran, Algeria and Turkey) represented only 1·3 per cent of total exports, and Canadian imports represented 3·9 per cent of imports (mainly from Iran and Saudi Arabia). The prospects of economic co-operation with the countries of the region are good, however, since Canada can supply substantial quantities of foodstuffs (notably cereals), agricultural machinery, fishing equipment, etc., as well as enter into association with local interests in major fields such as the paper and pulp sector. (A plant with a capacity of 150,000 tons per year is already to be constructed in northern Iran.) Canada is currently negotiating with Iran, Saudi Arabia and Turkey for the installation of nuclear power generating stations.

Australia – which is two-thirds self-sufficient in oil but has to import almost all its heavy crude requirements from the Gulf states – is making increasing efforts to gain a strong foothold in the Middle East. The region's share in total Australian exports comprised 4·4 per cent in 1974, as against 7·1 per cent in total Australian imports. Agricultural produce (especially wheat and wheat flour, wool, dairy products, meat and livestock) account for the greater part of Australian exports to the area, notably to the Gulf nations (Kuwait, Iran, Bahrain, the United Arab Emirates), Egypt and Saudi Arabia. Australian business is also developing outlets for manufactured goods, equipment, household and electrical appliances. Other very promising items that Australia expects to send to the Middle East include bauxite and iron ore for the aluminium smelters and iron and steel mills. The Australian-based international consortium ALCOA has already won a long-term contract to supply some 230,000 tons of bauxite a year to the ALBA aluminium smelter in Bahrain, and large quantities of Hammersley iron ore are being shipped to Kuwait.

Middle East nations have expressed interest in investing in Australian agriculture and her mining industry, and in attracting Australian participation in the development of the region. An agreement guaranteeing supplies of crude oil and the expansion of agricultural and industrial co-operation was concluded with Iran in 1974. The Shah attaches great importance to Australia as a potentially useful outlet for Iran's manufactures (petrochemicals, textiles, synthetic detergents, etc.). Australia could also support the increased co-operation which Iran plans to foster among the countries of the Indian Ocean area. In particular, Australia's decision to sell uranium to Iran and the setting up of a joint Iranian–Australian livestock venture emphasise the importance of this co-operation for both countries.

8.6 Economic co-operation with the European Economic Community

The EEC is by far the region's biggest trading partner, accounting for the largest share of both exports and imports (respectively 53·3 per cent and 46·5 per cent in 1972). Since Europe is heavily dependent on Middle East oil, the Nine yield a huge balance in favour of the oil-exporting countries of the region (to the tune of over $US 26 billion in 1974). In 1974, Middle East and North African markets represented for the EEC about 6 per cent of total exports (5 per cent in 1973) and about 15 per cent of total imports (9 per cent in 1973) – already a considerable amount. The relative importance of the Middle East outlet on the world total is greatest for Italy (10·2 per cent of exports), France (9·4 per cent) and the UK (7·4 per cent); then come the German Federal Republic (5·3 per cent), Holland (3·3 per cent), Denmark (3·2 per cent), Belgium (3·1 per cent) and, last, Ireland (0·7 per cent). Italy, France, the UK, Holland and the German Federal Republic are the countries most affected by imports from the region (representing respectively 23·6, 18·8, 15, 13·4 and 12 per cent of

Table 8.4
Middle East trade with the EEC in 1974 ('000 $US)

Middle East nations	German Federal Republic		France		UK		Italy		Holland(a)		Belgium - Luxembourg		Denmark		Ireland(a)		EEC Total	
	Exports	Imports	Exports	Imports	Exports	Imports	Exports	Imports	Exports	Imports	Exports	Imports	Exports	Imports	Exports	Imports	Exports	Imports
Algeria	482	1,087	1,297	957	128	83	325	269	73	20	129	70	19	32	-	1	2,453	2,519
Cyprus	40	15	26	3	90	72	58	5	26	3	9	1	9	2	1	2	259	103
Egypt	211	66	347	47	122	88	184	84	64	14	27	32	11	5	-	1	966	337
Lebanon	209	23	220	146	142	67	227	42	51	4	58	8	19	4	1	1	927	295
Libya	403	1,626	363	387	146	915	852	2,371	58	20	88	177	12	29	2	-	1,924	5,525
Mauritania	9	30	52	38	11	31	2	20	2	6	6	20	-	-	-	-	82	145
Morocco	166	152	524	449	66	123	82	151	40	48	46	117	9	16	-	22	933	1,078
Syria	175	89	136	43	49	48	128	150	29	3	38	5	8	-	-	-	563	338
Tunisia	92	94	349	189	27	14	120	176	24	16	27	12	10	1	4	1	653	503
Turkey	708	313	247	101	245	82	403	135	110	49	95	46	21	32	-	4	1,829	762
Mediterranean area	2,495	3,495	3,561	2,360	1,026	1,523	2,381	3,403	477	183	523	488	118	121	8	32	10,589	11,605
Bahrain	20	8	8	7	79	47	12	-	8	4	5	3	4	21	-	-	136	90
Jordan	48	-	16	-	48	4	21	-	12	-	15	-	3	-	-	-	163	4
Iran	1,140	1,241	258	716	653	1,203	281	1,120	123	2,852	111	333	37	349	3	44	2,606	7,858
Iraq	373	307	214	1,242	140	249	96	1,168	38	29	48	36	23	25	1	-	933	3,056
Kuwait	162	355	64	938	140	1,336	65	479	33	70	29	333	21	78	1	43	515	3,632
Oman	41	7	18	143	101	77	19	89	16	-	9	58	3	37	-	-	207	411
Qatar	20	92	9	264	52	389	11	208	7	7	4	32	2	36	-	-	105	1,022
United Arab Emirates	90	751	69	1,184	227	483	37	114	29	56	19	-	8	19	1	-	480	2,607
Gulf area	1,894	2,761	656	4,494	1,440	3,788	542	3,178	266	3,018	240	795	101	565	6	87	5,145	18,686
Saudi Arabia	287	2,043	120	3,027	280	2,761	133	3,036	98	290	88	1,246	20	92	2	94	1,028	12,589
Sudan	52	45	18	59	84	19	37	45	10	4	11	4	5	1	1	-	218	177
Yemen Democratic Republic	9	1	4	-	14	19	3	-	6	-	1	2	3	1	-	-	40	23
Yemen Arab Republic	15	-	8	1	14	3	5	2	7	1	1	-	4	-	-	-	50	7
Red Sea area	363	2,089	150	3,087	392	2,802	178	3,083	121	295	101	1,252	32	94	3	94	4,336	12,796
Middle East Total	4,752	8,345	4,367	9,941	2,858	8,113	3,101	9,664	864	3,496	864	2,535	251	780	17	213	17,070	43,087
World Total	89,245	69,593	46,460	52,900	38,634	54,132	30,227	40,894	25,811	26,063	28,165	29,628	7,718	9,878	2,389	3,529	268,649	286,617
Middle East % of World	5·3	12·0	9·4	18·8	7·4	15·0	10·2	23·6	3·3	13·4	3·1	8·5	3·2	7·9	0·7	6·0	6·3	15·0
Israel	485	169	203	104	516	184	217	62	94	45	162	69	18	11	5	7	1,700	651
% of World	0·5	0·2	0·4	0·2	1·3	0·3	0·7	0·1	0·4	0·2	0·6	0·2	0·2	0·1	0·2	0·2	0·6	0·3

Notes: [a]Data refers to the period January–November 1974.

Sources: IMF/International bank for reconstruction and development *Direction of Trade,* Washington DC, May 1975. Data for Holland and Belgium from their national bureaus of statistics.

total imports in 1974) followed by Belgium (8·5 per cent), Denmark (7·9 per cent) and Ireland (6 per cent).

The Community's exports are heavily *concentrated in the Mediterranean area* (notably in Algeria, Libya, Turkey, Egypt, Morocco, Lebanon, Tunisia and Syria). Thus, while the EEC trade links with the Mediterranean countries are fairly balanced (with France enjoying a comfortable trade surplus), the EEC trade deficit is quite large with the Gulf and Red Sea nations. It is, therefore, essentially with the oil-rich countries of the Gulf and the Red Sea areas that the Community must promote its exports and develop co-operation to readjust its trade balance with the region.

Italy has diversified export interest in the Mediterranean area, with Libya by far the most important outlet (27·5 per cent of total exports in 1974), while oil imports mainly come from Saudi Arabia (31·4 per cent of imports), Libya (24·5 per cent), Iraq 12·1 per cent), Iran (11·6 per cent) and Kuwait (5 per cent).

The Maghreb countries are *France's* most important market (with Algeria accounting for 29·8 per cent of total French exports to the region and 9·6 per cent of total imports; Morocco 12 per cent of exports and 4·5 per cent of imports; Tunisia 8 per cent of exports and 1·9 per cent of imports), importing essentially raw materials (notably oil, phosphates, iron ore) and exporting equipment, finished and semi-finished goods of all types, including armaments. The southernmost area of the region is also important, however, with oil imports from Saudi Arabia (30·4 per cent of French imports from the region), Iraq (12·5 per cent), the Emirates (11·9 per cent), Kuwait (9·4 per cent) and Iran (7·2 per cent).

The *UK*'s major trade is with the Gulf and Red Sea areas, especially Saudi Arabia (34 per cent of total imports), Kuwait (16·4 per cent of total imports), Iran (14·8 per cent of total imports and 22·8 per cent of total exports), the Emirates (5·9 per cent of total imports) and Qatar (4·8 per cent of total imports). Imports from Libya, in addition, rose considerably in 1974 accounting for 11·2 per cent of total imports.

The *German Federal Republic's* interests lie mainly in Saudi Arabia (24·4 per cent of total imports and 6 per cent of total exports); Iran (14·9 per cent of total imports and 24 per cent of total exports); Libya (19·5 per cent of total imports and 8·4 per cent of total exports); and Algeria (13 per cent of total exports and 10·4 per cent of total imports).

Holland relies on oil imports from Iran (81·6 per cent of total imports) and, to a much lesser extent, from Saudi Arabia (8·3 per cent). *Belgium* imports mainly from Saudi Arabia (49·1 per cent), Iran 13·1 per cent), Kuwait (13·1 per cent), Libya (6·9 per cent) and Morocco (4·6 per cent).

Denmark's trade links with the region are still at a low level and mainly consist of oil imports from Iran (44·7 per cent), Saudi Arabia (11·8 per cent) and Kuwait (10 per cent). Even smaller is the economic presence of *Ireland* which buys petroleum from Saudi Arabia, Iran and Kuwait.

Among the other Western European nations, the Middle East markets are of great importance to *Spain* (9·3 per cent of exports and 23·5 per cent of imports in 1974) and, to a lesser extent, *Switzerland* (5·6 per cent of exports and 4·1 per cent of imports), *Austria* (4·6 per cent of exports and 6·5 per cent of imports) and *Sweden* (3 per cent of exports and 4·5 per cent of imports). Spanish imports come mainly from Saudi Arabia (52·6 per cent of total imports from the region), Algeria (9·7 per cent), Iraq (7·5 per cent), Iran (7·2 per cent), Oman (5·7 per cent) and Kuwait (3·7 per cent). Though still at a modest level, Switzerland has a diversified export interest in the countries of the region, with special emphasis on Iran and Turkey, and enjoys a trade surplus. Swiss imports mainly come from the Emirates, Libya and Kuwait. Similarly, Sweden and Austria have diversified export interests in the region - at a level which still needs to be developed - and their imports mainly come from Iran and Iraq respectively. The *Israeli market* has no real consistency for EEC trade - British exports apart (which represented in 1974 1·3 per cent of the British world export total). However, the Community is Israel's leading customer and supplier, and the Israeli balance of trade shows a major deficit.

Despite the overriding importance of the region as a source of vital oil and gas supplies, the EEC action has been misleading. At the political level, the Europeans have deliberately abstracted themselves from any significant role in the Arab-Israeli conflict (leaving matters mainly to the superpowers). The one concession to the Arab side was the EEC aid programme to the United Nations Relief and Works Agency (UNRWA) for Palestine refugees. At the economic level, the most significant step on the oil front was merely the stockpiling of 65 days (then raised to 90 days) of reserves as a buffer in the event of crisis. And, on the trade field, the EEC was definitely passive in adopting - as requested by the Mediterranean countries - four types of preferential agreements (with Greece and Turkey aiming at full membership; with Morocco and Tunisia, as contemplated in the Treaty of Rome; with Malta and Cyprus, calling for a free trade area at the end of a second stage; with Spain, Israel, Egypt and Lebanon, calling for duty reductions and quota concessions in stages on both sides). In fact, according to two of the Eurocrats closely associated with the EEC negotiations in the Mediterranean, 'it is no exaggeration to say that each Mediterranean country considered separately had a European policy well before the

Community realised that it had a *de facto* Mediterranean policy'.[16]

Furthermore, the over-publicised and long-awaited Mediterranean policy has proved very frustrating (the size of the concessions varying between the various Mediterranean countries) and of limited scope (as the common agricultural policy made it extremely difficult to obtain special concessions for exports to the Common Market). In fact, with the exception of citrus fruit (which, up to 1972, was the cornerstone of the Mediterranean policy and for which the Community introduced a complex mechanism of reference prices whose merit has been highly questioned), the EEC has been unwilling even to discuss concessions on other agricultural products.

Concessions on industrial products, too, have been less generous than it appeared, any advantage to the Arab countries being limited by restrictive quotas for the so-called sensitive products and stringent Community rules of origin.[16] Some Arab countries such as Algeria have attacked the CAP, in the belief that 'European agriculture was being built at the expense of the developing nations'.[17] More recently, the leader of the Greek Socialist Party, Mr Papandreou, has called for an end to Greek co-operation with Europe.[18]

Further, in respect of the major oil-exporting countries of the region, the EEC failed to respond to attractive offers made by Algeria in March 1972 and Kuwait in April 1973 to guarantee oil supplies at a low price in return for adequate market access for their refined petroleum, and even concluded with Iran an outdated type of trade agreement, covering only dates, caviare, dried apricots and carpets, which was allowed to expire in November 1973.

Under pressure of the October 1973 oil crisis, the EEC – on 6 November 1973 – made a declaration of policy as to the Middle East, calling for complete Israeli withdrawal on the basis of UN Resolution 242 and recognition of Palestinian rights, and agreed on 4 March 1974 to start a European–Arab dialogue, aiming at long-term rural development, industrialisation, infrastructure, aid, trade, scientific, social, cultural and technical co-operation. On 23 July 1974 it was decided to enforce a 'global policy' with the countries bordering the Mediterranean, with the aim of establishing an industrial free trade area between the Community and each partner country; granting selective concessions in the agricultural sector; providing broad industrial co-operation, financial assistance and adequate guarantees for migrant workers). However, the most powerful stimulus to a change of policy was not provided by the EEC machinery (which failed to adopt a common energy policy), but by individual European member countries (notably, Italy, France, the

Table 8.5

Middle East trade with other major industrialised countries in 1974 ('000 $US)

Middle East nations	US		Japan		Canada		Australia		Switzerland		Sweden		Austria		Spain	
	Exports	Imports	Exports	Imports	Exports	Imports	Exports	Imports	Exports	Imports	Exports	Imports	Exports	Imports	Exports	Imports
Algeria	315	1,090	155	34	155	7	-	-	36	51	34	77	19	2	173	350
Cyprus	20	-	13	-	2	3	-	-	7	-	19	2	4	1	5	6
Egypt	455	68	74	169	14	1	199	1	34	14	34	7	14	10	22	22
Lebanon	287	28	94	3	45	14	10	-	45	4	22	4	35	3	44	5
Libya	139	-	234	364	6	31	5	-	36	92	34	-	20	104	111	275
Mauritania	11	-	7	39	-	-	-	-	-	1	1	-	-	-	4	32
Morocco	184	19	26	52	3	1	-	-	24	15	35	29	7	11	75	101
Syria	40	1	70	2	14	-	-	-	26	1	13	-	21	-	65	3
Tunisia	88	20	5	1	13	-	-	-	6	37	17	-	7	5	18	3
Turkey	463	140	212	34	52	3	18	2	102	35	36	39	65	35	28	31
Mediterranean area	2,002	1,366	890	698	304	60	232	3	316	250	245	158	192	171	545	828
Bahrain	80	59	61	375	1	-	30	151	5	-	2	6	3	-	2	1
Jordan	105	-	30	14	4	-	-	-	5	-	4	-	4	-	5	-
Iran	1,734	2,131	1,013	4,764	64	623	65	71	153	34	73	128	65	63	35	260
Iraq	285	-	473	202	18	37	38	108	34	2	62	53	29	340	20	273
Kuwait	209	11	279	2,132	5	66	36	220	26	60	19	82	8	-	25	134
Oman	37	20	44	378	-	-	10	-	5	-	10	54	1	-	6	207
Qatar	34	79	47	22	4	-	4	45	5	4	1	53	1	-	1	-
United Arab Emirates	230	365	309	2,115	5	84	21	7	44	190	8	61	6	-	-	-
Gulf area	2,714	2,665	2,256	10,002	101	810	204	602	277	290	179	437	117	403	94	875
Saudi Arabia	835	1,670	676	5,237	18	318	44	147	61	50	48	117	17	9	12	1,903
Sudan	64	26	53	27	3	-	1	2	6	8	7	3	4	3	4	9
Yemen Democratic Republic	12	5	14	15	9	109	2	31	-	-	1	1	-	-	-	-
Yemen Arab Republic	11	-	33	2	-	-	9	8	1	-	1	-	1	-	-	-
Red Sea area	922	1,701	776	5,281	30	427	56	188	68	58	57	121	22	12	16	1,912
Middle East total	5,638	5,732	3,992	15,981	435	1,297	492	793	661	598	481	716	331	586	655	3,615
World total	98,537	100,887	55,513	62,064	33,624	33,054	11,088	11,170	11,859	14,401	15,915	15,838	7,160	9,022	7,058	15,378
Middle East % of World	5·7	5·7	7·2	25·7	1·3	3·9	4·4	7·1	5·6	4·1	3·0	4·5	4·6	6·5	9·3	23·5
Israel	1,206	280	88	65	52	25	10	22	98	44	65	22	25	23	18	23
% of World	1·2	0·2	0·1	0·1	0·1	0·07	0·09	0·2	0·8	0·3	0·4	0·1	0·3	0·2	0·2	0·1

Sources: IMF/International bank for reconstruction and development, *Direction of Trade,* Washington DC, May 1975. Data from the Swiss National Bureau of Statistics.

German Federal Republic and the UK) which responded quickly to the market created in the Middle East by the sudden increase in wealth held by the oil-rich nations. Thus, Italy – whose state contractors are the most active in sizing up Middle East prospects and needs – has made a big deal for gas supplies with Algeria. In particular, ENI – the state oil and gas corporation – has signed a twenty-five year contract with Sonatrach for an annual supply of 11 billion m^3 of natural gas to be transported through a 1,550-mile pipeline running from Hassi R-Mel across the desert to Cap Bonn in Tunisia, where the pipe continues below the Mediterranean for 100 miles before surfacing in western Sicily. In addition, Siapem and Snam Progetti are building a $US 300 million oil refinery in Algeria, and Innocenti is building two tube mills. Other wide-ranging deals have also been concluded by Italy with Libya (which, in exchange for 30 million tons of crude oil, will receive adequate aid in several industrial projects, including petrochemicals, steel, oil refineries, agriculture and shipping); with Egypt (where the biggest Italian-backed project is the construction of the Suez–Mediterranean pipeline); with Saudi Arabia (where, in addition to an oil supply agreement for three years, a supply of a further 500 million tons of crude oil is envisaged over a fifteen-year period in exchange for technical know-how, training programmes, the construction of a large refinery, an ammonia plant, a car and truck assembly plant, etc.); with Iran (for the integrated construction of the Bandar Abbas region including the infrastructure projects, energy sources, etc., and a number of other projects in the textiles and clothing sectors, agriculture, agro-business, housing units, a fertiliser plant; participation in marketing and refining operations in Europe and Africa); with Iraq (to produce ethylene and polyethylene, establish a foundry, a power station, food processing units, a pipe plant and a tyre plant, and to undertake wide development projects in agriculture, especially land reclamation; also, to build a 650-km pipeline linking the northern and southern oilfields and to be extended to the Mediterranean); with Bahrain (to set up desalination plants); with Sudan (to undertake agricultural projects); and with Tunisia (to build a chlor plant near Gabes), etc.[19]

France – which enjoys a privileged position in the Arab World given its sympathy for the Arab cause – signed two agreements with Saudi Arabia in 1974, providing crude oil in exchange for industrial equipment (including Concorde, the Secam television system, etc.), technical aid (an industrial technical institute will be created at Jeddah) and armaments. The first agreement, which lasts three years, is now being implemented. The second, for a period of twenty years and 400 million tons of oil, has not yet been concluded. Saudi Arabia, moreover, has taken a stake in the

'Banque Arabe et Internationale d'Investissement' founded in Paris in 1973. Similarly, France has signed very important contracts with Iran (to set up a forty-mile subway system in Tehran, a special steel mill, 200,000 housing units, five nuclear plants, a factory initially producing 100,000 cars, agricultural development schemes, the manufacture of chemical products, a joint venture to transport liquefied natural gas and distribute Iranian petrochemical products, etc.); with Iraq (to build the Basra petrochemical complex, the Mosul Dam, an aluminium smelter, two sponge iron plants and a steelworks, etc.); with Libya (oil in exchange for nuclear power plants, refineries, arms and joint ventures); with Qatar (where two distillation complexes with a capacity of two million gallons of water per day are under construction); with Kuwait (where the Prime Minister has declared full priority for French products and granted the development of the petrochemical industry to Sofrapek); with the Emirates (notably in the petrochemical sector and in agriculture); with the Sudan (to create a road of 280 kms on the White Nile and develop the beef sector); and with Egypt (to participate in petrochemical complexes, an oil refinery in the Canal Zone, car assembly factories, food industries, a fertiliser plant at Suez, etc.). Moreover, France has considerably strengthened its economic presence in Algeria, Tunisia and Syria.[20]

The German Federal Republic, which is heavily oriented towards export markets and specialises in the selling of complete industrial plants, has also concluded important package deals with Saudi Arabia (with emphasis on building an airport near Jeddah, a Daimler–Benz truck factory, a Krupp desalination plant, a Korf and Demang steel mill, a Rheinstahl foundry, a Hoechst ammonium factory, etc.); with Iran (the major contracts involving a gas export venture of 10,000 million m^3 a year, a giant oil refinery of 25 million tons a year, two nuclear plants and a $US 800 million iron and steel works on the Gulf at Bushir); with Algeria (including the Oran steel plant, which will have a capacity of 10 million tons a year, exploitation of uranium in the Hoggar desert, utilisation of nuclear energy, expansion of the petrochemicals industry, and erection of an electricity power centre at Constantine, in which already 107 German firms are participating); with Libya (where the most important projects are a huge cement plant at Banghazi and a gas power station at Misurata); with Iraq (for the supply of 10,000 trucks); and with Egypt (for installation of a petrochemical complex by Bayer at Alexandria), etc.[21]

The United Kingdom – with emphasis on contracting, construction and cars – has made a wide-ranging deal with Iran (including the electrification of the Tehran–Tabriz railway, the supply of ships and trucks, the construction of silos, participation in programmes of port expansion, hospital development, etc.) and has strengthened its economic presence in the Gulf area and in Egypt (where British Leyland is to assemble Land Rovers).[22]

Despite these ventures, and although the prospects for an equal partnership based on mutal respect and mutual advantage seem good, given geographical proximity and complementary economies, it is unrealistic to hope for a co-ordinated approach between the EEC and the twenty countries of the Arab League. The European–Arab dialogue is still too much a fragile, tentative affair. Moreover, the Arab League is not as united or as monolithic as it pretends to be. And because of the disparate interests of the Nine - with Italy and France more dependent on Arab/Iranian oil, but Holland having enormous natural gas finds, the UK developing North Sea oil, and Belgium and the German Federal Republic having extensive coal industries - any systematic European response would seem to be precluded.

The best strategy for co-operation would therefore be to concentrate on the following fundamental goals:

1 The formation and mobilisation of European consortia to undertake vast development projects and to promote the commercialisation of the products obtained from joint ventures.[23] Such an objective could constitute one of the major tasks of the Euro-Arab dialogue, with a system of reciprocal guarantees, assurances, fiscal and financial incentives being agreed upon, thus rendering joint action much more attractive than separate bilateral deals. The EEC, moreover, could provide technical and other assistance for the use of Iranian/Arab capital, building up 'triangular operations', with arrangements giving all the appropriate guarantees to the countries holding the capital. Simultaneously a number of scientific, educational and cultural programmes should be drawn up at government level. In this framework a significant role could be played by the Association for Co-operation with the Arab World, which brings together parliamentarians representing virtually every country and major political movement of the EEC, and whose objectives include improved teaching of European languages and history in the Arab World (and vice versa) and the setting-up of two cultural centres, one in Europe and the other in an Arab country, to ensure that the culture, education and science of each region is more accessible to the other;[24]

2 The provision of basic foodstuffs (cereals, sugar, dairy products, etc.) through long-term supply contracts. Here the role of the EEC would lie in guaranteeing stable export aid to European operators for the duration of the contracts;

3 The provision of outlets in the Common Market, both for primary commodities such as oil, gas, minerals and certain agricultural products like wine, fruit and vegetables, and - more important - for the semi-finished and finished industrial goods that Middle East nations are hoping to produce from now on.

In this respect Algeria, Morocco, Tunisia, Egypt, Syria, Lebanon and Jordan await a satisfactory outcome of the already advanced negotiations in the context of the new Mediterranean 'global policy'. Hopes are intensified since the EEC/Israeli agreement establishing a reciprocal free trade area for most trade by 1977 came into force on 1 July 1975 (violating a 'parallelism' which would have been more appropriate from the political point of view); overall agreement was reached on 25 June 1975 by the EEC Ministers of Agriculture on the precautionary measures to be taken in the Community for wine, fresh and tinned fruit and vegetables, in order to forestall any harmful consequences for Italian and French farmers arising from the overall Mediterranean approach. Additionally, willingness has been expressed in Brussels to consider raising the ceilings for duty free imports of refined oil products (without automatic reintroduction of duties when these ceilings are exceeded), and the Lomé Convention has ruled out any trade reciprocity with the Community, but only treatment comparable with that of most favoured nation.

Problems arise, however, in regard to preferential schemes for the products resulting from joint Euro-Arab/Iranian companies and, even more so, for an eventual extension of the preferential trade régime to the oil-rich countries (specially to Iran, which France and Denmark - with the support of the German Federal Republic - view as a special case). Here, in fact, the Community is under strong pressures. In addition to the objections voiced internally by Italy and the Netherlands (which, having excess refining capacities, wish to maintain a Community preference for refined oil products), the oil-rich nations of the Gulf area (notably Iran) accuse the EEC of continued 'discrimination' against their exports and threaten to retaliate with measures against imports from the Community. Moreover, convinced that trade privileges for some of the wealthy members of OPEC could prejudice the consumer-producer dialogue and compromise the Tokyo Round, the US is ready to take action against the Community should it violate the assurances given in 1973 to confine its preferential agreements to the developing nations of the Lomé Convention, the Mediterranean countries and Jordan, and Britain's old EFTA partners.[25]

In respect of the oil-rich nations, therefore, the EEC Commission has suggested taking a more pragmatic approach, that of viewing the trade concessions in the context of the GSP scheme (which implies their extension to all developing nations). Such a solution is unsatisfactory, however, because of the autonomous nature of the generalised preferences and the constraints included in such a scheme (e.g. ceilings and tariff quotas). Moreover, the GSP system ends in 1980 and, although a further period of application is likely, it would be difficult to justify inclusion of the oil-rich nations. The only solution, therefore, is to provide a special régime - in particular *erga omnes* duty free access as proposed by the German Federal Republic - for products resulting from joint ventures with Community enterprises, as well as from long-term contracts by which reciprocal commitments are undertaken (e.g. oil supplies in exchange for foodstuffs). After all, as mentioned in Chapter 6, the principle of special tariff treatment is already generally accepted in East–West economic relations. Moreover, in a first stage, the special régime might cover only certain volumes of specific products on the basis of a gradual time schedule and could also take the form of special arrangements for simplifying customs procedures.

Finally, it is clear that peace in the Middle East is of foremost importance to the Community. Therefore, the Arab–Israeli conflict can no longer be managed with evasive tactics and policies. A European initiative is needed to exercise powers of persuasion on the Palestinians, as well as the Israelis, and to make a major contribution to maintaining peace while minimising the intervention of the two superpowers.

8.7 Economic co-operation with Japan

Although a latecomer to the Middle East scene, since the October War Japan has mounted a full-scale effort to strengthen its economic presence in the area. In particular, the issuing of an unequivocal official statement on 22 November 1973 in support of the Arab cause was followed by a flood of Japanese officials and businessmen to the Arab World.

Being the top world importer of petroleum (around 280 million tons in 1974), Japan is in fact a vulnerable target for the oil weapon. Over 80 per cent of the country's requirements for crude oil come from the Middle East, with the Arab countries supplying about 43 per cent of Japan's oil imports. It is therefore imperative for Japan to increase and promote its exports to the countries of the region to offset its staggering balance of trade deficit in the area ($US 11·9 billion in 1974), as well as to reduce its heavy dependence on the big international oil companies through direct deals with the oil-producing nations. In addition, Japan is aware of the enormous potential of the Middle East market, not only as a growing outlet for its products (given the ambitious industrialisation policies of the oil producers) but as a potential launching pad for European and other nearby export markets.

Although relevant to all countries of the region, Japan's economic interests are highly concentrated both in terms of their nature and location. In particular, Japan essentially exports manufactured goods, machinery and equipment (from cameras, transistor radios, watches, refrigerators and tape recorders to heavy industrial goods, passenger cars, trucks and other vehicles, tyres, textiles, synthetic fibres and scientific equipment) destined in large part to the Gulf and Red Sea areas; imports are oil, gas and crude materials (raw cotton, minerals, hides, etc.) mainly from the same areas. Similarly, almost 97 per cent of investment is in mining (predominantly oil) and is chiefly located in the Gulf states.[26]

Iran is the biggest outlet. In 1974 Iran, which accounts for 29·8 per cent of total Japanese imports from the region, purchased over $US 1 billion of Japanese goods, that is, 25·4 per cent of total Japanese exports to the region. Japan's investment interest in Iran is also considerable, notably in joint ventures to produce petrochemical products, exploit copper deposits and build up giant refineries. In the field of technical assistance, Japan admits Iranian trainees in agriculture and fisheries, the postal service, and construction and administration, and carries out feasibility surveys, e.g. the Iranian Economic Infrastructure Survey.

Among the Arab oil producers, Saudi Arabia, Kuwait, the Emirates and Oman are the fastest growing markets for Japanese goods. Saudi Arabia, in particular, is the most important trading partner, in 1974 accounting for 32·8 per cent of Japanese total imports from the region. And since Saudi Arabia has a quarter of the world oil reserves at its disposal, Japanese companies are keen to establish joint ventures in many fields. Thus, Mitsubishi Corporation has reached an agreement with Petromin to establish a $US 3,000 million petrochemical complex including an oil refinery (with an initial capacity of 250,000 barrels per day to be raised to 500,000 barrels per day) and an ethylene plant (with an annual capacity of 250,000 tons). Sumitomo Metal Industries is building a steel mill at Ad Damman and has created a joint enterprise with the Saudi Arabian Group Alireza for the manufacture of tubes for the petrochemical industry. Nissan Motor Co. is establishing a joint venture with Zahran Co. to produce 60,000 Datsun trucks per year. Nippon Mining Co. and Mitsui have concluded a deal with Petromin for a 4,000-square-mile concession in the Arabian Desert believed to be rich in copper, lead and zinc. A shipping company has been created by Saudi Arabia Tanker and Mitsui OSK. Further major investments by the Japanese are envisaged in other petro-industries, steel products, mining and shipping ventures involving Japanese giants such as Marubeni Trading Firm, Idemistu Kosan Oil Co., Nippon Kokan, Nippon Steel, etc.

In the United Arab Emirates – the second Arab market (13·2 per cent of total Japanese imports from the region) – Japanese industrial groups are actively engaged in the Abu Dhabi Marine Area Development (ADMA), in which they have a 12 per cent share, the Central Energy Development Company, eighteen oil tankers, an inter-state telecommunications centre and an Abu Dhabi oil refinery. In addition, the Japanese have 100 per cent ownership in the Abu Dhabi Oil Company Ltd, established in 1968.

Kuwait is Japan's third biggest Arab market (accounting in 1974 for 13·3 per cent of total Japanese imports from the region). Imports of Kuwait include silk, man-made fibres and woven fabrics, transistor radios, passenger cars, jeeps, buses, lorries and television sets. Apparently a large share of these items is re-exported as a result of the low customs tariffs imposed on imported goods in Kuwait. In addition to oil and liquefied petroleum gas (LPG), Kuwait exports shrimps to Japan. Japanese investments are primarily involved in the oil industry, desalination plants, power plants, a telecommunication project and other construction projects.

In 1974 Japan signed an ample economic and technical co-operation agreement with Iraq, under which it will supply 298 billion yen (about $US 1 billion) in loans to finance a number of Iraqi oil and industrial projects, including a liquefied gas plant, an oil refinery, chemical fertilisers, cement and aluminium factories and a petrochemicals complex. In return Iraq will supply Japan with 160 million tons of crude oil, LPG and other petroleum by-products over the next ten years. Moreover, Japanese business leaders have agreed to set up a private-sector Japan–Iraq Co-operation Committee to promote Japanese expertise and products. Already the Iraq National Oil Company (INOC) has concluded a deal with the Japanese firm Sumitomo and Associates for the purchase of four oil tankers (total tonnage: 500,000 dwt) to be delivered by 1977.

Japan's oil imports from Oman are increasing rapidly. In 1974 they represented 2·4 per cent of total Japanese imports from the region. Bahrain is exceptional in its trade relations with Japan since it exports more manufactured goods than oil. In Jordan the Japanese government has granted a long-term ten-million-dollar loan for the establishment of a new telecommunications system. Jordan's main imports from Japan are iron and steel plates, tyres and man-made fibres.

Libya and Turkey constitute the biggest markets for Japan in the Mediterranean area. Turkey imports textiles (excluding clothing), construction materials, rubber products, machinery and transport equipment. Japanese assistance in development projects in Turkey include the building of paper mills, an iron and steel plant, a petrochemical plant and the exploitation of mineral resources. Libya imports cast-iron tubes and pipes, radios, passenger cars, lorries and trucks. In addition to oil exploration and the building of tankers, Japanese companies are very interested in setting up joint ventures with Libyan firms. The first Libyan–Japanese venture was established at the end of 1974 to construct a carbon-paper manufacturing plant.

Among other Mediterranean countries foremost with the Japanese economic co-operation is Egypt, where a Japanese firm has a contract worth, $US 175 million to widen and deepen the Suez Canal to accommodate vessels of 250,000 to 300,000 dwt; exploitation of oil resources is proceeding, as is the refining and manufacture of oil products in the Cairo, Suez and Alexandria regions; the construction of a 700 km telecommunication network and of a monorail system in Cairo; the provision of technical assistance and aid in land reclamation; and other projects relating to transport, electronics and textiles. Similarly, in Algeria, in addition to supplying a variety of transport goods and equipment as well as manufactured articles in return for around ten milliard m^3 of gas per year, the Japanese are helping to increase the output of the El-Hadjar steel mill and hope to prospect new resources in the Sahara and establish joint ventures to open up new markets in Africa and Europe.

Lebanon is the headquarters of Japanese companies operating in the region. In view of the persistent trade deficit with Japan, the Lebanese Government is trying to persuade the Japanese to increase their imports of Lebanese products (namely citrus and other kinds of fruit), to invest in developmental projects and to establish joint ventures and give technical assistance for oil exploration. In Morocco Mitsui is said to be involved in a joint venture with Moroccan and French partners to prospect for copper deposits. In Syria the Japanese are building an oil refinery and a power station and have extended a 30-million-dollar loan for irrigation projects along the Euphrates.

Prospects for the growth of Japanese economic co-operation in the Middle East are therefore bright, with Japanese companies anxious to develop closer trade ties, more direct relationships to cut out the oil middlemen, and ambitious industrial and financial ventures. In fact, almost unlimited outlets exist in the region for Japanese capital goods and consumer durables so that trade ties are expected to increase sharply. The growth rate of Japan's trade with the region already exceeds those recorded by other industrialised countries. Moreover, Japan has decided to import, by 1978, as much as 40 per cent of its oil requirements through direct deals. The field of investment co-operation is also going to be greatly expanded to include: manufacturing industries in steel, food processing, synthetic fibres, motor vehicles, textiles, etc; mineral extraction and processing; oil and petrochemical industries; transport, particularly sea transport (oil and gas tankers, international commercial freight, etc.); infrastructure projects of a commercial nature (power supply, telecommunications, etc.).

In addition, there are excellent opportunities in the export of technology (notably for irrigation, artesian-well drilling, sand stabilisation) and in provision of technical assistance and training of Arab/Iranian technicians with Japanese firms. Although still newcomers in the financial field, the Japanese (to whom in 1974 Saudi Arabia granted a loan of $US 1 billion while Iran, Iraq and Kuwait deposited over $US 200 million in the London branches of Japanese banks) also have ample scope to take an active part in forming multinational combines in partnership with the Arabs (as with the Hong Kong based UBAN, a consortium of Arab–French–Japanese banks) to utilise some of their capital surpluses in South-East Asia, Latin America (Brazil); also to establish investment and finance companies which could finance projects in the Arab World and assist Japanese investors there. The main Japanese banks – Dai-Ichi Kangyo, Fuji Bank, the Industrial Bank of Japan, Mitsubishi, Sumitomo and Nippon Fudosan Bank, and Sanwa – have already established offices in Beirut and taken a stake in some local ventures, such as the minority share of the Mitsui Bank and Nomura Securities in Banque d'Investissement et de Financement, of Sumitomo Bank and Daiwa Securities in the Union Bank and of the Bank of Tokyo in the Arab Finance Corporation.

In their turn, Middle East countries – impressed by the efficiency and the rapid achievements of the Japanese economy – are well aware that the training of their technicians and the provision of Japanese know-how and assistance in the fields of petrochemicals, steel, textiles, plastics, fisheries, shipbuilding, etc. can make an important contribution to accelerated economic growth in the region. Furthermore, the policy of 'transforming technology to natural resources' (which is the cornerstone of Japan's economic policy towards the developing nations) meets the desire of the Arabs and Iranians to develop 'harmonious economic relationships' by welcoming Japanese heavy industry into the Middle East area in partnership with local interest.[27] In addition, Japan (like the European countries) is neither a military nor a political power and has no motives beyond the purely economic and financial.

Despite Japanese efforts, however, a certain lack of understanding persists. Thus, the Saudi Minister Chezik Omar Al Sakkaf has stressed that his country is not used to Japanese business procedures, while the Abu Dhabi Oil Minister has criticised the Japanese Government in regard to a statement concerning the price of oil.[28] Equally, Tehran does not favour massive Japanese assistance to Iraq, coupled with an unwillingness by Japan to participate in a petrochemical complex.

To improve their mutal understanding, a *sine qua non* to lasting and fruitful co-operation, Japan plans to participate - along with the oil-rich countries - in developmental projects in the less fortunate states of the region. Thus, for example, Japan, Kuwait and Libya are to finance certain industrial projects in Egypt. In addition, the strong economic federations (grouping various professional bodies and specialised associations in Japan) plan to take the initiative of exploring and promoting joint Arab–Iranian–Japanese investment, as well as identifying the elements of success or failure in joint ventures, so that later ones can be developed accordingly. Japan has also rightly emphasised that there must be a study and understanding of mutual cultures and societies in conjunction with economic co-operation. Thus it is expected that cultural and student exchanges will be increased in the near future.

Another problem for Japan is the keen competition of the other industrialised countries which - with the reopening of the Suez Canal - are certain to increase their economic presence in the Gulf and Red Sea areas. In this respect, Japan's tactic is to welcome multinational joint ventures.[29] Thus, for instance, Japan has entered into a joint venture agreement with an American firm for the exploitation and export of oil in North Yemen and the Gulf states. Similarly, the Japanese company, C. Itoh, is to enter into association with Companhia Vale Do Rio Doce (Brazil) and the German group Korf to set up, with participation by the Tunisian Government, an iron-ore enrichment complex in Tunisia. Situated on the Gulf of Gabes, the plant will have an annual capacity of 1 million tons, Korf Industrie supplying 1·5 million tons of iron-ore pellets a year, and C. Itoh taking charge of sales. Again, in Jordan, two Japanese companies - Nimmon Iryo Co. and Hiroshi Nakajima Sangyo KK in association with the British United Trading Co. - have established the Japanese-Arab Development Co. to study Arab economic growth and promote certain industrial projects. In addition, a petrochemicals complex is being built in Saudi Arabia by a Japanese–American–South Korean consortium, together with local interests.

Notes

[1] Good sources for an overall view of the structure of Middle East trade are: J. Rosen, 'Die wirtschaftliche Abhängigkeit der Arabischen Länder vom Westen', *Neue Zürcher Zeitung,* 21, 23, 24, 27 April 1974; E. Collard, 'The Place of the Middle East in World Trade, in *The Middle East,* edited by M. Adams, Praeger, New York 1971, pp. 465–75; L.E. Preston and K.A. Nashashibi, *Trade Patterns in the Middle East,* American Enterprise Institute for Public Policy Research, Washington DC, October 1970. See also: J.D. Coppock, *Foreign Trade of the Middle East: Instability and Growth,* American University of Beirut, Beirut, 1965. A good discussion of the area's internal trade problems is also contained in A.G. Musrey, *An Arab Common Market,* New York, 1969.

[2] ECWA, *Economic Co-operation and Integration Efforts in Selected Countries in the Middle East,* Beirut, April 1974.

[3] D. White, 'Open Field for Exports', *The Financial Times,* 5 December 1973.

[4] P. Labarde, 'Les fabuleux contrats avec les pays pétroliers: espérances et réalités, *Le Monde,* Paris, 21 January 1975.

[5] For a detailed list of the import regulations, see H.J. Budig and M. Süer, *Middle East and North Africa, Markets Review 1973–74,* op.cit.

[6] 'Business Candor Counts in the Arab World', *The Arab Economist,* September 1974, p. 45. However, local middlemen seem to be essential in securing orders from the national purchasing agencies. See 'Approaching the Syrian Market, The Distributor as Middleman', *Business Europe,* 24 March 1972.

[7[S. Topping, 'Huge Arab Development Push also Pressures on Israel', *International Herald Tribune,* 7 January 1975. According to Fuad Bseiso – author of a study published by the Central Bank of Jordan – the boycott rules are not implemented owing to interests of the individual states.

[8] IDCAS, *Development of Arab Industrial Exports,* 3rd Conference on Industrial Development for Arab States, Tripoli, 7–14 April 1974; G. Dziecielewski, 'Some possibilities for increasing exports of manufactured and semi-manufactured products from selected countries in the Middle East', paper submitted by UNIDO to the regional seminar on export promotion held in Beirut, 22–27 November 1971; EEC Commission, *Débouchés possibles en Europe Occidentale pour les produits des pays Mediterranéens,* Study prepared by CREDOC, Brussels, 1971.

[9] A. Alkazaz, *Measures for the Promotion of Arab Economic Integration,* German Foundation for Developing Countries, Berlin, 1972.

[10] J.S. Roucek, 'The US and USSR Confrontation in the Middle East and Eastern Mediterranean', *Il Politico,* anno XXXVIII, no. 3, September 1973; C. Campbell and H. Caruso, *The West and the Middle East,* Council on Foreign Relations, New York, 1972; G. Lenczowski (ed.), *United States Interests in the Middle East,* American Enterprise Institute for Public Policy Research, Washington DC, 1971.

[11] E. Rouleau, 'L'Oncle Sam au Proche-Orient: Les privilèges de la puissance', *Le Monde,* 23 April 1974; I. Smart, 'The Super-Powers and the Middle East', *The World Today,* January 1974.

[12] J.W. Anderson, 'Sources of US Oil Imports', *International Herald Tribune,* 24 January 1975.

[13] E. Rouleau, 'L'Oncle Sam au Proche-Orient, Une convergence d'intérêts, *Le Monde,* 13 June 1974.

[14] E. Rouleau, 'L'Oncle Sam au Proche-Orient, Les amitiés équivoques', *Le Monde,* 14 June 1974; 'US Middle East Policy and the National Interest', *Middle East International,* October 1974.

[15] G.P. Papa and J. Petit-Laurent, 'Commercial Relations between the EEC and the Mediterranean Countries: An Analysis of Recent Trends in Trade Flows', paper submitted at the conference on the Economic Relations between EEC and Mediterranean Countries organised by the University of Reading, December 1973.

[16] G.V. Vassiliou, 'Trade Agreements between EEC and Arab Countries of Eastern Mediterranean and Cyprus', paper submitted at the conference on the Economic Relations between EEC and Mediterranean Countries organised by the University of Reading, December 1973. F. Ellis, J. Marsh, C. Ritson, *Farmers and Foreigners, Impact of the Common Agricultural Policy on the Associates and Associables,* Overseas Development Institute, London, 1973.

[17] See editorial of the Algerian newspaper *El Moudjahid,* 6 January 1971.

[18] 'Papandreou Forms a Party', *International Herald Tribune,* 4 September 1974.

[19] *Italy and the Middle East,* a *Middle East Economic Digest* Special Report, London, 25 October 1974.

[20] 'France and the Arab World', *The Arab Economist,* August 1974; R. Dabernat, 'Le succès de l'industrie française en URSS et au Proche-Orient', *Le Soir,* 28 December 1974.

[21] P. Balta, 'La coopération germano-algérienne est promise à un bel avenir', *Le Monde,* 25 June 1974.

[22] 'Britain Lags with Exports to Middle East', *Middle East Economic Digest,* 13 September 1974.

[23] C. Cheysson, 'Towards a Relationship with the Mediterranean Countries', *Lo Spettatore Internationale,* vol. IX, no. 2, April–June 1974.

[24] C. Mayhew, 'Europe's Opportunity', *Middle East International,* October 1974.

[25] The total estimated US export loss through EEC preferential agreements is rather small. M.E. Kreinin, 'US Trade Interests and the EEC Mediterranean Policy', paper submitted at the conference on the Economic Relations between EEC and Mediterranean Countries organised by the University of Reading, December 1973.

[26] 'Japan in the Arab World', *The Arab Economist,* Special Survey, vol. VI, no. 69, October 1974; 'Japan Seeks to Strengthen Middle East Economic Ties', *Middle East Economic Digest,* 17 August 1973.

[27] 'Partnership is the Theme of Japan's Economic Drive', *Middle East Economic Digest,* 31 January 1975.

[28] 'Le Ministre du Pétrole d'Abou Dhabi reprouve les critiques du gouvernement japonais', *Le Monde,* 27 March 1973; P. Pons, 'Les Japonais essaient de séduire les producteurs de pétrole', *Le Monde,* 8 October 1974.

[29] 'Japan in the Arab World', *Monday Morning,* Beirut, 22 April 1974.

9 Conclusions

The prudence of assuming for the present that oil revenues may disappear in about a generation dictates the necessity for accelerated economic growth to ensure that industries and infrastructure are available for self-sustaining development. The Middle East countries are therefore committed to a race against time, having to achieve in 15 to 20 years what most Western countries have taken 150 to 200 years to attain. New discoveries of oil in commercial quantities, should they occur, might lessen the urgency for policy decisions, but would not warrant change of this strategy since, ultimately, oil is a depleting, non-renewable, resource.

Moreover, since the developed countries are committed to a policy of reducing their oil dependency on the Middle East and North Africa, the countries of the region have a unique chance to obtain a greater share of the power up to now experienced by the industrialised countries. But the region must first diversify its economy and create a modern, advanced industrial base - and in a relatively short period of time. The seventies and eighties should thus witness a real economic revolution.

In fact the region has already embarked on dramatic change. Almost everywhere, the scene which greets the new arrival or visitor is one of great activity on all fronts. In 1973–74, Qatar and Iran emerged with the highest rates of growth (37 per cent and 34 per cent in real terms), not only of the region, but of the world. And this performance is all but matched by the spectacular growth of Oman (30 per cent), the United Arab Emirates (28 per cent), Saudi Arabia (19·7 per cent), Libya (15 per cent), Kuwait and Iraq (each 12 per cent) and Bahrain (10 per cent). Although Egypt and Cyprus suffered a negative average growth rate in 1973–74 (because, respectively, of the demands of the armed forces and the Turkish invasion), higher rates of growth are also expected in the countries of the Mediterranean and Red Sea areas. Thus, the oil boom of the major oil-producing countries should also uplift the non-oil economies, attaining for the whole region a scale of economic growth without any parallel elsewhere in the world today.

Both the economic and social potential for the region are great. In the agricultural sector, cultivable land - rainsoaked or irrigated - could be raised from 15 million to more than 300 million acres and the average yield of crops, actually less than half of average world production, could be tripled, especially with regard to cereals and meat. Thus, the region could even establish successful export industries, for example in vegetable oils, textiles, ready-made clothing, vegetable and fruit canning, paper pulp, sugar and timber.

In the industrial sector, the availability of petroleum and natural gas for energy and as a feedstock could turn the region into the world's most important area for oil refining, petrochemical industries (including synthetic fibres and nitrogenous fertilisers) gas liquefaction plants, iron and steel mills based on the direct-reduction process, and smelters of imported ores. Moreover, the wav to many other major industrial projects is opened by the existence of other important raw materials (phosphates in Morocco, Jordan, Tunisia, Egypt, Iraq; chromium and chromite in Turkey and the Red Sea area; copper in Mauritania, Sudan and Cyprus; manganese in Oman, Bahrain, Sudan; cobalt in Morocco; iron ores in Mauritania, Algeria, Libya, Egypt, Syria, Sudan; uranium in Mauritania, Libya), with the likelihood also of other promising finds in the area. Equally important, the labour-intensive industries (glass making, ceramics, clothing, leather products, etc.) continue to offer ample opportunities for utilising the abundant labour force of Egypt, Algeria, Iraq, Tunisia, Morocco, Sudan and Turkey. Industrial development is also favoured by the fact that, being latecomers, the countries of the region can choose the best technological innovations developed by the major advanced countries through their own growth. Furthermore, as evident in the entrepôt areas which have sprung up in Lebanon, Bahrain and Dubai, the region could become one of the world's most important trading and banking centres providing all the necessary services for the Arab World as well as for the expanding economies of Africa, the Indian Ocean, South-East Asia and even the Far East. Such development is facilitated by the region's excellent geographical position, the low cost of electricity and the establishment of new free zones along the Suez Canal, the Arab peninsula and the Mediterranean coast.

On the social side, in addition to the pressures of an incredibly young population, the potential lies in the emergence of a new professional middle class of managers, technocrats, professors, writers and doctors, as distinct from the more traditional middle class - bureaucrats, bourgeoisie and clerics - which survived through family ties and similar allegiances. Often surprisingly dynamic, the new middle class firmly believe that their only hope of maintaining an independent identity and political existence lies in equipping themselves to compete effectively in economic and technical terms in the modern world. In fact, they are already having a growing effect on the decision making process, not only in the private enterprise oriented countries (notably Saudi Arabia and the Gulf states), but in the socialist countries (Egypt, Syria, Iraq) where the manifest insufficiency of the state economic organisations in the management of the economy both calls for reforms based on decentralisation and encouragement of the private sector, and for societal changes (e.g. worker participation, as in Democratic Yemen).

To be viable, the overall strategy of accelerated economic growth has to be based on adequate development policies. Otherwise, most of the countries under review may one day be in a situation worse than before the oil era – from the economic as well as the social viewpoint. In particular, three main objectives must be achieved: (a) self-sustained economic growth achieved by devoting a substantial part of oil revenues – while they exist – to the rapid development of the non-oil sectors; (b) dispersion of benefits from oil so that the money serves the region as a whole; (c) correction of the drawbacks and imbalances attached to fast economic growth.

For rapid development of the non-oil sectors, the emphasis of the major oil-producing countries of the region is on the 'Iranian/Algerian model' by which 'feeder' industries are established, to produce goods as inputs for other products. Thus, large-scale, highly capitalised industries with a high cash flow (oil refineries, petrochemical and fertiliser plants, natural gas liquefaction units, steel mills, etc.), employing a small but quite skilled labour force with the most modern technology – export-oriented and based on oil or natural gas – can service other intermediate industries which are less highly capitalised and more moderate in size. (These would produce, for example, engineering and mechanical machinery, electrical and electronic components.) Industrial development can thus be spread throughout the whole economic system.

Such a policy has remarkable advantages. First of all, it facilitates the emergence of a diversified economy, with control of locally available resources and greatly increased real returns from exports. Secondly, in addition to enhancing the powers of a new dynamic class of managers, it permits participation in an international redivision of labour in a manner that will ensure a more equitable share in the fruits of international specialisation. This policy, based on major capital-intensive industries, is especially attractive for the micro-states of the Gulf area, and for Saudi Arabia and Libya, because – though they have great financial resources from oil – they have only a relatively small indigenous population and cannot absorb a large number of immigrants whose presence could cause internal friction and resentment. Intensive industrialisation is also fairly successful in relatively large populations, like Algeria and Iran, where the establishment of integrated plants and of the industrial infrastructure is giving an enormous boost to the rapid development of alternative sources to oil and natural gas as the basis of the economy. Thus, by the eighties, Iran's ambition is to become the major industrial power in the region, while Algeria wants to become Africa's 'socialist Japan'. However, excessive reliance on capital-intensive industries cannot free the mass of the population from the underdevelopment cycle and solve the problem of the best allocation of the financial resources available. Despite Algeria's nationalisation of all major enterprises, the Algerian economy - like that of Iran - faces serious bottlenecks such as the lack of intermediate skilled labour and a heavy dependence on foreign technology. Moreover, economic dualism is aggravated by the neglect of the public services and of the agricultural sector. It is, therefore, essential that both in the major oil countries and in the more diversified economies facing a dramatic employment situation (e.g. Tunisia, Morocco, Egypt) intensive industrialisation is paralleled by the establishment of transnational ventures (e.g. the ALBA smelter of Bahrain which draws its fuel from locally available natural gas; alumina from Australia; technology, know-how and financial means from six international companies and the local government), of export-oriented labour-intensive industries producing parts for manufactured goods (electronic components, cement, glass, etc.) which can absorb some of the rapidly growing labour force, produce substitutes for imported goods and obtain substantial export earnings; and of agro-industries which can promote the modernisation of agriculture and lessen the heavy dependence on food imports.

Balanced growth could not rapidly solve the problems posed by the great gaps existing in the region between the oil and non-oil sectors, the rich and poor countries, the services and the production sectors. The adoption of eclectic and multifront development policies - involving capital-intensive plants, transnational ventures, export-oriented labour-intensive industries, agro-industries - does not therefore transgress the balanced versus unbalanced economic growth controversy, because, as stressed by R. El Mallakh, the economy of thc region 'cannot adhere strictly to either grouping'. However, since, by definition, accelerated growth leads to 'tensions, disproportions and disequilibrium', appropriate measures have to be worked out to reduce the growing inequalities between relatively rich and less developed countries, between urban and rural areas, economic sectors and population segments, and to halt the soaring inflation. For, if growth is fast but unjust, with the burden of development being placed on the shoulders of the masses to the profit of a few, a serious position could result, as the 'Lebanese model' has clearly shown. Of significance here is President Boumedienne's statement (to *Al Ahram,* 18 October 1974) that, 'we must now work out radical changes in the social plan and in the means of production'.

Particularly important is the problem of using the oil money effectively, to meet the development needs of the poorer countries of the region. In this respect, in the past, the governments of the oil-rich nations have acted cautiously, apart from repeated gifts of cash (from Saudi Arabia, Kuwait, Libya, Qatar and Abu Dhabi) to compensate Egypt, Syria, Jordan and Sudan for the war efforts of the Arab–Israeli conflicts and the closing of the Suez Canal. More recently, substantial aid has also been given for specific projects by the Kuwait Fund for Arab Economic Development, the Abu Dhabi Fund and by single governments (e.g. by Saudi Arabia, to help the infrastructure development of the Yemen Arab Republic). However, as the factoral distribution of the region (labour, capital and managerial skills) is extremely favourable, the course for the future is to establish ventures aiming at a complementary, industrialised and diversified regional economic structure. Thus, for example, Kuwait has built a 'satellite' chemical fertiliser plant in Turkey which is at present working relatively well, being near to the consumer market and enjoying cheap labour. A more advanced model of regional venture is the Suez–Mediterranean pipeline (SUMED) based on a mutually advantageous tripartite partnership by which oil-rich countries (Saudi Arabia, Kuwait, Abu Dhabi, Qatar) and Egypt finance 50 per cent of the $US 400 million capital of the company (the Arab Co. for Oil Pipeline SUMED), while the realisation of the project is entrusted to five Italian firms (Montubi, Cimi, Italsider, Saipem and Snam Progetti) and to the American company Bechtel for managerial supervision.

Thus, in addition to helping development of the poorer countries and relieving the already severe strains of the oil-rich nations (which suffer a dearth of trained manpower, too small domestic markets, the presence of too many immigrants, limited water and other resources), regional ventures have a far better chance of survival and growth since they allow economies of scale, increase productivity, improve product quality and reduce production costs, ultimately raising the prestige and competitiveness of Middle East products internationally. In order to speed the institution of various forms of regional ventures, a Pan-Arab Development Planning Authority should therefore be established. This would draft a comprehensive plan on an acceptably solid basis, granting facilities in regard to movement of skilled labour and set up standards for industrial production, under its aegis; a Pan-Arab Bank could be established also, in order to finance Arab industry.

The problem of rectifying the drawbacks surrounding accelerated growth cannot, however, be solved exclusively by massive investment in schools, universities, public housing, roads, desalination plants, medical centres, refuse disposal, gas, electricity, etc. New, pragmatic approaches are urgently needed to achieve a better equilibrium, especially in view of demographic pressures and of rising inflation (both phenomena causing a growing discontent in the whole region). Social policies must therefore be reformulated to meet the real needs of the region: (a) reorienting school systems, teaching methods and curricula; giving more emphasis to vocational and technical education, non-formal training for agriculture and industry; introducing new standards and practices; improving teacher training facilities; carrying out a massive regional programme aiming to eradicate illiteracy; financing study abroad on condition that governments approve the field of activity and students agree to accept a government assignment on their return; encouraging the return of highly qualified personnel working abroad; discouraging a 'brain drain' of scientists and skilled labour; creating new and sound scientific institutional bases; (b) replacing mere relief assistance to unemployed and poor families by productive programmes in which the assisted members receive training in certain skills under the supervision of social workers; (c) extending social security benefits to agricultural workers, the self-employed and domestic servants; (d) implementing effective labour legislation with emphasis on pensions, overtime, sickness, disability, and equality between men and women; (e) adopting community development programmes, in particular for the young (to promote their participation in developmental projects such as literacy campaigns) and for the nomadic populations of the steppe areas, as mentioned earlier for Saudi Arabia. In addition, well thought out anti-inflation programmes must be centred on: (a) low-cost housing; (b) stabilisation of prices for the most common foodstuffs, by means of state subsidies, increases in minimum wages and pensions, and state intervention on the free market following stockholding policies; (c) major structural efforts in the agricultural sector, such as redistribution of holdings, the strengthening of liberal-oriented co-operative structures; improvement of extension and technical services to farmers, supply of production requisites and credit.

Last but not least, a democratic management of the economy is of the utmost importance to enforce – on a decentralised basis – flexible and liberal-oriented planning, thus avoiding programmes dictated from above and generally not based on the needs of the population. In this respect, the establishment of a national assembly in Bahrain which, however, was dissolved on 24 August 1975, and in Kuwait, by means of general elections, provides a platform from which the government can be approached and, if necessary, criticised by the people through their representatives. Other vital moves towards liberalisation are under way in Egypt, Sudan and, to a lesser extent, Syria, and, if imitated by the other countries, could make a determinant contribution to the 'renaissance' of a region endowed with its own cultural identity and uniqueness.

However, should the official attitude towards such problems be maintained (as often underlined, for instance, by the Iranian Prime Minister, Amir Abbas Hoveyda) – that populations of the region must be patient while readjustment takes place in the economy – the political stability of the whole area could be threatened. For the working class (as well as the poor countries *vis-à-vis* the oil-rich states) now yearn to share the fruits of economic growth, and the Russian-inspired and oriented trend to revolt, on the pattern that is today found in Democratic Yemen, could spread throughout the region.

To achieve developmental targets within the next fifteen or twenty years, the countries of the region must: depend on the advanced technological know-how of the industrial countries; import the necessary equipment; ease the drastic shortage of technical skills; achieve economies of scale, obtaining outlets on world markets for exports of manufactured products, as well as achieving efficient commercialisation. Thus, to solve these problems, there must be constructive co-operation with the industrial countries. This should imply action for the mutual interest and benefit of both partners in a balanced manner. Thus, naïve formulae, whereby Arab and Iranian partners would have to provide the capital needed, cheap energy, cheap labour, and ask their governments to subsidise and protect exports and offer tax holidays – all in return for foreign technology and management – are out of the question, because the foreign investor's benefits (including royalties, management contract fees, majority rights, free repatriation of profits, etc.) would far outweigh his inputs. A policy of genuine international co-operation should aim at increasing trade and investment opportunities between Middle East nations and the industrial countries on the basis of a new and mutually fruitful relationship. In particular, it must involve a gradual shift – from Western countries to the Middle East and North Africa – of the production of 'first stage' basic products of energy-based industries, as well as a gradual removal of the industrial countries' import barriers levied on semi-finished and finished manufactures exported by these same industries. In fact, given the considerable difference in the price of basic raw materials, the cost of production, for example of ammonia, is lower in the Arab countries and in Iran. And such a difference is even wider for products like ethylene, because the costs of the ethane-based production in the Arab countries and Iran are three times lower than the costs of the naphtha-based production of Western Europe and Japan. Thus, as underlined by C. Robinson, President of the Marconi Co., which is heading a consortium to build a $US 500 million steel mill in Saudi Arabia, 'the Western World has to move the industry to raw materials rather than the raw materials to industry'. At the same time, Western nations must open up their markets also. And, despite the capital surpluses available, minority holdings of foreign capital are thought desirable by the Arabs and the Iranians on the grounds that these provide the 'best proof' of 'proper management', even if foreign investors are guaranteed freedom of movement of capital in and out of the region.

Although gradual, the redistribution of economic activities from the industrial countries to the developing nations of the Middle East and North Africa certainly raises problems of adjustment (e.g. for major exporters of oil-derived products, such as Italy and Holland). However, it is by the proposed 'diplomacy of resources' that long-delayed, inevitable, economic transformation can be carried out in the framework of multilateral long-range international planning, so that redundancies and closure of businesses are not dealt with in an improvised way but constructively, avoiding the breakdown of the world's trading system. Thus, the industrial countries – in return for the supply of a major part of their oil needs at an equitable, relatively stable, price for some definite period – would commit themselves to pay with a planned volume of goods and services and to open their own markets gradually to the imports of oil-derived products.

In addition, while the West must stay ahead technologically, concentrate on highest value-added sectors and give up the manufacture of products better suited to developing countries, the Middle East nations – and other developing countries entering tripartite deals with oil-rich states and multinational companies – could be more effectively helped if a substantial amount of the money currently spent on aid by the donor countries were used to cope with problems of industrial adjustment. On the other hand, in Western Europe there is a general consensus, as pointed out by the EEC's Commissioner for Development and Co-operation, C. Cheysson, that 'we have reached if not surpassed the maximum limits of imported labour'.

In fact, there are today about 10 million immigrants in the enlarged Common Market alone, excluding intra-EEC immigrants, a figure that, if it were not for the oil crisis of October 1973, could have reached 22 million by 1980, according to a UN forecast. Thus, to avoid industrial congestion and dangerous social tension (already mounting as evident in the anti-Turkish riots in Rotterdam in 1973 and the race riots in Marseilles in 1974 and 1975), it is necessary to build 'first stage' industries where raw materials, space and labour are plentiful, while retaining the production of the most elaborate and sophisticated goods. In particular, the Mediterranean–Arab–Persian Gulf area offers a complementary space for the European industries and presents sufficient comparative advantages to justify the setting up of Euro–Arab–Iranian ventures in many fields. The more so now that such a shift of economic activities is profitable, given the proximity to cheap and abundant raw materials and the very high transport costs of LNG shipments, for example.

In return, the industrial countries can be assured of a stable flow of 'direct deal' crude oil and of feedstock supplies for their worldwide activities; overcome the increasing difficulty of finding new plant sites at home (owing to soaring land prices, and more stringent environmental standards); participate in one of the fastest growing producing areas in the world; bypass the more stringent antipollution measures; and obtain capital at a reasonable cost.

Further, the production of energy-based products in the Middle East and North Africa will lead to the emergence of whole new, mutually advantageous industries. Indian ore, for instance, may be imported into Kuwait and Saudi Arabia in return for fertilisers. Australian raw material resources such as manganese can be profitably married with Arab/Iranian capital and energy as envisaged, for example, by Petromin, the state oil organisation of Saudi Arabia. Equally, there is the hope that benefits can also be distributed to those 'proletarian' nations that post-war prosperity has so far bypassed. As Mr Cheysson points out, 'this shift in riches may help open up completely new markets in the oil-producing nations themselves, in neighbouring countries such as Egypt and, most difficult of all, in countries that have no direct connection with the oil producers but where you have fantastic markets terribly short of money and terribly short of means for increased consumption.'

Because it lies closer to the Middle East region than the US and is both more eager to trade and more politically acceptable to the Arabs, Western Europe – by far the biggest trading partner of the countries of the region – can benefit greatly from a long-term partnership between oil-producer capital and European know-how based on:

1 The formation and mobilisation of consortia of a multinational character aiming at realising vast development projects for which a system

of reciprocal guarantees, assurances, fiscal and financial incentives should be agreed on.

2 A massive programme of technical, scientific and educative assistance.

3 The provision - through long-term contracts - of basic foodstuffs.

4 The provision of outlets through a satisfactory outcome of the new EEC Mediterranean 'global policy' (offering customs exemption for most goods, broad industrial co-operation, financial assistance and adequate guarantees for migrant workers with regard to Algeria, Morocco, Tunisia, Egypt, Syria, Lebanon and Jordan) as well as of the debated 'special régime' (allowing *erga omnes* duty free access) for the products obtained from joint ventures with Community enterprises and from long-term contracts where reciprocal commitments are undertaken.

At the same time, the EEC must widen its horizons by taking into consideration structural problems and general interests. In particular, within the framework of the new Mediterranean 'global policy', it is urgent that the Community promotes a concerted effort between all interested parties, since the maintenance of different rates of concession to various Mediterranean countries is likely to prove a continuing source of disagreement. Thus, agricultural meetings at the regional level are needed to control expansion of certain productions and to find new outlets (avoiding clashes between the farmers on both sides of the Mediterranean). Equally important is the establishment of a development fund to promote the growth of the less developed areas and a Mediterranean bank to foster investment in favour of small and medium-size enterprises.

Moreover, the EEC should extend its 'global approach' to the entire developing world, since the problems relating to essential raw materials concern the emerging nations as much as anyone. In this respect, the EEC can show the way by innovations such as stabilisation of export revenues, industrial co-operation and abolition of reverse preferences. This would be in accordance with the Lomé Convention, to be enforced early in 1976, in which two countries of the region (Sudan and Mauritania) already participate, and to which - as advocated by President Senghor - the oil-rich nations of the Middle East might also adhere, at least at a later stage when the Europe of the Nine has definitely and irrevocably chosen solidarity with the developing nations.

Finally, a political dimension is relevant. The Arab–Israeli conflict, and the enormous economic and strategic importance of the region generally, can no longer be managed by evasive tactics and policies. A European initiative is essential to exercise powers of persuasion, both on Israelis and Palestinians, and to make an important contribution towards peace in the

Arab–Persian Gulf, while minimising the intervention of the two superpowers. On both sides of the Mediterranean there exists the same longing for a less materialistic civilisation. One more sensitive and less utilitarian than those of the other side of the Atlantic, one more metaphysical than that hammered out in Eastern Europe. Between Western Europe and Middle East peoples there is a basic identity of views on the idea and reality of nationalistic passion.

Bibliography

Abdel-Malek, Belal A.-A. and Hanafi, H., *Renaissance du monde arabe,* Editions J. Duculot, 1972.

Adams, M., *The Middle East, A Handbook,* Praeger, 1971.

Adelman, M.A., *The World Petroleum Market,* Johns Hopkins University Press, Baltimore, 1972.

Ahmed, Y.L., *Oil Revenues in the Gulf,* OECD Development Centre, Paris, 1974.

Akins, J.E., 'The Oil Crisis: This Time the Wolf is Here', *Foreign Affairs,* April 1973.

Alamuddin, N., 'Co-operation will Lead to a Reformed World Economic Order', *Middle East Economic Digest,* London, 20 December 1974.

Al-Bazzaz, M., *The Petro-Dollar, Present and Future Oil Revenues, 1974–1985, and Their Use,* MEED Monographs, London, 1974.

Al-Hammad, A.Y., *Arab Funds and International Economic Co-operation,* a publication of the Kuwait Fund for Arab Economic Development, Kuwait, November 1973.

The American University of Beirut, 'Man, Food and Agriculture in the Middle East', symposium proceedings, Faculty of Agricultural Sciences, Beirut, 1969.

Amin, A., *Le maghreb moderne,* Les Editions de Minuit, Paris, 1970.

Amin, S., Faire, A., Hussein, M. and Massian G., *La crise de l'imperialisme,* Editions de Minuit, Paris, 1975.

Amuzegar, J. and Fekrat, A., *Iran: Economic Development under Dualistic Conditions,* University of Chicago Press, 1971.

The Arab Fund for Economic and Social Development, 'The General Frame of a Programme Designed to Effect an Increase in the Flow of Financial Resources with the Object of Economic Development in the Arab World', unpublished study in Arabic, Kuwait, February 1974.

The Arab Petroleum Research Center, *Arab Oil and Gas Directory,* Beirut, 1974.

Arab Planning Institute and Kuwait Economic Society, Seminar on Investment Policies of Arab Oil Producing Countries, Kuwait, 18–20 February 1974.

Barbour, K.M., *The Growth, Location and Structure of Industry in Egypt,* Praeger, New York, 1972.

Barthel, G., *Industrialisation in the Arab Countries of the Middle East,* Akademieverlag, Berlin, 1972.
de la Bastide, H., *Maghreb,* Editions Horizons de France, Paris, 1974.
Becker, A.S., Hansen, B. and Kerr, M.H., *The Economics and Politics of the Middle East,* Elsevier, New York, 1975.
de Bernis Destanne, G., 'Les hydrocarbures et l'industrialisation de l'Algérie', *Revue Algérienne,* vol. VI, Algiers, March 1969.
de Bernis Destanne, G., 'Industries industrialisantes et contenu d'une politique d'intégration régionale', *Economie Appliquée,* vol. XIX, nos. 3-4, Paris, 1966.
de Bernis Destanne, G., 'Les industries industrialisantes et les options algériennes', *Tiers Monde,* vol. XII, no. 47, Paris, July-September 1971.
Berque, J., *Les arabes d'hier à demain,* Editions du Seuil, Paris, 1969.
Berreby, J.-J., *Le pétrole dans la stratégie mondiale,* Casterman, Paris, 1974.
Bharier, J., *Economic Development in Iran 1900-1970,* Oxford University Press, 1971.
Blond, G., *La Méditerranée où se joue notre destin,* Librairie Académique Perrin, Paris, 1974.
Buchan, A., *The End of the Postwar Era,* Weidenfeld and Nicolson, London, 1974.
Budig, H.J. and Süer, M., *Middle East and North Africa Market Review 1973-74,* Gower Economic Publications, Epping, Essex, 1974.
Burdett, W.M., *Encounter with the Middle East,* André Deutsch, London, 1970.
Calchi Novati, G. (ed.), *La questione mediterranea, Le condizioni per lo sviluppo dei paesi dell'area mediterranea,* Ipalmo, Rome, 1973.
Campbell, J.C. and Caruso, H., *The West and the Middle East,* Council on Foreign Relations Inc., New York, 1972.
Canadian Institute of International Affairs, 'The Mediterranean', *International Journal,* vol. XXVII, no.4, Autumn 1972.
Casadio, G.P., 'External Relations of the EEC', *Journal of World Trade Law,* vol. 7, no. 4, July/August 1973.
Casadio, G.P., *I rapporti fra la politica agraria comunitaria ed i paesi del Mediterraneo,* Istituto di Tecnica Agraria, Rome, 1971.
Centre de Recherche Européennes, *Pour un nouvel équilibre mondial Nord-Sud,* Lausanne, 1973.
Chase World Information Corporation, *Agribusiness in the Middle East,* New York, 1975.
Chatelus, M., *Stratégies pour le Moyen-Orient,* Calmann-Lévy, Paris, 1974.

Chevalier, J.M., *Le nouvel enjeu pétrolier,* Calmann-Lévy, Paris, 1973.
Clarke, J.I. and Fisher, W.B., *Populations of the Middle East and North Africa, a geographical approach,* University of London Press Ltd., London, 1972.
Clawson, M., Landsberg, H.H. and Alexander, L.T., *The Agricultural Potential of the Middle East,* Elsevier, New York, 1971.
Connelly, P. and Perlman, R., *The Politics of Scarcity: Resource Conflict in International Relations,* Oxford University Press, 1975.
Cook, M.A. (ed.), *Studies in the Economic History of the Middle East: From the Rise of Islam to the Present Day,* Oxford University Press, 1970.
Cooper, C.A. and Alexander, S.S., *Economic Development and Population Growth in the Middle East,* Elsevier, 1972.
Corbet, H. and Jackson, R. (eds), *In Search of a New World Economic Order,* Croom Helm, London, 1974.
Cottrel, A. and Burrel, R.M., *Politics, Oil and the Western Mediterranean,* The Center for Strategic and International Studies, Georgetown University, Sage Publications Inc., London, 1973.
Crabb, C.V., 'The Energy Crisis, The Middle East and American Foreign', *World Affairs,* vol. 136, no. 1, Summer 1973.
CRESM, *Introduction à la Libye contemporaine,* Paris, CNRS, 1974.
Daniels, J., *Abu Dhabi: A Portrait,* Longman, London, 1974.
Dardoud, G. and Lacouture, J., *Les émirats mirages,* Editions Seuil, Paris, 1975.
Desjardins, T., *Cent millions d'Arabes,* Elsevier Sequoia, Brussels, 1974.
The Diebold Institute, *Business and Developing Countries, a study of the role of private enterprise in economic development,* Praeger Publishers, 1973.
Ellis, F., Marsh, J. and Ritson, C., *Farmers and Foreigners, Impact of the Common Agricultural Policy on the Associates and Associables,* Overseas Development Institute, London, 1973.
Ellis, H.S., *Private Enterprise and Socialism in the Middle East,* American Friends of the Middle East, Washington DC, 1970.
El Mallakh, R. and McGuire, C., 'Energy and Development', Proceedings of the International Conference on the Economics of Energy and Development, 9–11 May 1974, University of Colorado.
El Mallakh, R., *Kuwait, Economic Development and Regional Co-operation,* University of Chicago Press, Chicago, 1968.
El Sheikh, R., *Kuwait, Economic Growth of the Oil State, Problems and Policies,* University of Kuwait, 1972–73.
Europa Publications, *The Middle East and North Africa,* London, 1974.

European Commission, *Débouchés possibles en Europe Occidentale pour les produits des pays méditerranéens,* Brussels, 1971.
Evans, D., *The Politics of Trade,* Macmillan, London, 1974.
Evron, Y., *The Middle East, Nations, Superpowers and Wars,* Praeger, New York, 1974.
FAO, *Agricultural Development in the United Arab Emirates,* Cairo, 1973.
FAO, *L'horticulture dans la région méditerranéene,* Rome, 1968.
Fenelon, K.G., *The United Arab Emirates,* Longman, 1973.
Fisher, J.C., *Energy Crisis in Perspective,* Wiley Interscience Publication, New York, 1974.
Ford Foundation, *A Time to Choose,* Ballinger Publishing Co., Cambridge, Mass., October 1974.
Fried, J.J. and Edlund, M.C., *Desalting Technology for Middle Eastern Agriculture: An Economic Case,* Praeger, 1971.
Friedman, I., *Inflation, A World-Wide Disaster,* Hamish Hamilton, London, 1974.
Gasteyger, C., Lamanna, A., Tnani, C., Aliboni, R. and Berreby, J.J., *Cooperazione nel Mediterraneo occidentale,* Istituto Affari Internazionali, Rome, 1972.
Gendarme, R., 'Has the Industrialisation of the Developing Countries Always Properly Been Understood?', *Monde en Développement,* la Mediterranée et le Developpement, no. 2, Editions Techniques et Economiques, Paris, 1973.
General Union of Chambers of Commerce for Arab Countries, *Arab Economic Report,* Beirut, 1974.
Goux, C., 'Pour une nouvelle orientation de l'activé économique', *Le Monde Diplomatique,* Paris, November 1974.
Grine, O., *Possibilities of Industrial Co-operation between Italy and Arab Countries: Case of the Steel Industry,* University of Calabria/Ipalmo, Rome, 1974.
Halliday, F., *Arabia Without Sultans,* Pelican Books, London, 1974.
Hammond, P.Y. and Alexander, S.S. (eds), *Political Dynamics in the Middle East,* Elsevier, 1972.
Harputlu, K.B., *La Turquie dans l'impasse,* Editions Anthropos, Paris, 1974.
Henley Centre for Forecasting, *Middle East Economic Prospects: Forecasts to 1985,* Euromoney, London, 1975.
Hirschmann, I., *Red Star over Bethlehem: The Soviet Influence in the Middle East,* A. Barker, London, 1971.
Hitiris, T., *Trade Effects of Economic Association with the Common Market: The Case of Greece,* Praeger, 1972.

Hughes, E., *Prospects for Partnership, Industrialization and Trade Policies in the 1970s,* The Johns Hopkins University Press, 1973.

Hunaykaty, S., 'Countries of the Arab World Industrialize', *The Arab Economist,* Beirut, February 1975.

Hussein, M., *Les Arabes au present,* Editions du Seuil, Paris, 1974.

Iskandar, M., 'The Arab Oil Question', *Middle East Economic Consultant,* Beirut, 1974.

Istituto Affari Internazionali, 'Arabs and Europeans at the Milan Conference', *Lo Spettatore Internazionale,* vol. IX, no. 2, Rome, April–June 1974.

Istituto Affari Internazionali, *Conflitti e sviluppo nel Mediterraneo,* Rome, 1970.

Jabara, Abdeen and Terry, J. (eds), *The Arab World: From Nationalism to Revolution,* The Medina University Press International, 1971.

Jalal, F., *The Role of Government in the Industrialisation of Iraq 1950–1965,* F. Cass, London, 1972.

Jemain, A., 'Pétrole: Le grand affrontement', *Entreprise,* Paris, 2 February 1973.

Joshua, *Soviet Penetration into the Middle East,* National Strategy Information Center, Washington DC, 1971.

Kachachi, S., *Industrial Development and Projects, Industrial Planning in Iraq,* Ministry of Planning, Baghdad, July 1974.

Kreinin, M.E., 'US Trade Interests and the EEC Mediterranean Policy', paper submitted at the Conference on the Economic Relations Between EEC and the Mediterranean Countries, University of Reading, December 1973.

Labrousse, H., *Le Golfe et le Canal,* Presses Universitaires de France, Paris, 1973.

Laqueur, W., *Confrontation; The Middle East War and World Politics,* Wildwood, London, 1974.

Laroui, A., *La crise des intellectuels arabes,* F. Maspero, Paris, 1974.

Lenczowski, G., *US Interests in the Middle East,* American Enterprise Institute for Public Policy Research, Washington DC, 1968.

Lenczowski, G., *Soviet Advances in the Middle East,* American Enterprise Institute for Public Policy Research, Washington DC, 1972.

Lindbeck, A., *Possible Future International Conflicts in a Growing World Economy,* Institute for International Economic Studies, Stockholm, 1974.

Mabro, R., *The Egyptian Economy 1952–1972,* Clarendon Press, Oxford, 1974.

Mabro, R.E., 'Problems of Investment', paper submitted to the Seminar on Investment Policies of Arab Oil Producing Countries, Kuwait, 18–20 February 1974.

Mabro, R. and Monroe, E., 'Arab Wealth from Oil: Problems of its Investment', *International Affairs,* London, January 1974.

Madelin, H., *Pétrole et politique en Méditerranée occidentale,* A. Colin, Paris, 1973.

Makdisi, S.A., 'Arab Oil Revenues: Some Domestic and International Policy Aspects', paper submitted to the international meeting on Arab–Italian Economic Co-operation, Cetraro, Italy, 12–14 July 1974.

Makdisi, S., *Lebanon: Monetary Developments, Management and Performance in the Post-War Period up to 1972,* American University of Beirut, Economics Department, Beirut, 1974.

Mansfield, P., *The Middle East,* A Political and Economic Survey, Oxford University Press, 4th edition, 1973.

Merklein, H.A., 'Can Middle East Producers Preserve their Petro-Wealth?' *The Arab Economist,* Beirut, February 1975.

Mertz, R.A., 'Education and Manpower in the Arabian Gulf', a survey conducted for AFME, Washington DC, 1972.

Middle East Economic Digest, *Prospects for European Trade and Investment in the Middle East,* London, 1974.

Middle East Economic Digest, *The 1975 Middle East Business Strategies Conference,* Brussels, 1975.

Mikdashi, Z., *The Community of Oil Exporting Countries,* Allen and Unwin, London, 1972.

Minces, J., *Les travailleurs étrangers en France,* Editions du Seuil, Paris, 1973.

Mitchell, D., *Oil: The Shifting Balance of Power,* CAABU, London, 1974.

Monroe, E. and Mabro, R., 'Oil Producers and Consumers: Conflict or Co-operation', an international seminar report, the Center for Mediterranean Studies, American Universities Field Staff, Inc., New York, 1974.

Monroe, E., *The Changing Balance of Power in the Persian Gulf,* American Universities Field Staff Inc., Hanover, New Hampshire, 1974.

Nerfin, M., *Entretiens avec Ahmed Ben Salah,* F. Maspero, Paris, 1974.

Nightingale, R.W., 'National and Regional Applications of Agricultural Perspective Planning in the Near East', 7th regional seminar on perspective planning for agricultural development in the Near East, Beirut, 16–22 April 1974.

OECD, *Le développement de l'agriculture en Europe méridionale, Paris,*

1969.
OECD, Development Centre, *Oil Revenues in the Gulf,* Paris, 1974.
OECD Development Centre, *Agricultural and Industrial Development Policies in Turkey. A Review,* Paris, 1974.
Office Arabe de Presse et de Documentation, *Commerce Arabe et développement,* Damascus, 1971.
Office Arabe de Presse et de Documentation, *Etude sur les états du golfe arabe,* Damascus, 1973.
Office Arabe de Presse et de Documentation, *Rapport 1973/74 sur l'économie arabe,* Damascus, 1974.
Overseas Development Institute, *Britain, the EEC and the Third World,* London, 1971.
Oweiss, I., 'Petro-money and the International Monetary System', *Middle East International,* London, September 1974.
Oweiss, I., 'OPEC and the Oil Consumers, Deciding a Price', *Middle East International,* London, February 1975.
Owen, R.P., 'The Rebellion in Dhofar - A Threat to Western Interests in the Gulf', *The World Today,* London, June 1973.
Papa, J.P., and Petit-Laurent, J., *Commercial Relations Between the EEC and the Mediterranean Countries: an analysis of recent trends in trade flows,* University of Reading, December 1973.
Péan, P., *Pétrole, La troisième guerre mondiale,* Calmann-Lévy, 1974.
Peristiany, J.G. (ed.), *Mediterranean Kinship,* American Universities Field Staff Inc., Hanover, Hampshire, 1975.
Perroux, F., (ed.), *La méditerranée et le développement,* Editions techniques et économiques, Paris, 1973.
Preston, L.E. and Nashashibi, K.A., *Trade Patterns in the Middle East,* American Enterprise Institute for Public Policy Research, Washington DC, October 1970.
Ramazani, R.K., *The Persian Gulf, Iran's Role,* University Press of Virginia, Charlottesville, 1972.
Ramazani, R.K., *The Middle East and the European Common Market,* The University Press of Virginia, Charlottesville, 1964.
Raston, J.L., 'Systèmes alimentaires et firmes multinationales en Méditerranée', *Mondes en Développement,* no. 2, Ed. Techniques et Economiques, Paris, 1973.
Rifai, T., *The Pricing of Crude Oil,* Praeger, New York and Pall Mall Press, London, 1974.
Robana, A., *The Prospects for an Economic Community in North Africa,* Praeger, 1973.
Rossi, A., *Sulle conseguenze dell'ampliamento della CEE per le sue*

relazioni con i paesi del bacino mediterraneo, European Parliament, Luxembourg, 28 February 1973.

Rouhani, F., *A History of OPEC,* Praeger, 1971.

Said, E. and Suleiman, F., *The Arabs Today: Alternatives for Tomorrow,* Columbus, Ohio, Forum, 1973.

Sarkis, *Le pétrole à l'heure Arabe,* Stock, Paris, 1975.

Sarkis, C., 'Les pays arabes: de l'exploitation à la coopération, *Le Monde Diplomatique,* Paris, August 1973.

Shamsedin, M.E., *The Arab Oil Embargo and the United States Economy,* MEED Monographs, London, 1974.

Shwadran, B., *The Middle East, Oil and the Great Powers,* Israeli Universities Press, Jerusalem, 1974.

Sinha, R.P., 'Japan and the Oil Crisis', *The World Today,* London, August 1974.

Skeet, I., *Muscat and Oman: The End of an Era,* Faber and Faber, London, 1974.

Stephens, R., *The Arabs' New Frontier,* Temple Smith, London, 1973.

Tahtinen, D.R., *Arms in the Persian Gulf,* The American Enterprise Institute for Public Policy Research, Washington DC, 1974.

Taylor, D.C., *Research on Agricultural Development in Selected Middle Eastern Countries,* The Agricultural Development Council Inc., New York, 1968.

Thierry de Montbrial, *Le désordre économique mondial,* Calmann-Lévy Paris, 1974.

Tidafi, T., *L'agriculture algérienne et ses perspectives de développement,* F. Maspero, Paris, 1969.

Turner, L., 'Europe: The Politics of the Energy Crisis', *International Affairs,* vol. 50, no. 3, London, July 1974.

UNCTAD, *Problems of Raw Materials and Development,* New York, 1974. (Td/B/488)

UNIDO, *Les domaines industriels en Europe et au Moyen-Orient,* New York, 1969.

Uri, P. (ed.), *Israel and the Common Market,* Weidenfeld and Nicholson, Jerusalem, 1971.

US Senate, Committee on Finance, *Implications of Multinational Firms for World Trade and Investment and for US Trade and Labour,* Washington DC, February 1973.

US Tariff Commission, *World Oil Developments and US Oil Import Policies,* Washington, October 1973.

Vandermeulen, N., 'Les relations extérieures de la CEE avec les pays du bassin méditerranéen', doctorate thesis, Université Catholique de

Louvain, Institut des Sciences Politiques et Sociales, July 1972.
Vassiliou, G.V., *Trade Agreements between EEC and Arab Countries of the Eastern Mediterranean and Cyprus,* University of Reading, December 1973.
Vielle, P.M. and Banisadr, H., *Pétrole et violence,* Editions Anthropos, Paris, 1974.
Viratelle, G., *L'algérie algérienne,* Editions économie et humanisme, Les éditions ouvrières, Paris, 1970.
Wallace, D., 'International Control of Investment', The Düsseldorf Conference on Multinational Corporations, Praeger, 1974.
Yager, J. and Steinberg, E., *Energy and US Foreign Policy,* a study sponsored by the Ford Foundation, New York, 1975.
Yannopoulos, G., *Immigration from the Mediterranean Countries and its Impact on the Economies of the European Communities,* University of Reading, Department of Economics, December 1973.
Yar-Shater, E., *Iran Faces the Seventies,* Praeger, 1971.
Zevi, A., *Europa-Mediterraneo: Quale Cooperazione,* Istituto Affari Internazionali, Rome, 1975.

Index

Some references are to foot-note indices. Where a subject cannot be found on the page number given, the reader should look to the notes at the end of the chapter for a lead.

The author

Gian Paolo Casadio studied Economics at the University of Bologna and the London School of Economics. He has worked in various international organisations such as the OECD, UNIDO, GATT and UNCTAD, and is at present in charge of International Economic Organisation in the Faculty of Political Science at the University of Bologna.

Other SAXON HOUSE Studies

Hopwood, A. G.	*An accounting system and managerial behaviour*
Black, I. G., et al	*Advanced urban transport*
Pollock, N. C.	*Animals, environment and man in Africa*
McLean, A. T.	*Business and accounting in Europe*
Rogers, S. J., B. H. Davey	*The common agricultural policy and Britain*
Hermet, G.	*The communists in Spain*
Klingen, J. S.	*Company strategy*
Chrzanowski, I.	*Concentration and centralisation of capital in shipping*
Bailey, R. V., J. Young (eds)	*Contemporary social problems in Britain*
Mack, J. A.	*The crime industry*
Sjølund, A.	*Daycare institutions and children's development*
Lewis, C.	*Demand analysis and inventory control*
Jambrek, P.	*Development and social change in Yugoslavia*
Macmillan, J.	*Deviant drivers*
Richards, M. G., M. E. Ben-Akiva	*A disaggregate travel demand model*
Teff, H.	*Drugs, society and the law*
Snickers, F. et al (eds)	*Dynamic allocation of urban space*
Ellison, A. P., E. M. Stafford	*The dynamics of the civil aviation industry*
Birnbaum, K. E.	*East and West Germany*
Masnata, A.	*East-West economic co-operation*
Ghosh, D.	*The economics of building societies*
Richardson, H. W.	*The economics of urban size*
Starkie, D. N., D. M. Johnson	*The economic value of peace and quiet*
John, I. G. (ed.)	*EEC policy towards Eastern Europe*
More, W. S. (ed.)	*Emotions and adult learning*
Grassman, S.	*Exchange reserves and the financial structure of foreign trade*
Thompson, M. S.	*Evaluation for decision in social programmes*
von Geusau, F.A.M.A. (ed.)	*The external relations of the European Community*
Bergmann, T.	*Farm policies in socialist countries*
Ash, J. C. K., D. J. Smyth	*Forecasting the U.K. economy*
Blank, S.	*Government and industry in Britain*
Buttler, F. A.	*Growth pole theory and economic development*
Richardson, H. W., et al	*Housing and urban spatial structure*
van Duijn, J. J.	*An interregional model of economic fluctuations*
Brittain, J. M., S. A. Roberts (eds)	*Inventory of information resources in the social sciences*
Fukuda, H.	*Japan and world trade*
Jackson, M. P.	*Labour relations on the docks*
Stephenson, I. S.	*The law relating to agriculture*
Hess, H.	*Mafia and Mafiosi*
Vodopivec, K.	*Maladjusted youth*
Hovell, P. J., et al	*The management of urban public transport*
Funnell, B. M., R. D. Hey (eds)	*The management of water resources in England and Wales*
Martin, M. J. C.	*Management science and urban problems*
Rhenman, E.	*Managing the community hospital*
Giddings, P. J.	*Marketing boards and ministers*
Klaassen, L. H., P. Drewe	*Migration policy in Europe*
Chapman, C. B.	*Modular decision analysis*

Hodges, M.	*Multinational corporations and national governments*
Liggins, D.	*National economic planning in France*
Friedly, P. H.	*National policy responses to urban growth*
Madelin, H.	*Oil and politics*
Tilford, R. (ed.)	*The Ostpolitik and political change in Germany*
Friedrichs, J., H. Ludtke	*Participant observation*
Fitzmaurice, J.	*The party groups in the European parliament*
Brown, J., G. Howes (eds)	*The police and the community*
Lang, R. W.	*The politics of drugs*
Denton, F. T., B. G. Spencer	*Population and the economy*
Dickinson, J. P. (ed.)	*Portfolio analysis*
Wilson, D. J.	*Power and party bureaucracy in Britain*
Wabe, J. S.	*Problems in manpower forecasting*
Willis, K. G.	*Problems in migration analysis*
Farnsworth, R. A.	*Productivity and law*
Shepherd, R. J.	*Public opinion and European integration*
Richardson, H. W.	*Regional development policy and planning in Spain*
Sant, M. (ed.)	*Regional policy and planning for Europe*
Thorpe, D. (ed.)	*Research into retailing and distribution*
Dickinson, J. P.	*Risk and uncertainty in accounting and finance*
Hey, R. D., T. D. Davies (eds)	*Science, technology and environmental management*
Britton, D. K., B. Hill	*Size and efficiency in farming*
Buchholz, E., et al	*Socialist criminology*
Paterson, W. E.	*The SPD and European integration*
Blohm, H., K. Steinbuch (eds)	*Technological forecasting in practice*
Piepe, A., et al	*Television and the working class*
Goodhardt, G. J., et al	*The television audience*
May, T. C.	*Trade unions and pressure group politics*
Labini, P. S.	*Trade unions, inflation and productivity*
Casadio, G. P.	*Transatlantic trade*
Whitehead, C. M. E.	*The U.K. housing market*
Balfour, C.	*Unions and the law*